P9-CAH-456

Especially for
From
Date

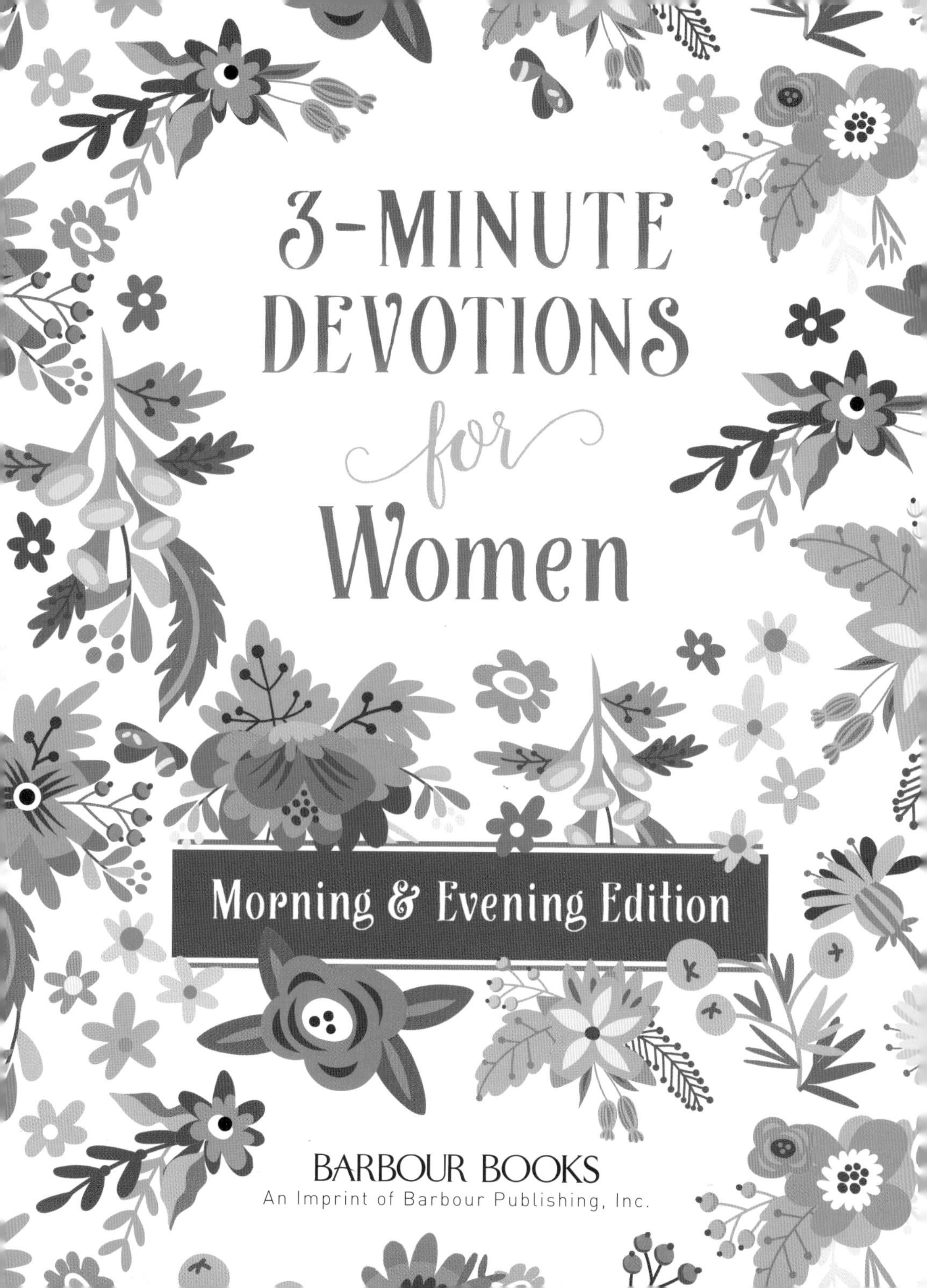

3-MINUTE DEVOTIONS for Women

Morning & Evening Edition

BARBOUR BOOKS
An Imprint of Barbour Publishing, Inc.

Text originally appeared in *Choose Hope: 3-Minute Devotions for Women*, *Choose Joy: 3-Minute Devotions for Women*, *Daily Wisdom: 3-Minute Devotions for Women*, and *Today God Wants You to Know. . .You Are Blessed.*

Print ISBN 978-1-68322-610-9

Published by Barbour Books, an imprint of Barbour Publishing, Inc., 1810 Barbour Drive, Uhrichsville, Ohio 44683, www.barbourbooks.com

Our mission is to inspire the world with the life-changing message of the Bible.

Printed in China.

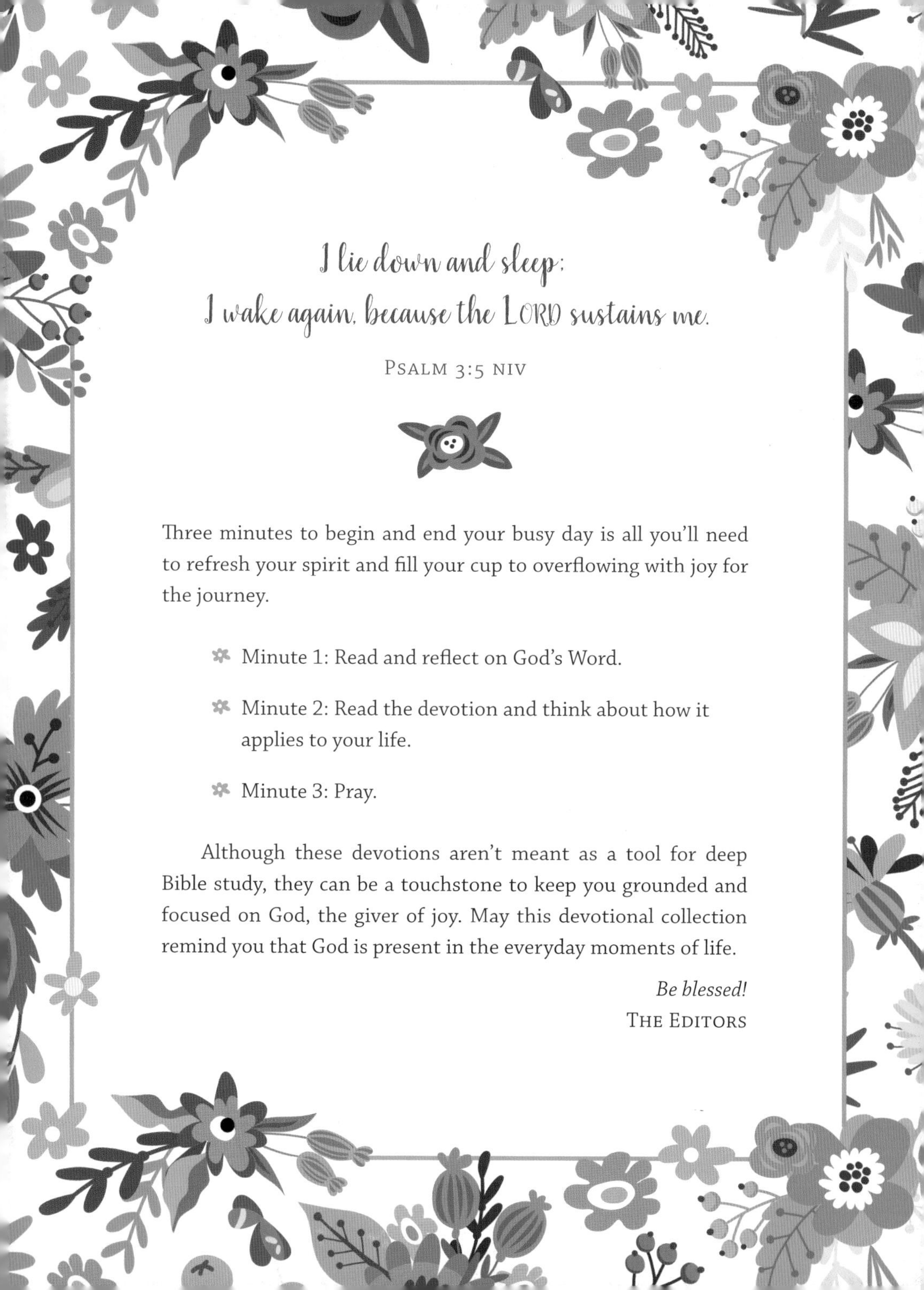

I lie down and sleep;
I wake again, because the LORD sustains me.

PSALM 3:5 NIV

Three minutes to begin and end your busy day is all you'll need to refresh your spirit and fill your cup to overflowing with joy for the journey.

- Minute 1: Read and reflect on God's Word.
- Minute 2: Read the devotion and think about how it applies to your life.
- Minute 3: Pray.

Although these devotions aren't meant as a tool for deep Bible study, they can be a touchstone to keep you grounded and focused on God, the giver of joy. May this devotional collection remind you that God is present in the everyday moments of life.

Be blessed!
THE EDITORS

DAY 1

MORNING
Our Rock and Savior

"The LORD lives! Praise be to my Rock! Exalted be my God, the Rock, my Savior!"

2 SAMUEL 22:47 NIV

Throughout the Psalms, we read that David not only worshipped and praised God, he also complained to Him, was honest with God about what he was feeling, and even admitted to being angry at God. Perhaps the most amazing thing about David, though, was his constant devotion and reliance on his Creator. Even though David is the powerful king of Israel, he praises God in 2 Samuel 22:47, calling Him his Rock and Savior. David knew that God was alive, and he also knew that he needed Him more than anything else in the world. It's the same for us today!

Dear Lord, You are my Rock and my Savior. You are alive, and I praise You as God above all else. Thank You for Your love and power. Amen.

EVENING
John 3:16

For God so loved the world, that he gave his only begotten Son, that whosoever believeth in him should not perish, but have everlasting life.

JOHN 3:16 KJV

If you grew up going to Sunday school, you probably know this verse by heart. The words may have become *too* familiar, so take a moment to think about what this verse really means. It's the message of the Gospel all wrapped up in a nutshell: God loves you. . .God gives you His Son. . .through Jesus you have life. . .in Him you'll never die.

God, thank You for giving me so much—love, life, and most of all Your Son, Jesus. May the knowledge of Your love sink into my heart and mind. Amen.

DAY 2

MORNING
Even More!

Now unto him that is able to do exceeding abundantly above all that we ask or think, according to the power that worketh in us. . .

EPHESIANS 3:20 KJV

"Above all that we ask or think" is just that. Imagine every good thing that God has promised in His Word—or things you've only dreamed about. Think of wonderful things that exceed the limits of human comprehension or description then imagine that God is able and willing to do even more!

The last part of this verse indicates that the Holy Spirit works within the Christian's life to accomplish the seemingly impossible. Our highest aspirations are within God's power—but like Paul, we must pray. When we do, God does far more for us than we could ever guess.

Oh Lord, You accomplish things I perceive as impossible. You know my hopes and dreams, and I believe that You are able to exceed my greatest expectations. Amen.

EVENING
Sense of Belonging

"All that the Father gives Me will come to Me, and the one who comes to Me I will by no means cast out."

JOHN 6:37 NKJV

We belong to Christ. When the Father calls us to come to Jesus, we belong to Him. This is an irrevocable transaction. We are His, given to Him by the Father. He does not refuse to save us. He will not refuse to help us. No detail of our lives is unimportant to Him. No matter what happens, He will never let us go. Like the enduring love of a parent—but even more perfect—is the love of Christ for us. He has endured all the temptations and suffered all the pain that we will ever face. He has given His very life for us. We can live peacefully and securely knowing we belong to Him.

Lord Jesus, I confess I often forget that I belong to You and how much You love me. Help me to rest in Your everlasting love and care. Amen.

DAY 3

MORNING
The Fruit of the Spirit

But the fruit of the Spirit is love, joy, peace, patience, kindness, goodness, faithfulness, gentleness, self-control; against such things there is no law. Now those who belong to Christ Jesus have crucified the flesh with its passions and desires. If we live by the Spirit, let us also walk by the Spirit.

GALATIANS 5:22–25 NASB

When we become Christians, we receive spiritual gifts as a result of our inward relationship with Jesus Christ. These gifts are known in the Bible as the fruit of the Spirit, but what does that really mean?

Inventoried in today's scripture are qualities that, apart from God's power, would not likely be displayed in our character.

Why is God showering us with these gifts? Because they prove that He can enter a human life and affect her or him with change, so that others might also be won to Christ as they observe this miracle.

Lord, my greatest gift from You is salvation; Your grace enables me to begin life with a fresh start. And with this transformation of character, spiritual fruit becomes the yield, shared as I serve the body of believers with my unique spiritual gifts. Amen.

EVENING
The Shadow of Death

"The people living in darkness have seen a great light; on those living in the land of the shadow of death a light has dawned."

MATTHEW 4:16 NIV

Death is the great mystery, the dark unknown that shadows all life. For us, death means sorrow. It means losing the people we love. For us, it may mean fear, even terror. And there's no escaping it. Everyone we love will die, and our dying day will come to each one of us. But Jesus let us know that death is not the end. Night may fall—but a new dawn will come.

Jesus, I am so grateful that I do not have to face death alone. When loved ones die, Your love will be my strength and comfort. And when my time comes to leave this world, and I have to venture into the dark, You'll walk with me. Amen.

DAY 4

MORNING

Reveal the Hope

In your hearts revere Christ as Lord. Always be prepared to give an answer to everyone who asks you to give the reason for the hope that you have. But do this with gentleness and respect.

1 PETER 3:15 NIV

Isn't the relevance of God's Word amazing? Peter gives three parts of advice with several key words. First, Peter advises, set God apart from everything else in your heart; in other words, "sanctify," or recognize God's holiness, and treat Him with deserved awe. Second, be prepared to explain your hope in Christ and eternal life, having a full grasp of what and in whom you believe. Finally, remember *how* you say something is equally important to *what* you say. In other words, we must walk the walk before we can reveal the hope we have in Jesus Christ.

Dear God, please prepare me to explain my hope in Christ and eternal life. Teach me to explain it in a way that honors You with gentleness and respect. Amen.

EVENING

Blessings Now

The LORD shall increase you more and more, you and your children.

PSALM 115:14 KJV

Eternal life waits for us on the other side of death—but it also expands our lives right now. It makes them fuller, wider, deeper. It gives us *more* life than we ever knew was possible. And this promise of eternal blessing isn't only ours. It's so big that it spreads out from us. It reaches our children, too. The Lord's blessings have no limits.

Thank You, Lord, that I don't have to wait to enter eternity. Help me to remember that it's all around me, right now. Give me eyes to see and a heart to know Your blessing. Amen.

DAY 5

MORNING
Seasons of Change

The Spirit of God, who raised Jesus from the dead, lives in you. And just as God raised Christ Jesus from the dead, he will give life to your mortal bodies by this same Spirit living within you.

Romans 8:11 NLT

Change can be exciting or fearsome. Changing a habit or moving beyond your comfort zone can leave you feeling out of control. The power of God that formed the world, brought the dry land above the waters of the sea, and raised Jesus from the dead is alive and active today. Imagine what it takes to overcome the natural laws of gravity to put the earth and seas in place. Imagine the power to bring the dead to life again. That same power is available to work out the details of your life.

Lord, I want to grow and fulfill all You've destined me to be. Help me to accept change and depend on Your strength to make the changes I need in my life today. Amen.

EVENING
Good Things

Every good gift and every perfect gift is from above, and cometh down from the Father of lights.

James 1:17 KJV

Somewhere along the way, quite a few Christians got the idea that anything we enjoy is a temptation to sin. And it's true: anything we put ahead of God can become our little-*g* god. But that doesn't mean that the things we like most are sin in and of themselves. All the good things in our lives come directly from God. They're a part of the eternal life He's blessed us with right now.

Giver of all things good, I thank You for all the joys with which You've blessed me. May they never separate me from You, but instead, bring me always closer to You. Amen.

DAY 6

MORNING
Peace Despite Our Trials

Therefore, having been justified by faith, we have peace with God through our Lord Jesus Christ, through whom also we have obtained our introduction by faith into this grace in which we stand; and we exult in hope of the glory of God. . . . For while we were still helpless, at the right time Christ died for the ungodly.

ROMANS 5:1–2, 6 NASB

People have scoured every nook and cranny of the globe in search of peace. From yoga and transcendental meditation to new age tranquility tapes and self-empowerment courses, people will try just about anything. But do these methods work?

Of course not! Instead, each new road eventually leads to the dead ends of dissatisfaction and emptiness. "I have seen all the works which have been done under the sun, and behold, all is vanity and striving after wind" (Ecclesiastes 1:14 NASB). The promises of peace that this world has to offer are nothing more than vapors of an expensive fragrance.

Enduring tranquility cannot be found outside a relationship with Christ.

Lord, I know the only true and lasting peace comes from Jesus Christ. Amen.

EVENING
Strength in Hope

I say to myself, "The Lord is my portion; therefore I will wait for him."

LAMENTATIONS 3:24 NIV

In this verse, the writer declares that the Lord is his portion. The Lord is our portion, too. But when will we fully receive this inheritance and celebrate with Him? We know it is coming, but it's difficult to wait. Hope gives us strength as we anticipate our return to God. We belong to God and know someday we will worship Him face-to-face in His presence. Knowing God will keep his promise, we can say with confidence, "The Lord is my portion; therefore I will wait."

What an amazing promise You have made to me, Father, that one day I will be with You in heaven. My hope is in You as I wait for that day. Amen.

DAY 7

MORNING
Sweating the Small Stuff

*Blessed are all who fear the LORD,
who walk in obedience to him. You will
eat the fruit of your labor; blessings
and prosperity will be yours.*

PSALM 128:1–2 NIV

The Lord showers us with many blessings each day—family, friends, education, jobs, good health, and a beautiful earth. But despite the gifts He gives, it's easy to get bogged down in the little things that go wrong. We're all human, and we sometimes focus on all the negatives rather than the positives in life. Next time you're feeling that "woe is me" attitude, remember that you are a child of God. Spend some time counting all the wonderful blessings that come from the Lord rather than the headaches from this earth.

*Father, thank You that I am Your child.
Remind me each day to count the
many blessings You shower upon me,
rather than focusing on the
negatives of this world. Amen.*

EVENING
Everlasting Love

*"I have loved you, my people, with an
everlasting love. With unfailing love
I have drawn you to myself."*

JEREMIAH 31:3 NLT

God's love never ends. It never fails. It's unconditional. It's broader and deeper than anything we could ever comprehend, because it has no limits, no boundary lines it refuses to cross. Wherever we go, it follows us. It pulls at our hearts, because somewhere inside us all, we know God's love is the source of all our joy. God's everlasting love isn't a part of eternity. It *is* eternity.

*Lover of my soul, thank You that I can
never go beyond Your endless love.
There is no place Your love will
not follow me. Amen.*

DAY 8

MORNING

Gomer, a Picture of Israel

The LORD said to Hosea, "Go, take to yourself a wife of harlotry and have children of harlotry; for the land commits flagrant harlotry, forsaking the LORD." So he went and took Gomer the daughter of Diblaim, and she conceived and bore him a son.

HOSEA 1:2–3 NASB

Why would God ask the prophet Hosea to enter into an unwholesome alliance? Because He wanted Israel to understand what it was like to observe the one to whom they were betrothed go off and play the harlot. When Israel entered into the covenant with God, the people had promised fidelity to Him. But this beloved nation had "prostituted" themselves in worship of false gods, forsaking their true God.

The book of Hosea reveals the brokenness of God's own heart as He watched Israel wander away. Now God was forced to take action against the people He loved, in order to bring them back to Him.

"And I will say to those who were not My people, 'You are My people!'" (Hosea 2:23 NASB). Lord, thank You for Your unique invitation. Amen.

EVENING

Planted Deep

Fix these words of mine in your hearts and minds; tie them as symbols on your hands and bind them on your foreheads.

DEUTERONOMY 11:18–20 NIV

Memorizing Bible verses isn't a fashionable trend in today's world, but learning key verses plants the Word of God deeply in our hearts. We draw strength and nourishment in dark times from remembering what God told us in the Bible. In times of crisis we recall God's promises of hope and comfort. In our everyday moments, repeating well-known verses reminds us that God is always with us—whether we feel like it or not.

What an awesome gift You have given me, God—the Bible! I will fix Your words in my mind and heart and carry them with me wherever I go. Amen.

DAY 9

MORNING
Prayer

Jesus often withdrew to lonely places and prayed.
Luke 5:16 NIV

Jesus is our perfect role model. If He withdrew often to pray, shouldn't we? Do we think we can continually give to others without getting replenished ourselves? Make prayer a priority. Recognize that the Lord must daily fill your cup so that you will have something to give. Set aside a specific time, a specific place. Start slow. Give Him five minutes every day. As you are faithful, your relationship with Him will grow. Over time you will crave the time spent together as He fills your cup to overflowing. Follow Jesus' example and pray!

Dear Lord, help me set aside time to pray each day. Please fill my cup so that I can share with others what You have given me. Amen.

EVENING
Abundant Blessing

From his abundance we have all received one gracious blessing after another.
John 1:16 NLT

God can give us abundant blessings because He Himself is rich with abundance. When we enter into a relationship with God, we experience His endless wealth. We become aware that we live in a stream of blessing that never ends. God's blessings will carry us all our lives—and they will carry us through death and into the world beyond.

Abundant God, take away my fears for the future, my worries that I won't have enough of what I need. Give me eyes to see the limitless blessings You have poured out into my life. Amen.

DAY 10

MORNING

Michael Stands Guard

"Now at that time Michael, the great prince who stands guard over the sons of your people, will arise. And there will be a time of distress such as never occurred since there was a nation until that time; and at that time your people, everyone who is found written in the book, will be rescued."

DANIEL 12:1 NASB

Those whose names are written in the book will be spared. God writes the names in His book. It's called the Lamb's book of life.

It is these, whose names are written in the book, who will be rescued from destruction: "These are the ones who come out of the great tribulation, and they have washed their robes and made them white in the blood of the Lamb. For this reason, they are before the throne of God; and they serve Him day and night in His temple; and He who sits on the throne will spread His tabernacle over them" (Revelation 7:14–15 NASB).

Lamb of God, who takes away sin, I want to know my name is written in Your book! Amen.

EVENING

But What about the Jews?

For if Abraham was justified by works, he has something to boast about, but not before God. For what does the Scripture say? "ABRAHAM BELIEVED GOD, AND IT WAS CREDITED TO HIM AS RIGHTEOUSNESS."

ROMANS 4:2–3 NASB

Salvation is not based on our "goodness," but rather on Christ's. For no matter how diligently we try to keep those Ten Commandments, we're going to fail. God made Abraham, the one the Jews claim as their father, a promise and he believed God.

His belief wasn't merely an intellectual assent. The supreme God of the universe, who made absolutely everything that Abraham now saw in his world, had deigned not only to speak to him, but He promised him an heir. The reason that Abraham could place his trust in God was because God kept His promises. No matter how impossible the situation looks, God always comes through.

I thank You that I worship a God whose word can be trusted. I know Jesus will always be there for me. Amen.

DAY 11

MORNING

Know the Hope

I pray that the eyes of your heart may be enlightened in order that you may know the hope to which he has called you, the riches of his glorious inheritance in his holy people, and his incomparably great power for us who believe.

EPHESIANS 1:18–19 NIV

Our heart is central when it comes to God. It's not only vital for our physical life but our spiritual life as well. It's the thinking apparatus of our soul, containing all our thoughts, passions, and desires. Why was Paul so anxious for Christians to make heartfelt spiritual progress? Because of the payoff! God freely offers us his incomparably great power along with a rich, glorious inheritance. We just have to see our need for a little surgery.

Instill in me a new heart, God. Fill it with Your unrivaled power and love. Place within it the priceless gift of Jesus' sacrifice and the promise of eternal life in heaven. Amen.

EVENING

All the King's Horses

Solomon amassed chariots and horsemen.

2 CHRONICLES 1:14 NASB

Solomon's horses were the finest that money could buy. But they weren't just for pleasure. These valiant steeds helped defend his kingdom and also provided revenue as they were sold or loaned to other kings.

Solomon's horses were stationed in strategic cities, ready to guard and protect the kingdom. And in 1 Kings 4:26 (NASB) we see that "Solomon had 40,000 stalls of horses for his chariots". He also had deputies who "brought barley and straw for the horses and swift steeds to the place where it should be, each according to his charge" (v. 28).

Long before Israel even had a king, the Lord had established certain standards for this monarch. He was not to multiply horses for himself, nor cause the people to return to Egypt to get horses (Deuteronomy 17:14–16). God didn't want the king's heart to turn away from following Him.

Had Solomon followed God's commands, his kingdom would have been assured of survival. Lord, help me to remain faithful. Amen.

DAY 12

MORNING

Smile, Smile, Smile

"I will forget my complaint, I will change my expression, and smile."

JOB 9:27 NIV

Days may not go just as planned. We are all human, and we can't always control our circumstances. What we can control, however, is our attitude. Remember each day that you are a representative of Jesus Christ. As a Christian and a woman, it is important to model a godly attitude at all times. Even a small look or smile can help show others the love of God. Just because we don't feel like having a good attitude doesn't mean we shouldn't try. God tells us to praise Him always—in good times and in bad. Let that praise show on your face today.

Lord, I know I can choose my attitude. Help me to show Your love to others by having a positive attitude each day. Let Your glory show on my face. Amen.

EVENING

Unfolding God's Tablecloth

Not a day goes by without his unfolding grace.

2 CORINTHIANS 4:16 MSG

Imagine a tablecloth folded tightly into a small square, only a few inches across. As you start to unfold it, however, you realize it's not small at all; it's actually long and wide. The more you unfold it, the longer and wider it becomes. God's blessings are like that: not a day goes by that He's not unfolding new expressions of His grace in your life. His tablecloth of blessing is longer and wider than anything you can imagine!

I praise You, God, for the grace that keeps unfolding in my life—Your love expressing itself to me in ever-wider, ever-deeper, ever-richer ways. Amen.

DAY 13

MORNING

I love the Lord *because he hears*
my voice and my prayer for mercy.

Psalm 116:1 nlt

Psalm 116:1 is a wonderful verse that should not be missed. It is neither lament nor praise, as are many of the other psalms. But it is a strong assurance of hope. Whether we are offering our praise to God or falling at His feet with our struggles, we know from these few words that God hears us. Isn't that mind blowing? The almighty God of the universe who created and assembled every particle in existence hears us when we come before Him.

I have so many reasons to love You, Lord, so many reasons to worship and praise You. How grateful I am that You hear my voice! I love You, Lord. Amen.

EVENING

Saul and Stephen

They went on stoning Stephen as he called on the Lord and said, "Lord Jesus, receive my spirit!" Then falling on his knees, he cried out with a loud voice, "Lord, do not hold this sin against them!" Having said this, he fell asleep. Saul was in hearty agreement with putting him to death. And on that day a great persecution began against the church in Jerusalem.

Acts 7:59–60; 8:1 nasb

After the stoning of Stephen, Saul entered home after home and dragged Christians off to prison. And then the powerful hand of the Lord God intervened.

"Suddenly a light from heaven flashed around him; and he fell to the ground and heard a voice saying to him, 'Saul, Saul, why are you persecuting Me?' And he said, 'Who are You, Lord?' And He said, 'I am Jesus whom you are persecuting, but get up and enter the city, and it shall be told you what you must do' " (Acts 9:3–6 nasb).

Thank You, God, for changing Saul into Paul! Amen.

DAY 14

MORNING

Renewed Hope and Faith

I am Alpha and Omega, the beginning and the end, the first and the last.

REVELATION 22:13 KJV

In the Old Testament, the Lord God called Himself a shepherd, the Alpha and Omega, the Beginning and the End, and the Almighty. He is called the First and the Last. In the New Testament, we find the same titles given to Jesus. The Bible is unique because in it God fully reveals who He is. Since Jesus is fully God, let it renew our hope and faith in our Savior. He who created all things out of nothing will re-create this world into a paradise without sin.

Jesus, I learn how to live by Your human example, and I trust in You as my God—Father, Son, and Holy Spirit—three persons, one God, one perfect You! Amen.

EVENING

Antichrist, the Ruler to Come

"In his place a despicable person will arise, on whom the honor of kingship has not been conferred, but he will come in a time of tranquility and seize the kingdom by intrigue."

DANIEL 11:21 NASB

The antichrist is a real person who will one day deviously slither onto the scene right on cue. He will appear indispensable at a time of worldwide, unsolvable chaos. His allies will be the foes of God.

His deception will be so great that people will fail to see his face of evil until "the ABOMINATION OF DESOLATION" takes place (Matthew 24:15 NASB). Three and one-half years after he comes on the scene, the antichrist will enter the rebuilt temple in Jerusalem, declare himself god, and demand worship and allegiance from the world. Jesus Himself warned the Jews about this diabolical person, telling them that when they saw him, "those who are in Judea must flee to the mountains" (Mark 13:14 NASB).

Lord, compel me with new urgency to study Your powerful Word, that I might bring it to others. Amen.

DAY 15

MORNING
A True Mother's Love

"So give Your servant an understanding heart to judge Your people to discern between good and evil. For who is able to judge this great people of Yours?"

1 KINGS 3:9 NASB

Shortly after King Solomon had asked the Lord for wisdom, two harlots brought their case before him. Each woman stated that one particular infant belonged to her.

As they stood arguing and shouting, Solomon said, " 'Get me a sword.' So they brought a sword before the king. The king said, 'Divide the living child in two, and give half to the one and half to the other' " (1 Kings 3:24–25 NASB). Solomon knew that the child's true mother would come to the baby's defense.

Within minutes the issue was resolved and the real mother held her child again. "When all Israel heard of the judgment which the king had handed down, they feared the king, for they saw that the wisdom of God was in him to administer justice" (1 Kings 3:28 NASB).

Lord, how I pray that such wisdom would be given to lawmakers. I also need Your guidance for my family. Help me remember to turn to You in my dilemmas. Amen.

EVENING
Fruit Trees

Blessed is the one. . .whose delight is in the law of the LORD. . . . That person is like a tree planted by streams of water, which yields its fruit in season and whose leaf does not wither.

PSALM 1:1–3 NIV

When God gives us the blessing of His life, we thrive. We put down strong roots. God's life flows into us, the way trees pull water up from the earth into their branches and leaves. Even though we experience all the effects of this world's time, eternity keeps us green. Our lives are rich and fruitful.

Lord, I delight in Your ways. You are an endless source of love and joy and life. You make my life fruitful, and You keep my heart evergreen, no matter how many years go by. Amen.

DAY 16

MORNING
Hope Thrives

"For I know the plans I have for you," declares the LORD, "plans to prosper you and not to harm you, plans to give you hope and a future."

JEREMIAH 29:11 NIV

Hope thrives in the fertile soil of a heart restored by a loving gesture, a compassionate embrace, or an encouraging word. It is one of God's most precious gifts. God *wants* to forgive our sins and lead us on the paths of righteousness—just as He did for the Israelites of old. He has great plans for us. That's His promise, and our blessed hope.

Father, You provide hope when all seems hopeless. Trusting in Your plans for me brings me joy. My future is in Your hands, so how can it be anything but good? Amen.

EVENING
Your Glorious Future

" 'What no eye has seen, what no ear has heard, and what no human mind has conceived'—the things God has prepared for those who love him."

1 CORINTHIANS 2:9 NIV

God's promise for our future is so magnificent we can't even comprehend it. He has great plans for each of us, but we often become paralyzed by fear. Why? Because the past seems more comfortable. Because the future is uncertain. While God doesn't give us a map of what our future is like, He does promise that it will be more than we could ever ask or imagine. What steps of faith do you need to take today to accept God's glorious future for your life?

God, Your ways are not my ways and Your plans are too wonderful for me to even comprehend. Help me to never be satisfied with less than Your glorious plans for my life. Amen.

DAY 17

MORNING
A Dance in the Fiery Furnace

"O peoples, nations and men of every language. . .you are to fall down and worship the golden image that Nebuchadnezzar the king has set up."

DANIEL 3:4–5 NASB

King Nebuchadnezzar had slipped into total egotism, making an image of gold that represented himself and then demanding worship from the people. The king's advisers used this proclamation to entrap Daniel's friends who refused to bow down to any king but the Lord. Therefore, Shadrach, Meshach, and Abednego were bound and then thrown into a fiery furnace.

But when the king looked into the furnace he saw a fourth person in the midst of the fire. "Look! I see four men loosed and walking about in the midst of the fire without harm, and the appearance of the fourth is like a son of the gods!" (Daniel 3:25 NASB). So the king ordered them out again.

Jesus was with Daniel's friends in the fire.

Lord, be my faithful God, just as You were to Daniel's friends. Keep me from harm as I walk through the fires in my own life. Amen.

EVENING
God's Forever House

Surely your goodness and unfailing love will pursue me all the days of my life, and I will live in the house of the LORD forever.

PSALM 23:6 NLT

When my mother taught me this psalm long ago, it was one of her greatest gifts to me. In every difficult moment of my life, I repeat it. Its words ran through my head as I sat by my mother's deathbed—and I knew she was already living in the Lord's house, and she always would. God's love is always chasing us, always welcoming us, even in the valley of the shadow of death.

Lord, Your love has pursued me ever since I was born—and I know it won't fail me when I reach the end of my life. You both proceed and follow me. You are in my past, in my future, and in my "now." Amen.

DAY 18

MORNING
Baptism of Repentance

"Repent, and each of you be baptized in the name of Jesus Christ for the forgiveness of your sins; and you will receive the gift of the Holy Spirit."
ACTS 2:38 NASB

Many of us were christened or baptized as infants. While this is a beautiful as well as meaningful service, such a rite does not cleanse a person from sin.

Jesus said, "The time is fulfilled, and the kingdom of God is at hand; repent and believe in the gospel" (Mark 1:15 NASB). There's no getting around His meaning here. One first has to come face-to-face with her need for salvation before she can receive this great gift. How can an infant make such a choice?

Also, it's critical to note that the Holy Spirit is given at the moment of repentance (Acts 2:38). In the Gospel of Mark, quoted above, we know for certain that God's timetable for obtaining salvation has begun.

Lord, I thank You that those who lived before Jesus came to earth were given the same Gospel message through the prophets. I thank You that You have always provided a way to salvation. Amen.

EVENING
Our Confidence

Have no fear of sudden disaster or of the ruin that overtakes the wicked, for the LORD will be at your side and will keep your foot from being snared.
PROVERBS 3:25–26 NIV

Whether our loved ones are in harm's way daily or not, all of us live in a dangerous world. And while we should take physical precautions, our best preparation is spiritual. When we spend time with God and learn about His love for us and our families, we begin to realize that He will give us His grace when we need it. He promises to never leave us, and the more we come to know His love, the more we will rest in that promise.

God, thank You that You promise Your peace to those who seek You. Help me to rest in Your love for my family and me. Amen.

DAY 19

MORNING
Confident Hope

*For you have been my hope, Sovereign LORD,
my confidence since my youth.*

PSALM 71:5 NIV

Internal clues suggest that the psalmist wrote Psalm 71 during a troublesome time. In the midst of recounting his situation, he asserted that God had been his hope and confidence since his youth. As Paul later outlined in Romans 5, his previous experiences built that hope. . . . Confidence in the Lord allows us to face disasters without fear (Proverbs 3:25–26), to live in peace (Isaiah 32:17), and to approach God (Ephesians 3:12). In an unpredictable world, we serve an unchanging God who has earned our confidence.

Father, in this ever-changing, fast-paced world, I find comfort knowing that You never change. My confidence is in You with a good outcome guaranteed. Amen.

EVENING
David's Rock, Fortress, and Deliverer

"The LORD is my rock and my fortress and my deliverer; my God, my rock, in whom I take refuge, my shield and the horn of my salvation, my stronghold and my refuge; my savior, You save me from violence."

2 SAMUEL 22:2–3 NASB

David depended on the Lord as his Rock of faith. "Let the words of my mouth and the meditation of my heart be acceptable in Your sight, O LORD, my rock and my Redeemer" (Psalm 19:14 NASB).

However, to those who choose not to believe, Christ becomes only a stumbling block. "But Israel, pursuing a law of righteousness, did not arrive at that law. Why? Because they did not pursue it by faith, but as though it were by works. They stumbled over the stumbling stone, just as it is written, 'BEHOLD, I LAY IN ZION A STONE OF STUMBLING AND A ROCK OF OFFENSE, AND HE WHO BELIEVES IN HIM WILL NOT BE DISAPPOINTED' " (Romans 9:31–33 NASB).

*I praise You only, Jesus,
my Rock of faith and Redeemer. Amen.*

DAY 20

MORNING
Redemption

Put your hope in the LORD, for with the LORD is unfailing love and with him is full redemption.

PSALM 130:7 NIV

When God permits a redemption, or "buying back," of lost years and relationships, we get a black-and-white snapshot of the colorful mural of God's redemption of us in Christ. When we one day stand in His presence, we'll understand more clearly the marvelous scope of God's redeeming love. In ways we cannot now begin to imagine. In broken relationships we thought could never be restored.

I praise You, Father, for Your awesome redemption. Thank You that I've yet to see the scope of it all. Amen.

EVENING
He Enjoys You

"The LORD your God is in your midst, a mighty one who will save; he will rejoice over you with gladness; he will quiet you by his love; he will exult over you with loud singing."

ZEPHANIAH 3:17 ESV

Zephaniah's words remind us that God is our loving parent. Our mighty Savior offers us a personal relationship, loving and rejoicing over us, His children, glad that we live and move in Him. He is the Lord of the universe, and yet He will quiet our restless hearts and minds with His tender love. He delights in our lives and celebrates our union with Him. We can rest in His affirmation and love, no matter what circumstances surround us.

Lord, help me remember that You are always with me and that You delight in me. Remind me that I am Your child and that You enjoy our relationship. Amen.

DAY 21

MORNING
A False Peace

"So My hand will be against the prophets who see false visions and utter lying divinations. They will have no place in the council of My people, nor will they be written down in the register of the house of Israel, nor will they enter the land of Israel, that you may know that I am the Lord GOD. It is definitely because they have misled My people by saying, 'Peace!' when there is no peace."

EZEKIEL 13:9–10 NASB

People today get sick of hearing modern doomsday forecasters who shout, "Turn or burn." Those living in Ezekiel's day reacted the same way. They preferred to listen to those who preached a message of peace rather than the need for repentance.

Just as Ezekiel could not remain complacent in the midst of false peace givers, those of our own day who know the truth are obligated to bring the message of repentance and salvation to others. How else will they hear and respond?

Lord, help me to share Your truth or assist others to do so, even in the midst of an apathetic and, yes, hostile world. Amen.

EVENING
Pour Out Prayers

Trust in Him at all times, you people; pour out your heart before Him; God is a refuge for us.

PSALM 62:8 NKJV

The psalmist tells us to trust the Lord at all times and to pour out our hearts to Him. There is nothing we think or feel that He does not already know. He longs for us to come to Him, spilling out our thoughts, needs, and desires. God invites us to an open-ended conversation. He made us for relationship with Him. He never tires of listening to His children. The Lord is our Helper. He is our Refuge. He knows the solutions to our problems and the wisdom we need for living each day.

Lord, remind me of Your invitation to pour out my problems to You. You are my Refuge and my Helper. Help me to trust You with every detail of my life. Amen.

DAY 22

MORNING
A New Day

GOD, treat us kindly. You're our only hope.
First thing in the morning, be there for us!
When things go bad, help us out!

ISAIAH 33:2 MSG

Every day is a new day, a new beginning, a new chance to enjoy our lives—because each day is a new day with God. We can focus on the things that matter most: worshipping Him, listening to Him, and being in His presence. No matter what happened the day before, we have a fresh start to enjoy a deeper relationship with Him. A fresh canvas, every twenty-four hours.

Before I get out of bed in the morning, let me say these words and mean them: "This is the day that the LORD has made; let us rejoice and be glad in it" (Psalm 118:24 ESV). Amen.

EVENING
Expectant Hope

In the morning, LORD, you hear my voice;
in the morning I lay my requests before
you and wait expectantly.

PSALM 5:3 NIV

God fulfills His side of the bargain to hear our prayers. Then we take off on our merry way, trying to solve our dilemma without Him. We leave His presence without lingering with the Lord to listen and to worship Him in the silence of our heart. Then later we return with more demands and *gimmes*. God knows our human hearts and understands. He gently waits to hear from us—and He delights when we keep our end of the bargain and linger in His light with hearts full of anticipation and hope.

Dear God, my hope is in You. Thank You for listening to my prayers and knowing exactly what I need. I wait patiently, expectantly, knowing that You will answer me. Amen.

DAY 23

MORNING
Always a Remnant

" 'So as I live,' declares the Lord God, 'surely, because you have defiled My sanctuary with all your detestable idols. . .therefore I will also withdraw, and My eye will have no pity and I will not spare.' "

EZEKIEL 5:11 NASB

Only the nation of Israel has managed to survive being scattered all over the globe and then come back to become a world power. How is this possible? God always preserves a remnant of His people. And it will be so until the end of time on this earth.

But how do we know this cycle will continue? Four angels stand ready to execute God's judgment on the world. And they are restrained from action until "one hundred and forty-four thousand [were] sealed from every tribe of the sons of Israel" (Revelation 7:4 NASB). Twelve thousand from each of the tribes of Israel will be marked by God's own hand.

Many plagues and judgments will take place upon the earth. However, God will bring this remnant of Israel safely through it all.

Father, I rejoice in Your Word: "And then He will send forth the angels, and will gather together His elect. . .from the farthest end of the earth to the farthest end of heaven" (Mark 13:27 NASB). Amen.

EVENING
Lasting Treasure

"Beware! Guard against every kind of greed. Life is not measured by how much you own."

LUKE 12:15 NLT

The Lord never meant for us to be satisfied with temporary treasures. Earthly possessions leave us empty because our hearts are fickle. Once we gain possession of one thing, our hearts yearn for something else. Lasting treasure can only be found in Jesus Christ. He brings contentment so that the treasure chests of our souls overflow in abundance. Hope is placed in the Lord rather than our net-worth statement. Joy is received by walking with the Lord, not by chasing some fleeting fancy. Love is showered upon us as we grab hold of real life—life that cannot be bought, but that can only be given through Jesus Christ.

Dear Lord, may I be content with what You have given me. May I not wish for more material treasures, but seek eternal wealth from You. Amen.

DAY 24

MORNING
Sweet Aroma

The heartfelt counsel of a friend
is as sweet as perfume and incense.

PROVERBS 27:9 NLT

Whether it's over coffee, dessert, or even on the phone, a cherished friend can offer the encouragement and God-directed counsel we all need from time to time. Friendships that have Christ as their center are wonderful relationships blessed by the Father. Through the timely, godly advice these friends offer, God speaks to us, showering us with comfort that is as sweet as perfume and incense. So what are you waiting for? Make a date with a friend and share the sweet aroma of Jesus!

Jesus, Your friendship means the world to me. I value the close friendships You've blessed me with, too! Thank You for the special women in my life. Show me every day how to be a blessing to them, just as they are to me. Amen.

EVENING
Ezekiel's Call

On the fifth of the month in the fifth year
of King Jehoiachin's exile, the word of
the LORD came expressly to Ezekiel
the priest, son of Buzi.

EZEKIEL 1:2–3 NASB

Sometimes God's plans are so different from what we expect to be doing with our lives that it's really astonishing.

Although he was only eighteen years old when some of the nobles and princes were captured by King Nebuchadnezzar and taken from Judah to Babylon, Ezekiel had already been groomed for the priesthood.

Ezekiel's life plan became forever altered ten years later, in 597 BC, when he was among those taken in Nebuchadnezzar's second siege against Jerusalem. Never again would he view the temple where he had hoped to serve God. However, when he was thirty years old, the Lord gave him a vision of a new temple and another Jerusalem. His call was to prophesy concerning Judah and Jerusalem, Israel's coming restoration, and the temple.

Ezekiel's visions parallel those John recorded in Revelation. These dreams showed that no matter how bleak Israel's present situation might be, their future would be bright.

Lord, as I read the prophecies of Ezekiel, fill me with expectation! Amen.

DAY 25

MORNING
Love Song of Forgiveness

"In that day," declares the LORD,
"you will call me 'my husband';
you will no longer call me
'my master.'"
HOSEA 2:16 NIV

God wants *our* hearts. He desires a relationship with us based on love and forgiveness. He enters into a covenant with us, like the marriage between Hosea and Gomer. God is the loving, faithful husband, constantly pursuing us no matter what we do or where we roam. Though it is difficult to grasp how much He loves us, we find hope in His promise. God will keep His commitment to us. His love song to us is forgiveness, and His wedding vow is unconditional love.

Thank You for loving me so fully and unconditionally, God. I find comfort knowing that as much as any man on earth could love me, You love me more. Amen.

EVENING
The New Me

Therefore, if anyone is in Christ,
the new creation has come:
The old has gone, the new is here!
2 CORINTHIANS 5:17 NIV

Are you in Christ? Is He consistently Lord of your life? Then you are a new creation. *Everything* is new. What's history is done and over—and Jesus has replaced your old with His new: new peace, new joy, new love, new strength. Since God Himself sees us as a new creation, how can we do any less? We need to choose to see ourselves as a new creation, too. And we can, through God's grace. Be glad. Give thanks. Live each day as the new creation you have become through Jesus.

Father, I'm so thankful that You are a God of grace—and I thank You that I am a new creation. Please give me the spiritual eyes to see myself as a new creation, looking past the guilt of yesterday's choices. Amen.

DAY 26

MORNING
I Lift My Eyes

I lift up my eyes to the mountains—where does my help come from? My help comes from the LORD, the Maker of heaven and earth.

PSALM 121:1–2 NIV

Adulthood is a time when decisions can be the most crucial. Challenges, failures, doubts, and fears may cloud decisions and cripple us into inaction because the end result is unknown. Career paths, relationships, and financial decisions are only some of the areas that cause concern. In all of those things, and in all of life, we shouldn't keep our eyes fixed on the end result, and we shouldn't keep our heads down and simply plow through. Instead, we must lift our eyes to the Lord. If we fix our focus on Jesus, we will see that He is prepared to lead and guide us through all of life's challenges.

Lord, I lift up my eyes to You. Please help me and guide me down the path of life. Let me never become so focused on my own goals or so busy about my work that I forget to look to You, for You are my Help. Amen.

EVENING
David Learns of Saul's Death

"Saul and Jonathan his son are dead also."

2 SAMUEL 1:4 NASB

A young Amalekite man had related to David that Saul and Jonathan were dead. Then he confessed that Saul had been impaled on his own sword and begged him to kill him. After complying with this request, the Amalekite then removed the crown from Saul's head and the bracelet that was on his arm and brought these royal ornaments to David.

First, David led Israel in a time of mourning for Saul (2 Samuel 1:11–12). Following this expression of sorrow came a time of retribution (2 Samuel 1:14–15).

David poured forth his personal anguish by writing a song for Saul and Jonathan. One verse reads, "Saul and Jonathan, beloved and pleasant in their life, and in their death they were not parted; they were swifter than eagles, they were stronger than lions" (2 Samuel 1:23 NASB).

Lord, what an example David was, as he refused to gloat over Saul's death. David turned to You and requested guidance, and You gave him a fresh call to leadership. I rejoice! Amen

DAY 27

MORNING
Unchained!

The Spirit you received does not make you slaves, so that you live in fear again; rather, the Spirit you received brought about your adoption to sonship. And by him we cry, "Abba, Father."

Romans 8:15 niv

Do you struggle with fear? Do you feel it binding you with its invisible chains? If so, then there's good news. Through Jesus, you have received the Spirit of sonship. A son (or daughter) of the most high God has nothing to fear. Knowing you've been set free is enough to make you cry, "Abba, Father!" in praise. Today, acknowledge your fears to the Lord. He will loose your chains and set you free.

Lord, thank You that You are the great chain breaker! I don't have to live in fear. I am Your child, Your daughter, and You are my Daddy God! Amen.

EVENING
Always Thinking of You

What is man that You are mindful of him, and the son of man that You visit him?

Psalm 8:4 nkjv

Have you ever wondered what God thinks about? *You* are always on His mind. In all you think and do, He considers you and makes intercession for you. He knows the thoughts and intents of your heart. He understands you like no other person can. He knows your strengths and weaknesses, your darkest fears and highest hopes. He's constantly aware of your feelings and how you interact with or without Him each day. God is always with you, waiting for you to remember Him—to call on Him for help, for friendship, for anything you need.

Lord, help me to remember You as I go throughout my day. I want to include You in my life and always be thinking of You, too. Amen.

DAY 28

MORNING

Only Believe

While Jesus was still speaking, some people came from the house of Jairus, the synagogue leader. "Your daughter is dead," they said. "Why bother the teacher anymore?"

MARK 5:35 NIV

When the odds are stacked against us and circumstances riddle us with hopelessness, our tendency is to manage our burdens as well as we can and stop praying. Doubtful, we wonder: Can God restore an unhappy marriage? Can He heal cancer? Can He deliver me from financial ruin? *Will* He? Jesus knows the way out. Only believe; have faith in Him and never lose hope.

Jesus my hope is in You. Even when it appears that all hope is lost, I will hold on to the hope that You will deliver me. Amen.

EVENING

People Pleaser versus God Pleaser

We are not trying to please people but God, who tests our hearts.

1 THESSALONIANS 2:4 NIV

When we allow ourselves to be real before God, it doesn't matter what others think. If the God of the universe has accepted us, then who cares about someone else's opinion? It is impossible to please both God and man. We must make a choice. Man looks at the outward appearance, but God looks at the heart. Align your heart with His. Let go of impression management that focuses on outward appearance. Receive God's unconditional love, and enjoy the freedom to be yourself before Him!

Dear Lord, may I live for You alone. Help me transition from a people pleaser to a God pleaser. Amen.

DAY 29

MORNING

James, Bond Servant of God

James, a bond-servant of God and of the Lord Jesus Christ, to the twelve tribes who are dispersed abroad: Greetings. Consider it all joy, my brethren, when you encounter various trials, knowing that the testing of your faith produces endurance.

JAMES 1:1–3 NASB

James had taken Christ for granted. Jesus' sinless life had been lived out before him and yet James had not responded to the invitation for salvation.

James finally understood his position in Christ, that of a servant. He had successfully journeyed from a place of hindering the Gospel, unaware of the time constraints Christ had with the Father, to a place of understanding the true source of wisdom (John 7:1–5). The apostle Paul relates that James, along with Peter and John, became one of the chief leaders of the church in Jerusalem (Galatians 2:9).

How grateful I am, Lord, that You're not willing that any should perish, especially those of Your own family. Amen.

EVENING

He Will Send Help

"The waves of death swirled about me; the torrents of destruction overwhelmed me. . . . In my distress I called to the LORD. . . . From his temple he heard my voice; my cry came to his ears."

2 SAMUEL 22:5, 7 NIV

God never asked us to do life alone. When the waves of death swirl around us, and the pounding rain of destruction threatens to overwhelm us, we can cry out to our heavenly Father, knowing that He will not let us drown. He will hear our voice, and He will send help. So, next time you feel that you can't put one foot in front of the other, ask God to send you His strength and energy. He will help you to live out your purpose in this chaotic world.

Lord, thank You for strengthening me when the "dailyness" of life, and its various trials, threatens to overwhelm me. Amen.

DAY 30

MORNING

His Healing Abundance

"Behold, I will bring it health and healing; I will heal them and reveal to them the abundance of peace and truth."

JEREMIAH 33:6 NKJV

If we confess our sins to God, He will bring relief to our souls. When we're distressed, we have Jesus, the Prince of Peace, to give us peace. When our emotions threaten to overwhelm us, we can implore Jehovah-Rapha—the God who Heals—to calm our anxious hearts. When we're physically sick, we can cry out to Jesus, our Great Physician. Whether our problems affect us physically, spiritually, mentally, or emotionally, we can trust that God will come to us and bring us healing. And beyond our temporal lives, we can look forward with hope to our heavenly lives. There we will be healthy, whole, and alive—forever.

Jehovah-Rapha, thank You for healing me. Help me do my part to seek health and the abundance of peace and truth You provide. Amen.

EVENING

Jonathan, Faithful to the End

Now the Philistines were fighting against Israel, and the men of Israel fled from before the Philistines and fell slain on Mount Gilboa. The Philistines overtook Saul and his sons; and the Philistines killed Jonathan and Abinadab and Malchi-shua the sons of Saul.

1 SAMUEL 31:1–2 NASB

Who has faithfully stood beside you through life's triumphs and tragedies? For David, this person was Jonathan.

Jonathan walked a tightrope, remaining faithful to God, to Saul, his father, and to David. Considering Saul's obsession with killing David, this task took on monstrous proportions.

Father, help me to be a faithful, loving, and unforgettable friend. Amen.

DAY 31

MORNING

Seeking God's Plan

For we are His workmanship,
created in Christ Jesus for good works,
which God prepared beforehand
that we should walk in them.

EPHESIANS 2:10 NKJV

How can you know God's plans for your life? First, you should meet with Him in prayer each day and seek His will. Studying the Bible is also important. Often, God speaks to us directly through His Word (Psalm 119:105). Finally, you must have faith that God *will* work out His plan for your life and that His plan is good. Jeremiah 29:11 (NIV) says, " 'For I know the plans I have for you,' declares the LORD, 'plans to prosper you and not to harm you, plans to give you hope and a future.' " Are you living in Christ's example and seeking God's plan for your life?

Father, what is Your plan for me? I know that it is good. Reveal it to me, Lord. Speak to me through prayer and Your Word. Amen.

EVENING

Shake It Up!

The LORD had said to Abram, "Leave your
native country, your relatives, and your
father's family, and go to the land that
I will show you. . . . I will bless you. . .
and you will be a blessing to others."

GENESIS 12:1–2 NLT

In God's wisdom, He likes to shake us up a little, stretch us out of our comfort zone, push us out on a limb. Yet we resist the change, cling to what's known, and try to change His mind with fat, sloppy tears. Are you facing a big change? God wants us to be willing to embrace change that He brings into our lives. Even unbidden change. You may feel as if you're out on a limb, but don't forget that God is the tree trunk. He's not going to let you fall.

Holy, loving Father, in every area of my life, teach me to trust You more deeply. Amen.

DAY 32

MORNING
Release the Music Within

Those who are wise will find a time and a way to do what is right.

ECCLESIASTES 8:5 NLT

It has been said that many people go to their graves with their music still in them. Do you carry a song within your heart, waiting to be heard?

Whether we are eight or eighty, it is never too late to surrender our hopes and dreams to God. A wise woman trusts that God will help her find the time and manner in which to use her talents for His glory as she seeks His direction. Let the music begin.

Dear Lord, my music is fading against the constant beat of a busy pace. I surrender my gifts to You and pray for the time and manner in which I can use those gifts to touch my world. Amen.

EVENING
Crown of Mockery

Pilate then took Jesus and scourged Him. And the soldiers twisted together a crown of thorns and put it on His head, and put a purple robe on Him; and they began to come up to Him and say, "Hail, King of the Jews!" and to give Him slaps in the face.

JOHN 19:1–3 NASB

They pretended to shower Him with all the outward trappings of royalty. But this homage was one of cruel mockery. The thorns were razor-sharp briars about an inch and a half long. We can only imagine the taunting voices of these men, triumphant sneers spreading across their faces as they pressed this crown into Christ's head until blood ran down His face.

Lord, on my behalf You withstood extreme torture. Am I adding new but invisible wounds each time I refuse to crown You King of my own life? Amen.

DAY 33

MORNING
The Perfect Reflection

"Give careful thought to your ways."
HAGGAI 1:7 NIV

As we give careful thought to our ways, we should first look back to where we have come from and reflect on God's work in our lives. We are on a journey. Sometimes the road is difficult; sometimes the road is easy. We must consider where we were when God found us and where we are now through His grace. Even more importantly, we must think about the ways our present actions, habits, and attitudes toward God reflect our lives as Christians. Only when we are able honestly to assess our lives in Christ can we call on His name to help perfect our reflection.

Dear Lord, help me to look honestly at the ways I live and make changes where necessary. Amen.

EVENING
Good News

These are evil times, so make every minute count.
EPHESIANS 5:16 CEV

While it may seem tempting to crawl back into bed and hide beneath the covers of denial instead of facing the harsh reality of the world, God has a different idea. Every minute counts because we, as believers, carry an eternal hope that the world needs to hear. Bad things do happen to good people, but ever present in the trials of this world is a loving God who cares deeply for His children. Who will you share this good news with today?

Dear God, how should I share the good news with those who have suffered at the hand of evil? Show me ways to encourage them that You love and care for them. Amen.

DAY 34

MORNING
Joel and a Plague of Locusts

What the gnawing locust has left,
the swarming locust has eaten. . .
and what the creeping locust has left,
the stripping locust has eaten.

JOEL 1:4 NASB

Joel's words could provide a great plotline for a sci-fi thriller. Other catastrophes would follow.

The apostle Peter explained Pentecost in light of Joel's prophecy: "This is what was spoken of through the prophet Joel: 'AND IT SHALL BE IN THE LAST DAYS,' God says, 'THAT I WILL POUR FORTH OF MY SPIRIT. . . and they shall prophesy. AND I WILL GRANT WONDERS IN THE SKY ABOVE AND SIGNS ON THE EARTH BELOW. . .BEFORE THE GREAT AND GLORIOUS DAY OF THE LORD SHALL COME. AND IT SHALL BE THAT EVERYONE WHO CALLS ON THE NAME OF THE LORD WILL BE SAVED' " (Acts 2:16–21 NASB).

The information contained in the book of Joel is referred to as eschatology, or a study of the end times, and it parallels other passages in scripture. When Jesus spoke to His disciples, He too quoted this prophetic passage, providing additional clarity.

Lord, I rejoice in Your Word. Amen.

EVENING
Confidence

For I know that my redeemer liveth,
and that he shall stand at the latter day
upon the earth: and though after
my skin worms destroy this body,
yet in my flesh shall I see God.

JOB 19:25–26 KJV

Although we experience various difficulties throughout life, we can still look forward to the blessed future we have. No matter what our struggles are, our Lord controls. Job had no idea what the purpose of his trial was, but he faced his troubles with confidence, knowing that ultimately he would emerge victorious. Too many times we view our own situations with self-pity rather than considering God's strength and trusting that His plan is perfect. What peace God offers when we finally cast our cares on Him and with great conviction declare, "I know that my redeemer liveth!"

Oh great Redeemer, in You I have confidence
even when I don't understand life's trials.
Please help me to live victoriously. Amen.

DAY 35

MORNING
A Promise of Unity

"At that time they shall call Jerusalem 'The Throne of the LORD,' and all the nations will be gathered to it."

JEREMIAH 3:17 NASB

In the year 586 BC, Solomon's temple was utterly destroyed. At the same time, the ark of the covenant was lost. God's glory had departed from Israel. For this reason, God's confirmation that Jerusalem would once again become the center for worship became critically important. During King Herod's reign the temple was rebuilt, fulfilling part of this prophecy. And when Jesus Christ came, it had once again become the center of worship.

True peace will reign in Israel when Christ returns again to earth (Matthew 24:29–39). Lord, help me wait! Amen.

EVENING
Simply Silly

A cheerful disposition is good for your health.

PROVERBS 17:22 MSG

Imagine the effect we could have on our world today if our countenance reflected the joy of the Lord all the time: at work, at home, at play. Jesus said, "I have told you this so that my joy may be in you and that your joy may be complete" (John 15:11 NIV). Is your cup of joy full? Have you laughed today? Not a small smile, but laughter. Maybe it's time we looked for something to laugh about and tasted joy. Jesus suggested it.

Lord, help me find joy this day. Let me laugh and give praises to the King. Amen.

DAY 36

MORNING
Abiding Peace

He himself is our peace.

EPHESIANS 2:14 NIV

Regardless of life's circumstances, hope and peace are available if Jesus is there. You do not have to succumb to getting buffeted and beaten by the storms of life. Seek refuge in the center of the storm. Run to the arms of Jesus, the Prince of Peace. Let Him wipe your tears and calm your fears. Like the eye of the hurricane, His presence brings peace and calmness. Move yourself closer. Desire to be in His presence. For He Himself is your peace. As you abide in His presence, peace will envelop you. The raging around you may not subside, but the churning of your heart will. You will find rest for your soul.

Dear Lord, thank You for being our peace in the midst of life's fiercest storms. Amen.

EVENING
What Constitutes Dynamic Faith?

You see that faith was working with his works, and as a result of the works, faith was perfected; and the Scripture was fulfilled which says, "AND ABRAHAM BELIEVED GOD, AND IT WAS RECKONED TO HIM AS RIGHTEOUSNESS," and he was called the friend of God.

JAMES 2:22–23 NASB

Abraham's faith was evident by his actions. The very foundation of Abraham's faith was the Word of God. And no matter what God required of him, Abraham obeyed God. Therefore, all of his actions were born out of the call God had on his life.

"So faith comes from hearing, and hearing by the word of Christ" (Romans 10:17 NASB). This kind of dynamic faith involves the whole person. If someone professes his or her belief in God and yet does not take the Word to others, and refuses to attend a weekly Bible study, and can't be bothered to help those in obvious need, it makes me wonder whether that faith is real. For there has to be some outward manifestation of the change that takes place inwardly.

Lord, show me by Your Word how to reflect dynamic faith. Amen.

DAY 37

MORNING
Behind the Scenes

Now faith is confidence in what we hope for and assurance about what we do not see.

HEBREWS 11:1 NIV

Be encouraged today that no matter what takes place in the natural—what you see with your eyes—it doesn't have to be the final outcome of your situation. If you've asked God for something, then you can trust that He is working out all the details behind the scenes. What you see right now, how you feel, is not a picture of what your faith is producing. Your faith is active, and God is busy working to make all things come together and benefit you.

Heavenly Father, what I see today is not what I'm going to get. Thank You for working behind the scenes to bring about the very best for my life. Amen.

EVENING
Anxious Anticipations

I am not saying this because I am in need, for I have learned to be content whatever the circumstances.

PHILIPPIANS 4:11 NIV

Have you ever been so eager for the future that you forgot to be thankful for the present day?

Humans have a tendency to complain about the problems and irritations of life. It's much less natural to appreciate the good things we have—until they're gone. While it's fine to look forward to the future, let's remember to reflect on all of *today's* blessings—the large and the small—and appreciate all that we do have.

Thank You, Lord, for the beauty of today. Please remind me when I become preoccupied with the future and forget to enjoy the present. Amen.

DAY 38

MORNING
Refreshing Gift

For we have great joy and consolation in your love, because the hearts of the saints have been refreshed by you, brother.

PHILEMON 1:7 NKJV

Jesus always took the time for those who reached out to Him. In a crowd of people, He stopped to help a woman who touched Him. His quiet love extended to everyone who asked, whether verbally or with unspoken need. God brings people into our path who need our encouragement. We must consider those around us. Smile and thank the waiter, the cashier, the people who help in small ways. Cheering others can have the effect of an energizing drink of water so that they will be able to finish the race with a smile.

Jesus, thank You for being an example of how to encourage and refresh others. Help me to see their need and to be willing to reach out. Amen.

EVENING
Focus Time

In the morning, LORD, you hear my voice; in the morning I lay my requests before you and wait expectantly.

PSALM 5:3 NIV

What is the first thing you do each morning? Many of us hit the ground running, armed with to-do lists a mile long. While it doesn't ensure perfection, setting aside a short time each morning to focus on the Father and the day ahead can help prepare us to live more intentionally. During this time we, like Jesus, gain clarity, so that we can invest our lives in the things that truly matter.

Father, help me to take time each morning to focus on You and the day ahead. Align my priorities so that the things I do will be the things You want me to do. Amen.

DAY 39

MORNING

Infinite and Personal

Am I a God at hand, saith the LORD, and not a God afar off? . . . Do not I fill heaven and earth?

JEREMIAH 23:23–24 KJV

God says that He is both close at hand and over all there is. Whether your day is crumbling around you or is the best day you have ever had, do you see God in it? If the "sky is falling" or the sun is shining, do you still recognize the One who orders all the planets and all your days? Whether we see Him or not, God tells us He is there. And He's here, too—in the good times and bad.

Lord, empower me to trust You when it's hard to remember that You are near. And help me to live thankfully when times are good. Amen.

EVENING

Question the Witnesses

The high priest then questioned Jesus about His disciples, and about His teaching. Jesus answered him, "I have spoken openly to the world; I always taught in synagogues and in the temple, where all the Jews come together; and I spoke nothing in secret. Why do you question Me? Question those who have heard what I spoke to them; they know what I said."

JOHN 18:19–21 NASB

Jesus Christ didn't come for a few souls; He presented the Gospel message openly for all to hear. Teaching in the Jewish temple, which was frequented not only by those who sought knowledge but also those in search of an explanation of the truth, Jesus provided both.

As we go out into a world that is hostile to the Gospel message, there are those who listen to our testimony and then draw near to its refreshing waters. Others vow that nothing will force them to make a life change. And then there are those who deny the metamorphosis has even taken place. Their hearts are closed to receive the truth.

Lord, break down my walls of stubbornness that prevent me from hearing, seeing, and rallying to Your message. Amen.

DAY 40

MORNING
The Breath of God

Every part of Scripture is God-breathed and useful one way or another—showing us truth, exposing our rebellion, correcting our mistakes, training us to live God's way.

2 TIMOTHY 3:16 MSG

Do you spend time in God's Word each day? Do you let the breath of God wash over you and comfort you? Are you allowing His Word to penetrate your heart and show you where you've been wrong? If not, you are missing out on one of the most important ways that God chooses to communicate with us today. Ask the Lord for the desire to spend more time in His Word. Don't feel you have the time? Consider purchasing the Bible on CD, and listen to God's Word as you drive to work or school.

Father, Your Word is so important to me. Please give me the desire to spend more time in the Bible each day. Amen.

EVENING
Chosen

"Before I formed you in the womb I knew you [and approved of you as My chosen instrument], and before you were born I consecrated you."

JEREMIAH 1:5 AMP

God said that before He formed Jeremiah in his mother's womb, He knew him. God separated him from everyone else to perform a specific task, and He consecrated him for that purpose. We can be sure that if God did that for Jeremiah, He did it for each one of us. Nothing about us or our circumstances surprises God. He knew about everything before we were born. And He ordained that we should walk in those ways because we are uniquely qualified by Him to do so. What an awesome God we serve!

Father, the thought that You chose me before the foundation of the world and set me apart for a specific calling is humbling. You are so good. May I go forward with a renewed purpose in life. Amen.

DAY 41

MORNING

Releasing Your Hold on Anxiety

Search me, God, and know my heart;
test me and know my anxious thoughts.
See if there is any offensive way in me,
and lead me in the way everlasting.

PSALM 139:23–24 NIV

What is it that weighs you down? Financial issues? An unhealthy relationship? Your busy schedule? Surrender these misgivings to a God who wants to take them from you. Ask Him to search your heart for any and all anxieties, for any and all signs that you have not truly put your trust in Him. Find the trouble spots in your life to which you direct most of your thoughts and energy, and then hand these troubles over to the One who can truly address them. Realize that you are only human, and that God is infinitely more capable of balancing your cares than you are.

Lord, take from me my anxieties, big and small. May I remember to give these to You daily so that I will not find myself distracted by the things of this world. Amen.

EVENING

God in the Details

"When we heard of it, our hearts melted and
everyone's courage failed because of you,
for the LORD your God is God in heaven
above and on the earth below."

JOSHUA 2:11 NIV

Sometimes—when our lives seem to be under siege from the demands of work, bills, family, whatever—finding the work of God amid the strife can be difficult. Even though we acknowledge His power, we may overlook the gentle touches, the small ways in which He makes every day a little easier. Just as the Lord cares for the tiniest bird (Matthew 10:29–31), so He seeks to be a part of every detail in your life. Look for Him there.

Father God, I know You are by my side every day, good or bad, and that You love and care for me. Help me to see Your work in my life and in the lives of my friends and family. Amen.

DAY 42

MORNING
Praying with Confidence

For we do not have a high priest who is unable to empathize with our weaknesses, but we have one who has been tempted in every way, just as we are—yet he did not sin. Let us then approach God's throne of grace with confidence, so that we may receive mercy and find grace to help us in our time of need.

HEBREWS 4:15–16 NIV

There is no one like a sister. A sister is someone who "gets you." But even a sister's love cannot compare to Christ's love. However you're struggling, help is available through Jesus. Our Savior walked on this earth for thirty-three years. He was fully God *and* fully man. He got dirt under His fingernails. He felt hunger. He knew weakness. He was tempted. He felt tired. He "gets it." Go boldly before the throne of grace as a daughter of God. Pray in Jesus' name for an outpouring of His grace and mercy in your life.

Father, I ask You boldly in the name of Christ to help me. My hope is in You alone. Amen.

EVENING
Sealed by the Holy Spirit

In Him, you also, after listening to the message of truth, the gospel of your salvation—having also believed, you were sealed in Him with the Holy Spirit of promise, who is given as a pledge of our inheritance, with a view to the redemption of God's own possession, to the praise of His glory.

EPHESIANS 1:13–14 NASB

The apostle Paul penned the letter to the Ephesians between AD 60 and 62 while he was a prisoner in Rome. Ephesus, the fourth largest city in the Roman Empire, was steeped in idolatrous worship.

Into this spiritual darkness God sent Paul. The Lord desired to use this cultural setting to call out for Himself a church so that He could shine the light of truth upon this evil place.

Lord, there are dark places today that cry out for Your redeeming light. Lead me to share Your Word where it is needed desperately. Amen.

DAY 43

MORNING

He Has Chosen You

Therefore, as God's chosen people, holy and dearly loved, clothe yourselves with compassion, kindness, humility, gentleness and patience.

COLOSSIANS 3:12 NIV

No matter how athletic, beautiful, popular, or smart you are, you've probably experienced a time when you were chosen last or overlooked entirely. Being left out is a big disappointment of life on earth. The good news is that this disappointment isn't part of God's kingdom. Even when others forget about us, God doesn't. He has handpicked His beloved children now and forever. The truth is that Jesus died for *everyone*—every man, woman, and child who has ever and will ever live. The Father chooses us all. All we have to do is grab a glove and join the team.

Father, thanks for choosing me. I don't deserve it, but You call me Your beloved child. Help me to remember others who may feel overlooked or unloved. Let Your love for them shine through me. Amen.

EVENING

Practicality versus Passion

Leaving her water jar, the woman went back to the town and said to the people, "Come, see a man who told me everything I ever did. Could this be the Messiah?"

JOHN 4:28–29 NIV

Practicality gave way to passion the day the woman at the well abandoned her task, laid down her jar, and ran into town. Everything changed the day she met a man at the well and He asked her for a drink of water. Although they had never met before, He told her everything she had ever done, and He offered her living water that would never run dry. Do you live with such passion, or do you cling to your water jar? Has an encounter with Christ made an impact that cannot be denied in your life?

Lord, help me to lay down anything that stifles my passion for sharing the good news with others. Amen.

DAY 44

MORNING
Power Packed and Personal

Thou hast magnified thy word above all thy name.

PSALM 138:2 KJV

Of all the wonderful graces and gifts God has given humankind, there's nothing that touches the power and truth of that all-time bestseller, the Bible. The Bible provides healing, hope, and direction (Psalm 107:20; 119:74, 133). If we want wisdom and the desire to do things the right way, God's Word equips us (2 Timothy 3:16–17). From the scriptures we can make sense of a confusing world. We can get a hold on real truth. God has given us His eternal Word to know Him and to know ourselves better.

Teach me not only to read, but also to obey Your living, powerful Word every day, Lord God. Amen.

EVENING
Fences

"If you keep My commandments, you will abide in My love, just as I have kept My Father's commandments and abide in His love."

JOHN 15:10 NKJV

God's commandments are much like the pasture fence. Sin is on the other side. His laws exist to keep us in fellowship with Him and to keep us out of things that are harmful to us that can lead to bondage. We abide in the loving presence of our heavenly Father by staying within the boundaries He has set up for our own good. He has promised to care for us and to do the things needful for us. His love for us is unconditional, even when we jump the fence into sin. But by staying inside the boundaries, we enjoy intimacy with Him.

Father, help me to obey Your commandments that are given for my good. Thank You for Your love for me. Amen.

DAY 45

MORNING

Now the word of the LORD came to me saying, "Before I formed you in the womb I knew you, and before you were born I consecrated you; I have appointed you a prophet to the nations."

JEREMIAH 1:4–5 NASB

Jeremiah prophesied prior to and during Babylon's three sieges of Judah. Revival came when the Word of the Lord was found in the house of God and Josiah, one of the last kings of Judah, called the people to repentance. However, following this great time of worship, Israel's disobedience once again set in, bringing upon them yet again God's heavy hand of judgment. And Jeremiah the prophet wept.

Lord, I pray for answers to the dilemmas that plague our society. Not knowing whom You have called for special service, let me respect and revere each life with hope, anticipation, and gratitude. Amen.

EVENING

Marvelous Plans

LORD, you are my God; I will exalt you and praise your name, for in perfect faithfulness you have done wonderful things, things planned long ago.

ISAIAH 25:1 NIV

God has a "promised land" for us all—a marvelous plan for our lives. Recount and record His faithfulness in your life in the past, because God has already demonstrated His marvelous plans to you in so many ways. Then prayerfully anticipate the future journey with Him. Keep a record of God's marvelous plans in a journal as He unfolds them day by day. You will find God to be faithful in the smallest aspects of your life and oh so worthy of your trust.

Oh Lord, help me to recount Your faithfulness, record Your faithfulness, and trust Your faithfulness in the future. For You are my God, and You have done marvelous things, planned long ago. Amen.

MORNING

"The Lord will fight for you;
you need only to be still."
Exodus 14:14 NIV

Moses commanded the Israelites to stop panicking and stand still. Then God held back the waters of the Red Sea, and the Israelites were able to walk across on dry ground! When the Egyptians tried to follow them, the waters rushed in and drowned them all. Sometimes when we stress and panic, we rack our brains trying to figure out solutions to our problems; and instead of standing still and praying to God, we become even more panicked. Moses' words still apply to us today. When we face our fears we should be still, trusting in God and relying on Him to bring us through the struggle.

Dear Lord, please teach me to be still and to trust in You. Thank You for Your constant faithfulness. Amen.

EVENING

Christ Is Risen Today!

"He isn't here! He is risen from the dead!"
Luke 24:6 NLT

The power God used to raise Christ from the dead is the same power we have available to us each day to live according to God's will here on earth. What happened on Easter gives us hope for today and for all eternity. If you haven't accepted Jesus Christ as your personal Savior, take the time right now and start your new life in Christ.

Dear Jesus, thank You for dying on the cross for me and taking away all my sin. You are alive and well, and I praise You today for all You are and all You have done. Amen.

DAY 47

MORNING

Wives, be subject to your own husbands, as to the Lord. For the husband is the head of the wife, as Christ also is the head of the church, He Himself being the Savior of the body. But as the church is subject to Christ, so also the wives ought to be to their husbands in everything.

EPHESIANS 5:22–24 NASB

It's critical to remember that God intended marriage to be a partnership. We need to build one another up. "So husbands ought also to love their own wives as their own bodies" (Ephesians 5:28). If men truly loved their wives to this degree, there probably isn't a woman alive who'd run from it.

So what can we do to make things better? Pray. . .every single day. But especially when things are out of kilter. Know that God is vitally interested in the success of your marriage, and act accordingly.

Lord, I know that only You are capable of loving perfectly. So the next time my marriage feels like a 90/10 proposition, please remind me that You're giving 100 percent. Amen.

EVENING

Life Preservers

My comfort in my suffering is this: Your promise preserves my life.

PSALM 119:50 NIV

In the difficulties of life, God is our life preserver. When we are battered by the waves of trouble, we can expect God to understand and to comfort us in our distress. His Word, like a buoyant life preserver, holds us up in the bad times. But the life preserver only works if you put it on *before* your boat sinks. God will surround you with His love and protection—even if you're unconscious of His presence. He promises to keep our heads above water in the storms of living.

Preserving God, I cling to You as my life preserver. Keep my head above the turbulent waters so I don't drown. Bring me safely to the shore. Amen.

DAY 48

MORNING
Why Not Me?

God gave Paul the power to perform unusual miracles. When handkerchiefs or aprons that had merely touched his skin were placed on sick people, they were healed.

ACTS 19:11–12 NLT

When his fellow missionary, Trophimus, fell sick, Paul was given no miracle to help him. When Timothy complained of frequent stomach problems, Paul had no miracle-working handkerchief for Timothy's misery. Paul himself suffered from an incurable ailment (2 Corinthians 12:7), yet he was willing to leave it with God. We, too, may be clueless as to why God miraculously heals some and not others. Like Paul, we must trust God when there's no miracle. Can we be as resilient as Job, who said, "Though he slay me, yet will I trust in him" (Job 13:15 KJV)? We can—waiting for the day when health problems and bad accidents and death cease forever (Revelation 21:4).

When healing doesn't come, Lord Jesus, give me grace to trust You more. Still I choose hope. Amen.

EVENING
A Shadow of the Past

"Only Rahab the prostitute and all who are with her in her house shall be spared, because she hid the spies we sent."

JOSHUA 6:17 NIV

Rahab wasn't trapped by her past. It didn't hold her back. She was used by God. Her name has come down to us centuries later because of her bold faith. We all have to deal with a past. But God is able to bring good from a painful past. By the grace and power of God we can make choices in the present that can affect our future. There is transforming power with God. We have hope, no matter what lies behind us.

Holy Spirit, You are always at work. Don't ever stop! Show me a new way, Lord. Help me to make healthier choices for myself and my family. Thank You for Your renewing presence in my life. Amen.

DAY 49

MORNING
The Blues

Why, my soul, are you downcast?
Why so disturbed within me? Put your
hope in God, for I will yet praise
him, my Savior and my God.

PSALM 42:11 NIV

Everyone experiences times when frustrations seem to outweigh joy, but as Christians, we have an unending source of encouragement in God. *That's great,* you may think, *but how am I supposed to tap into that joy?* First, pray. Ask God to unburden your spirit. Share your stress, frustrations, and worries with Him. Don't hold back; He can take it. Make a list of the blessings in your life and thank the Provider of those blessings. Choose to not focus on yourself; instead, praise Him for being Him. Soon you'll feel true, holy refreshment—the freedom God wants you to live out every day.

Rejuvenate my spirit, Lord! You alone can take away the burden I feel. You are my hope and my Redeemer forever. Amen.

EVENING
Peter, an Apostle of Jesus Christ

Peter, an apostle of Jesus Christ, to those
who reside as aliens. . .who are chosen
according to the foreknowledge of God the
Father, by the sanctifying work of the Spirit,
to obey Jesus Christ and be sprinkled with
His blood: May grace and peace be
yours in the fullest measure.

1 PETER 1:1–2 NASB

The only true "superhero" is Jesus Christ, who will never fail us. He alone was fully God and fully man. Therefore, He alone possesses perfectly all the characteristics we most admire. For He remains faithful, just, loving, omnipotent, and eternal.

Peter never seeks position or power. Instead, he humbly admonishes his hearers to "obey Christ," on whom Peter also depends.

The name Peter, or petra, *means "rock." Help my faith, Lord, to be rock solid and unwavering. Amen.*

DAY 50

MORNING
Be Still

Thou wilt keep him in perfect peace,
whose mind is stayed on thee:
because he trusteth in thee.

Isaiah 26:3 KJV

Longing for His children to know His peace, God sent prophets like Isaiah to stir up faith, repentance, and comfort in the hearts of the "chosen people." God's message is just as applicable today as it was back then. By keeping our minds fixed on Him, we can have perfect, abiding peace even in the midst of a crazy world. The path to peace is not easy, but it is simple: Focus on God. As we meditate on His promises and His faithfulness, He gets bigger, while our problems get smaller.

God, when I focus on the world, my mind and heart feel anxious. Help me to keep my mind on You, so that I can have hope and peace. Amen.

EVENING
Setting Priorities

Cause me to hear Your lovingkindness in the morning, for in You do I trust; cause me to know the way in which I should walk, for I lift up my soul to You.

Psalm 143:8 NKJV

Twenty-four hours. That's what we all get in a day. Though we often think we don't have time for all we want to do, our Creator deemed twenty-four-hour days sufficient. How do we decide what to devote ourselves to? The wisdom of the psalmist tells us to begin the day by asking to hear the loving voice of the One who made us. We can lay our choices, problems, and conflicts before Him in prayer. He will show us which way to go. Psalm 118:7 (NIV) says, "The LORD is with me; he is my helper." Hold up that full plate of your life to Him, and allow Him to decide what to keep and what to let go.

Lord, make me willing to surrender my choices and activities to You. Cause me to desire the things You want me to do. Amen.

DAY 51

MORNING
Charm Bracelet

But the fruit of the Spirit is love, joy, peace, patience, kindness, goodness, faithfulness, gentleness, self-control; against such things there is no law.

GALATIANS 5:22–23 NASB

A charm bracelet is a beautiful way to commemorate milestones or special events. Consider your spiritual charm bracelet. If you had a charm to represent your growth in each of the traits from Galatians 5, how many would you feel comfortable attaching to your bracelet in representation of that achievement? Ask your Father which areas in your Christian walk need the most growth. Do you need to develop those traits more before you feel comfortable donning your bracelet?

Lord, please show me which milestones of Christian living I need to focus on in order to have the full markings of the Holy Spirit in my life. Please help me to grow into the Christian woman You call me to be. Amen.

EVENING
Rock Solid

"Therefore everyone who hears these words of mine and puts them into practice is like a wise man who built his house on the rock. The rain came down, the streams rose, and the winds blew and beat against that house; yet it did not fall, because it had its foundation on the rock."

MATTHEW 7:24–25 NIV

Prepare for tomorrow's storms by laying a solid foundation today. Rain and wind are guaranteed to come. It is only a matter of time. We need to be ready. When our foundation is the Rock, Jesus Christ, we will find ourselves still standing when the storm has passed. Rain will come. Winds will blow and beat hard against us. Yet, when our hope is in the Lord, we will not be destroyed. We will remain steadfast because our feet have been firmly planted. Stand upon the Rock today so that your tomorrows will be secure.

Dear Lord, help me build my foundation today upon You so I can remain steadfast in the storms of life. Amen.

DAY 52

MORNING
God Cares for You

"Consider how the wild flowers grow. They do not labor or spin. Yet I tell you, not even Solomon in all his splendor was dressed like one of these. If that is how God clothes the grass of the field, which is here today, and tomorrow is thrown into the fire, how much more will he clothe you—you of little faith!"

LUKE 12:27–28 NIV

If God makes the flowers, each type unique and beautiful, and if He sends the rain and sun to meet their needs, will He not care for you as well? He made you. What the Father makes, He loves. And that which He loves, He cares for. We were made in His image. Humans are dearer to God than any of His other creations. Rest in Him. Trust Him. Just as He cares for the birds of the air and the flowers of the meadows, God is in the business of taking care of His sons and daughters. Let Him take care of you.

Father, I am amazed by Your creation. Remind me that I am Your treasured child. Take care of me today as only You can do. Amen.

EVENING
Board God's Boat

Then, because so many people were coming and going that they did not even have a chance to eat, he said to them, "Come with me by yourselves to a quiet place and get some rest."

MARK 6:31 NIV

The disciples ministered tirelessly—so much so, they had little time to eat. The Lord noticed that they had neglected to take time for themselves. Sensitive to their needs, the Savior instructed them to retreat by boat with Him to a solitary place of rest. Often we allow the hectic pace of daily life to drain us physically and spiritually, and in the process, we deny ourselves time alone to pray and read God's Word. Meanwhile, God patiently waits. So perhaps it's time to board God's boat to a quieter place!

Heavenly Father, in my hectic life I've neglected time apart with You. Help me to board Your boat and stay afloat through spending time in Your Word and in prayer. Amen.

DAY 53

MORNING

A New Name for Israel

For Zion's sake I will not keep silent, and for Jerusalem's sake I will not keep quiet, until her righteousness goes forth like brightness, and her salvation like a torch that is burning. The nations will see your righteousness, and all kings your glory; and you will be called by a new name which the mouth of the LORD will designate.

ISAIAH 62:1–2 NASB

Whenever God sets about to perform a work of regeneration, He also provides a new name. For instance, Abraham was known simply as Abram prior to God's promise that he would be the father of a "multitude of nations" (Genesis 17:1, 5–6 NASB).

Similarly, God changed Jacob's name to Israel, and he became the father of the twelve tribes of Israel (Genesis 32:28).

Lord, my name remains the same, but my heart is forever changed by Your love. Amen.

EVENING

A Child in Need

"For all those things My hand has made, and all those things exist," says the LORD. "But on this one will I look: on him who is poor and of a contrite spirit, and who trembles at My word."

ISAIAH 66:2 NKJV

A humble child of God with a need catches His eye. Though He is always watching over all of us, He is drawn to a child who needs Him. We may need forgiveness, wisdom, courage, endurance, patience, health, protection, or even love. God promises to come to our aid when He sees us with a hand up, reaching for His assistance.

What needs do you have in your life today? Raise your hand in prayer to God. He'll take care of your needs, and then some—blessing your life in ways you can't even imagine!

Father, thank You for caring about the needs of Your children. Help me to remember to always seek You first. Amen.

DAY 54

MORNING
God's Work

The LORD will perfect that which concerns me; Your mercy, O LORD, endures forever; do not forsake the works of Your hands.

PSALM 138:8 NKJV

The psalmist offers hope when he tells us the Lord will complete things that concern us. We are the work of His hands and He has enduring mercy toward our failures. He is as active in our sanctification as He is in our salvation. Philippians 1:6 (NKJV) says, "Being confident of this very thing, that He who has begun a good work in you will complete it until the day of Jesus Christ." The power to change or to see difficult things through to the end comes from the Lord who promises to complete the work He begins.

Lord, remind me of this word when I am discouraged by my lack of progress. Help me remember Your eternal love and mercy to me. Give me confidence that You will complete me. Amen.

EVENING
Jesus, the True Vine

"I am the true vine, and My Father is the vinedresser. Every branch in Me that does not bear fruit, He takes away; and every branch that bears fruit, He prunes it so that it may bear more fruit. You are already clean because of the word which I have spoken to you. Abide in Me, and I in you. As the branch cannot bear fruit of itself unless it abides in the vine, so neither can you unless you abide in Me. I am the vine, you are the branches; he who abides in Me and I in him, he bears much fruit, for apart from Me you can do nothing."

JOHN 15:1–5 NASB

Christ used word pictures to clarify concepts for His followers. And this parable about the vine and the branches was extremely familiar to them.

This same offer to abide in the vine is extended to all who hear the Gospel message. Have you responded? And how diligently are you abiding?

Lord, help me to abide in You. Amen

DAY 55

MORNING
The Secret of Serendipity

A happy heart makes the face cheerful.

PROVERBS 15:13 NIV

Can you remember the last time you laughed in wild abandon? Better yet, when was the last time you did something fun, outrageous, or out of the ordinary? Perhaps it is an activity you haven't done since you were a child, like slip down a waterslide, strap on a pair of ice skates, or pitch a tent and camp overnight. A happy heart turns life's situations into opportunities for fun. When we seek innocent pleasures, we glean the benefits of a happy heart. So try a bit of whimsy just for fun. And rediscover the secret of serendipity.

Dear Lord, because of You, I have a happy heart. Lead me to do something fun and spontaneous today! Amen.

EVENING
Holding On to Hope

"In this world you will have trouble. But take heart! I have overcome the world."

JOHN 16:33 NIV

Christ tells us to hold on to the hope we have in Him. He tells us to "*take heart*" because the trials of this world have already been won, the evil has already been conquered, and He has already overcome the world. Live your life as a statement of hope, not despair. Live like the victor, not the victim. Live with your eye on eternity, not the here and now. Daily remind yourself that you serve a powerful and gracious God, and decide to be used by Him to act as a messenger of grace and healing to the world's brokenness.

Lord, forgive my doubts. Forgive me for growing discouraged and not placing my full trust in You. May I learn to trust You better and to live my life as a statement of hope. Amen.

DAY 56

MORNING
Abide in the Vine

"I am the vine; you are the branches. If you remain in me and I in you, you will bear much fruit; apart from me you can do nothing."

JOHN 15:5 NIV

The fruit we bear is consistent with Christ's character. Just as apple trees bear apples, we bear spiritual fruit that reflects Him. Spiritual fruit consists of God's qualities: love, joy, peace, patience, kindness, goodness, faithfulness, gentleness, and self-control. The fruit of the Spirit cannot be grown by our own efforts. We must remain in the vine. How do we abide in Him? We acknowledge that our spiritual sustenance comes from the Lord. We spend time with Him. We seek His will and wisdom. We are obedient and follow where He leads. Abide in the vine and be fruitful!

Dear Lord, help me abide in You so that I may produce fruit as a witness to Your life within me. Amen.

EVENING
Jesus' Last Passover

Jesus, knowing that the Father had given all things into His hands, and that He had come forth from God and was going back to God, got up from supper, and laid aside His garments; and taking a towel, He girded Himself. Then He poured water into the basin, and began to wash the disciples' feet.

JOHN 13:3–5 NASB

In this one paragraph we are given reams of information about the last supper Jesus shared with His disciples. How difficult it must have been for Christ to say good-bye to them, knowing they still didn't fully comprehend His impending death! So Jesus set about to love them. By His example, He wanted to show them that they were called likewise to be servants.

Christ began washing the dust from the disciples' feet. Usually a servant would administer this kindness to those who came in for the banquet supper. But the God who had created them desired that His followers know the depth of His humility.

Lord, help me to cultivate the heart of a true servant. Amen.

DAY 57

MORNING

A Very Important Phrase

And it came to pass. . .
FOUND NEARLY 400 TIMES
IN THE KING JAMES BIBLE

There are times in life when we think we can't bear one more day, one more hour, one more minute. But no matter how bad things seem at the time, they are temporary. What's really important is how we handle the opportunities before us today, whether we let our trials defeat us or look for the hand of God in everything. Every day, week, and year is made up of things that "come to pass"—so even if we fail, we needn't be disheartened. Other opportunities—better days—will come. Let's look past those hard things today and glorify the name of the Lord.

Lord Jesus, how awesome it is that You send or allow these little things that will pass. May we recognize Your hand in them today and praise You for them. Amen.

EVENING

No Matter What

Be thankful in all circumstances, for this is God's will for you who belong to Christ Jesus.
1 THESSALONIANS 5:18 NLT

Jesus enables us to be thankful, and Jesus is the cause of our thankfulness. *No matter what happens,* we know that Jesus has given up His life to save ours. He has sacrificed Himself on the cross so that we may live life to the fullest. And while "to the fullest" means that we will experience pain as well as joy, we must *always* be thankful—regardless of our circumstances—for the love that we experience in Christ Jesus.

Dear Lord, thank You for Your love. Please let me be thankful, even in the midst of hardships. You have blessed me beyond measure. Amen.

DAY 58

MORNING
The White Knight

Then I will rejoice in the LORD.
I will be glad because he rescues me.
PSALM 35:9 NLT

We're all waiting for someone to rescue us. We wait and wait and wait. . . . The truth is, God doesn't want you to exist in a perpetual state of waiting. Live your life—your whole life—by seeking daily joy in the Savior of your soul, Jesus Christ. And here's the best news of all: He's already done the rescuing by dying on the cross for our sins! He's the *true* white knight who secured your eternity in heaven. Stop waiting; seek His face today!

Jesus, I praise You because You are the rescuer of my soul. Remind me of this fact when I'm looking for relief in other people and places. You take care of my present and eternal needs, and for that I am grateful. Amen.

EVENING
Rescued

God rescued us from dead-end alleys and dark dungeons. He's set us up in the kingdom of the Son he loves so much, the Son who got us out of the pit we were in, got rid of the sins we were doomed to keep repeating.
COLOSSIANS 1:13–14 MSG

The message of the Gospel doesn't leave us trapped in our sin and misery without hope. God sent the rescuer, Christ, who plucked us out of the dungeons of despair and into His kingdom of light and strength to overcome the dragons of sin. It's by the Father's grace that we are not stuck in our habitual ruts and dead-end alleys, living without purpose and fulfillment. We walk in His kingdom—a kingdom that goes counter to the world's ideas. We are out of the pit, striding confidently in Him, enjoying life to its fullest.

Glory to You, Jesus! You have rescued me from the pit and lifted me to Your kingdom of real life and victory. Help me to walk in that fact today. Amen.

DAY 59

MORNING
The Meaning of True Christian Fellowship

I thank my God in all my remembrance of you, always offering prayer with joy in my every prayer for you all, in view of your participation in the gospel from the first day until now.

PHILIPPIANS 1:3–5 NASB

Paul's joy is not dependent upon circumstances. Rather, it overflows from the content of his heart, where the true source of joy resides, Jesus Christ. And because of this indwelling, Paul senses a oneness with other believers despite the fact that they are far from him. It is the love of Christ that binds them together.

Paul's only aim in life was to be where God wanted him—so that he might spread the Gospel to all who would listen. And if this aspiration required suffering and isolation on his part, then Paul gladly paid the price.

Lord, might I pray as Paul, "I press on toward the goal for the prize of the upward call of God in Christ Jesus" (Philippians 3:14 NASB*). Amen.*

EVENING
My Life

I long for your salvation, LORD*, and your law gives me delight. Let me live that I may praise you, and may your laws sustain me.*

PSALM 119:174–175 NIV

Can you really do laundry to please God? Can you really go to work to please God? Can you really pay the bills and make dinner to please God? The answer is a resounding *yes*! Doing all the mundane tasks of everyday life with gratitude and praise in your heart for all that He has done for you is living a life of praise. As you worship God through your day-to-day life, He makes clear His plans, goals, and dreams for you.

Dear Father, let me live my life to praise You. Let that be my desire each day. Amen.

DAY 60

MORNING

Is Anyone Listening?

"And I will ask the Father, and He will give you another Helper (Comforter, Advocate, Intercessor—Counselor, Strengthener, Standby), to be with you forever."

John 14:16 AMP

Our heavenly Father wants to hear from us. He cares so much that He sent the Holy Spirit to be our Counselor, our Comforter. When we pray—when we tell God our needs and give Him praise—He listens. Then He directs the Spirit within us to speak to our hearts and give us reassurance. Our world is filled with noise and distractions. Look for a place where you can be undisturbed for a few minutes. Take a deep breath, lift your prayers, and listen. God will speak—and your heart will hear.

Dear Lord, I thank You for Your care. Help me to recognize Your voice and to listen well. Amen.

EVENING

Joyful, Patient, and Faithful

Be joyful in hope, patient in affliction, faithful in prayer.

Romans 12:12 NIV

Faithfulness in prayer requires discipline. God is faithful regardless of our attitude toward Him. He never changes, wavers, or forsakes His own. We may be faithful to do daily tasks around the house. We feed the cat, wash the clothes, and empty the trash. But faithfulness in the quiet discipline of prayer is harder. There are seemingly no consequences for neglecting our time with the Lord. Oh, what a myth this is! Set aside a daily time for prayer, and see how the Lord blesses you, transforming your spirit to increase your joyful hope, your patience, and your faithfulness.

Faithful God, find me faithful. Stir up the hope and joy within me. Give me the grace I need to wait on You. Amen.

DAY 61

MORNING

A Comfortable Place

Don't you realize that your body is the temple of the Holy Spirit, who lives in you and was given to you by God? You do not belong to yourself.

1 CORINTHIANS 6:19 NLT

We take the time to make our homes comfortable and beautiful when we know visitors are coming. In the same way, we ought to prepare our hearts for the Holy Spirit who lives inside of us. We should daily ask God to help us clean up the junk in our hearts. We should take special care to tune up our bodies through exercise, eating healthful foods, and dressing attractively and modestly. Our bodies belong to God. Taking care of ourselves shows others that we honor God enough to respect and use wisely what He has given us.

Dear Lord, thank You for letting me belong to You. May my body be a comfortable place for You. Amen.

EVENING

Being of One Mind

Do nothing from selfishness or empty conceit, but with humility of mind regard one another as more important than yourselves; do not merely look out for your own personal interests, but also for the interests of others.

PHILIPPIANS 2:3–4 NASB

As Christians, we are called to encourage one another in the faith. Paul, who spent so much of his own life in prison, had a deep understanding of the need for the reassurance and hope that the Lord richly supplies. This reliance on God's abundant source of blessings overflowed from his heart, spilling out to his fellow Christians.

What if in church we used the greeting time during the worship service to find out the specific needs within the body of Christ? Many of our brothers and sisters are wounded, both physically and spiritually. Yet they come to Sunday services with a deceptive smile on their faces, their return trip home as lonely as the rest of their week will probably be. Do you care?

Who is my source of strength? Lord, help me encourage others. Amen.

DAY 62

MORNING
All You Need

For your Maker is your husband—the LORD Almighty is his name—the Holy One of Israel is your Redeemer; he is called the God of all the earth.

ISAIAH 54:5 NIV

God is the great "I Am." He is all things that we need. He is our Maker. He is our husband. He is the Lord Almighty, the Holy One, the Redeemer, the God of all the earth. . . . He is not a god made of stone or metal. He is not unreachable. He is present. He is near, as close as you will let Him be, and He will meet your needs as no earthly relationship can. Seek the fullness of God in your life. Call upon Him as your Prince of Peace and your King of Glory. He is all that you need—at all times—in all ways.

Oh, Father, be close to me. Fill the empty spots in my heart. Be my husband, my Redeemer, and my best friend. Amen.

EVENING
One Thing Is Needed

"Martha, Martha," the Lord answered, "you are worried and upset about many things, but few things are needed—or indeed only one."

LUKE 10:41–42 NIV

We are each given twenty-four hours in a day. Einstein and Edison were given no more than Joseph and Jeremiah of the Old Testament. Since God has blessed each of us with twenty-four hours, let's seek His direction on how to spend this invaluable commodity wisely—giving more to people than things, spending more time on relationships than the rat race. In Luke, our Lord reminded dear, dogged, drained Martha that only one thing is needed—Him.

Father God, oftentimes I get caught up in the minutia of life. The piled laundry can appear more important than the people around me. Help me to use my time wisely. Open my eyes to see what is truly important. Amen.

DAY 63

MORNING

Who Helps the Helper?

The LORD is my strength and my shield; my heart trusted in him, and I am helped: therefore my heart greatly rejoiceth; and with my song will I praise him.

PSALM 28:7 KJV

Helping can be exhausting. The needs of young children, teens, grandchildren, aging parents, our neighbors and fellow church members—the list is never ending—can stretch us until we're ready to snap. And then we find that *we* need help. Who helps the helper? The Lord does. When we are weak, He is strong. When we are vulnerable, He is our Shield. When we can no longer trust in our own resources, we can trust in Him. He is always there, ready to help. Rejoice in Him, praise His name, and you will find the strength to go on.

Father, I'm worn out. I can't care for all the people and needs You bring into my life by myself. I need Your strength. Thank You for being my Helper and my Shield. Amen.

EVENING

His Light Dispels Darkness

And Jesus cried out and said, "He who believes in Me, does not believe in Me but in Him who sent Me. He who sees Me sees the One who sent Me. I have come as Light into the world, so that everyone who believes in Me will not remain in darkness."

JOHN 12:44–46 NASB

How people can read the Word of God and reach such faulty conclusions mystifies me. If you have a question about one verse of scripture, first, you need to pray that God's Spirit will provide enlightenment. Then, get a good study Bible that has cross-referencing indexed on each page along with the text.

Next, invest in or borrow a theological text from your church library that deals with the Bible book you are studying. Ask your pastors or ministers for their personal recommendations. With such guidance, God's Word becomes clearer and your faith is sure to deepen.

Your truth is readily available, Lord. Therefore, I know with certainty that I will one day see You face-to-face. Deepen my faith so that I might penetrate the spiritual darkness around me. Amen.

DAY 64

MORNING
What's in Your Heart?

Delight thyself also in the LORD:
and he shall give thee the
desires of thine heart.

PSALM 37:4 KJV

Too many times we look at God's promises as some sort of magic formula. We fail to realize that His promises have more to do with our own relationship with Him. It begins with a heart's desire to live your life in a way that pleases God. Only then will fulfillment of His promises take place. The promise in Psalm 37:4 isn't intended for personal gain—it is meant to glorify God. God wants to give you the desires of your heart when they line up with His perfect plan. As you delight in Him, His desires will become your desires, and you will be greatly blessed.

Lord, I know You want to give me the desires of my heart. Help me live in a way that makes this possible. Amen.

EVENING
Unbroken Promise

In hope of eternal life which God,
who cannot lie, promised before time began.

TITUS 1:2 NKJV

God always keeps His word. The Bible is filled with the promises of God—vows to us that we can trust will be completed. God never lies. Lying is not in Him. He sees us as worthy of His commitment. The promise of eternal life—given even before time began—is one of God's most wonderful gifts. No matter how disappointed we are with ourselves or with others, we only have to look at the pledge God has made to be filled with a heart of praise and gladness.

God, thank You that Your Word is trustworthy and true. I praise You for the promise of eternal life. Amen.

DAY 65

MORNING
Stand Firm and Receive the Crown

Therefore, my beloved brethren whom I long to see, my joy and crown, in this way stand firm in the Lord, my beloved. I urge Euodia and I urge Syntyche to live in harmony in the Lord.

PHILIPPIANS 4:1–2 NASB

Evidently, two of the women at the church in Philippi, Euodia and Syntyche, were less than harmonious. Therefore, Paul admonished them.

It is significant that Paul took the time to address this issue. Left unchecked, such arguing would wreak havoc in the church. Perhaps you have encountered someone who, although she professes belief in Christ, has treated you without charity or love. Fast, pray for guidance, and then go to her and pray again. Failure to do so gives Satan an opportunity to get a foothold within the church as the argument escalates and people choose sides.

Lord, help me to remember that You surrendered all Your rights that I might know true freedom. Please show me how to persevere, make amends, and live in harmony. Amen.

EVENING
Magnifying Life

My soul makes its boast in the LORD; let the humble hear and be glad. Oh, magnify the LORD with me, and let us exalt his name together!

PSALM 34:2–3 ESV

Mary knew she was the object of God's favor and mercy. That knowledge produced humility. Try as we might, we can't produce this humility in ourselves. It is our natural tendency to be self-promoters. . .to better our own reputations. We need the help of the Spirit to remind us that God has favored each of us with His presence. He did not have to come to us in Christ, but He did. He has chosen to set His love on us. His life redeemed ours, and He sanctifies us. We are recipients of the action of His grace.

Christ Jesus, help me remember what You have done for me and to desire for others to see and know You. Amen.

DAY 66

MORNING
No More Sting

O death, where is thy sting?
O grave, where is thy victory?
1 CORINTHIANS 15:55 KJV

We have a choice to make. We can either live life in fear or live life by faith. Fear and faith cannot coexist. Jesus Christ has conquered our greatest fear—death. He rose victorious and has given us eternal life through faith. Knowing this truth enables us to courageously face our fears. There is no fear that cannot be conquered by faith. Let's not panic but trust the Lord instead. Let's live by faith and experience the victory that has been given to us through Jesus Christ, our Lord.

Lord, You alone know my fears. Help me to trust You more. May I walk in the victory that You have purchased for me. Amen.

EVENING
Well Watered

"The LORD will guide you always; he will satisfy your needs in a sun-scorched land and will strengthen your frame. You will be like a well-watered garden, like a spring whose waters never fail."
ISAIAH 58:11 NIV

We need a downpour of God's Word and the Holy Spirit's presence in our parched spirits. Not an occasional sprinkle, but a soul soaking to replenish our frazzled bodies and weary minds. We know this soaking comes from consistent Bible study, the necessary pruning of confessed sin, and prayer time. These produce a well-watered garden, fruitful and lush, mirroring God's beauty, creating a life to which others are drawn to come and linger in His refreshing presence.

Eternal Father, strengthen my frame, guide my paths, and satisfy my needs as only You can. Make my life a well-watered garden, fruitful for You and Your purposes. Amen.

DAY 67

MORNING
Guidance in the Midst of Strife

To everything there is a season,
a time for every purpose under heaven.
ECCLESIASTES 3:1 NKJV

Only one thing in our lives never changes: God. When our world swirls and threatens to shift out of control, we can know that God is never surprised, never caught off guard by anything that happens. Just as He guided David through dark nights and Joseph through his time in prison, God can show us a secure way through any difficulty. He can turn the roughest times to good. Just as He supported His servants in times past, He will always be with us, watching and loving.

Lord, help me remember Your love and guidance when my life turns upside down. Grant me wisdom for the journey and a hope for the future. Amen.

EVENING
A Matter of Priorities

"So in everything, do to others what
you would have them do to you."
MATTHEW 7:12 NIV

Jesus took responsibilities, commitments, and obligations seriously. In fact, Jesus said, "All you need to say is simply 'Yes' or 'No'; anything beyond this comes from the evil one" (Matthew 5:37 NIV). Satan desires for us to be stressed out, overcommitted, and not able to do anything well. Satan delights when we treat others in an unkind, offensive manner. However, God, upon request, will help us prioritize our commitments so that our "yes" is "yes" and our "no" is "no." Then in everything we do, we are liberated to do to others as we would have them do to us.

Lord, please prioritize my commitments to enable me in everything to do to others as I would desire for them to do to me. Amen.

Then Hannah prayed and said, "My heart exults in the LORD; my horn is exalted in the LORD, my mouth speaks boldly against my enemies, because I rejoice in Your salvation. There is no one holy like the LORD, indeed, there is no one besides You."

1 SAMUEL 2:1–2 NASB

Hannah spent her time in the temple, praying and serving others. And God granted the deepest longing of her heart, despite the fact that she was just a sinner who could offer God nothing but her brokenness and yielded spirit.

Hannah refers to her Savior as a "God of knowledge" for she revered or honored His Word (1 Samuel 2:3 NASB). She took to heart all that God had done for her people in the past and accepted that He alone could change her circumstances. To whom do you turn for solutions?

Lord, You alone can lift me from the depths of despair and set me on high places. Amen.

EVENING

Put on a Happy Face

He restoreth my soul: he leadeth me in the paths of righteousness for his name's sake.

PSALM 23:3 KJV

Our God is not a God of negativity but of possibility. He will guide us through our difficulties and beyond them. Today we should turn our thoughts and prayers toward Him. Focus on a hymn or a praise song and play it in your mind. Praise chases away the doldrums and tips our lips up in a smile. With a renewed spirit of optimism and hope we can thank the giver of all things good. Thankfulness to the Father can turn our plastic smiles into real ones, and as the psalm states, our souls will be restored.

Father, I'm down in the dumps today. You are my unending source of strength. Gather me in Your arms for always. Amen.

DAY 69

MORNING
Remember This

Keep your eyes on Jesus, who both began and finished this race we're in.

HEBREWS 12:2 MSG

When our heads are spinning and tears are flowing, there is only one thing to remember: focus on Jesus. He will never leave you nor forsake you. When you focus on Him, His presence envelops you. Where there is despair, He imparts hope. Where there is fear, He imparts faith. Where there is worry, He imparts peace. He will lead you on the right path and grant you wisdom for the journey. When the unexpected trials of life come upon you, remember this: focus on Jesus.

Dear Lord, I thank You that nothing takes You by surprise. When I am engulfed in the uncertainties of life, help me remember to focus on You. Amen.

EVENING
One Step at a Time

With your help I can advance against a troop; with my God I can scale a wall.

PSALM 18:29 NIV

We often become discouraged when we face a mountain-size task. Whether it's weight loss or a graduate degree or our income taxes, some things just seem impossible. And they often *can't* be done—not all at once. Tasks like these are best faced one step at a time. One pound at a time. Chipping away instead of moving the whole mountain at once. With patience, perseverance, and God's help, your goals may be more attainable than you think.

Dear Father, the task before me seems impossible. However, I know I can do it with Your help. I pray that I will trust You every step of the way. Amen.

DAY 70

MORNING
Mirror Image

Behold, thou art fair, my love; behold, thou art fair; thou hast doves' eyes.

Song of Solomon 1:15 KJV

No matter how hard we try, when the focus is on self, we see shortcomings. Our only hope is to see ourselves through a different mirror. We must remember that as we grow as Christians we take on the characteristics of Christ. The more we become like Him, the more beautiful we are in our own eyes and to those around us. God loves to behold us when we are covered in Christ. The mirror image He sees has none of the blemishes or imperfections, only the beauty.

Oh God, thank You for beholding me as being fair and valuable. Help me to see myself through Your eyes. Amen.

EVENING
Stop and Consider

"Listen to this, Job; stop and consider God's wonders. Do you know how God controls the clouds and makes his lightning flash? Do you know how the clouds hang poised, those wonders of him who has perfect knowledge?"

Job 37:14–16 NIV

"Stop and consider My wonders," God told Job. Then He pointed to ordinary observations of the natural world surrounding Job—the clouds that hung poised in the sky, the flashes of lightning. "Not so very ordinary" was God's lesson. Maybe He was trying to remind us that there is no such thing as ordinary. Let's open our eyes and see the wonders around us.

Oh Father, teach me to stop and consider the ordinary moments of my life as reminders of You. Help me not to overlook Your daily care and provisions that surround my day. Amen.

DAY 71

MORNING
Jesus Raises Lazarus

Now a certain man was sick, Lazarus of Bethany. . . . So the sisters sent word to Him, saying, "Lord, behold, he whom You love is sick."

JOHN 11:1, 3 NASB

Lazarus was about to breathe his last. And yet Christ seemed to be denying the gravity of the situation. Jesus took His time getting there, four days as a matter of fact. And when He did arrive, Lazarus had been buried! Now Christ was only a few miles away from Bethany. It probably took all the human restraint He possessed not to run to Lazarus's aid. But Jesus had, as always, a greater purpose.

At the tomb of His friend Jesus called: "Lazarus, come forth" (John 11:43 NASB). And Lazarus arose from the tomb and walked out, his grave clothes dangling from his body. Have you allowed Christ to exercise His authority to bring you forth to new life?

Lord, strengthen my faith so that when tragedy strikes, I know that You are the Resurrection and the Life. Amen.

EVENING
Isaiah, a Major Prophet

The vision of Isaiah the son of Amoz concerning Judah and Jerusalem, which he saw during the reigns of Uzziah, Jotham, Ahaz and Hezekiah, kings of Judah. Listen, O heavens, and hear, O earth; for the LORD speaks, "Sons I have reared and brought up, but they have revolted against Me. . . . My people do not understand."

ISAIAH 1:1–3 NASB

Reading Isaiah provides a necessary heart check. Like Israel, if we fail to turn from our defiant ways, we must ask, "Where will you be stricken again, as you continue in your rebellion? The whole head is sick, and the whole heart is faint. From the sole of the foot even to the head there is nothing sound in it, only bruises, welts and raw wounds, not pressed out or bandaged, nor softened with oil" (Isaiah 1:5–6 NASB).

Lord, this book of prophecy displays Your promises and prophecies. Open my mind to receive Your truth. And keep me from confusion, that I might know You as both Messiah and Lord. Amen.

DAY 72

MORNING
Unswerving Faith

Let us hold unswervingly to the hope we profess, for he who promised is faithful.

HEBREWS 10:23 NIV

The author of Hebrews challenges us to hold *unswervingly* to our hope in Christ Jesus. Certainly we fail to do this at times, but life is much better when we keep our eyes fixed on Him. Sometimes just a whisper from Satan, the father of lies, can cause shakiness where once there was steadfastness. Place your hope in Christ alone. He will help you to resist the lies of this world. Hold *unswervingly* to your Savior today. He is faithful!

Jesus, You are the object of my hope. There are many distractions in my life, but I pray that You will help me to keep my eyes on You. Thank You for Your faithfulness. Amen.

EVENING
Rejoicing with Friends

"Then he calls his friends and neighbors together and says, 'Rejoice with me; I have found my lost sheep.' "

LUKE 15:6 NIV

Think of all the reasons you have to celebrate. Are you in good health? Have you overcome a tough obstacle? Are you handling your finances without much grief? Doing well at your job? Bonding with friends or family? If so, then throw yourself a party and invite a friend. Better yet, call your friends and neighbors together, as the scripture indicates. Share your praises with people who will truly appreciate all that the Lord is doing in your life. Let the party begin!

Lord, thank You that I'm created in the image of a God who knows how to celebrate. I have so many reasons to rejoice today. Thank You for Your many blessings. And today I especially want to thank You for giving me friends to share my joys and sorrows. Amen.

DAY 73

MORNING
Why Me?

I am Alpha and Omega, the beginning and the ending, saith the Lord, which is, and which was, and which is to come, the Almighty.

REVELATION 1:8 KJV

When God spoke our world into existence, He called into being a certain reality, knowing then everything that ever was to happen—and everyone who ever was to be. That you exist now is cause for rejoicing! God made *you* to fellowship with Him! If that fellowship demands trials for a season, rejoice that God thinks you worthy to share in the sufferings of Christ—and, eventually, in His glory. Praise His holy name!

Father, I thank You for giving me this difficult time in my life. Shine through all my trials today. I want You to get the glory. Amen.

EVENING
Faith, the Emotional Balancer

No man is justified by the law in the sight of God, it is evident: for, The just shall live by faith.

GALATIANS 3:11 KJV

Emotions mislead us. One day shines with promise as we bounce out of bed in song, while the next day dims in despair and we'd prefer to hide under the bedcovers. It has been said that faith is the bird that feels the light and sings to greet the dawn while it is still dark. The Bible instructs us to live by faith—not by feelings. Faith assures us that daylight will dawn in our darkest moments, affirming God's presence so that even when we fail to pray and positive feelings fade, our moods surrender to song.

Heavenly Father, I desire for my faith, not my emotions, to dictate my life. I pray for balance in my hide-under-the-cover days so that I might surrender to You in song. Amen.

DAY 74

MORNING
Samuel Is Born

It came about in due time, after Hannah had conceived, that she gave birth to a son; and she named him Samuel, saying, "Because I have asked him of the LORD."

1 SAMUEL 1:20 NASB

Hannah, a woman of real faith, wanted to keep her promise to God. After Samuel was born and she had weaned him, she took him promptly to the temple.

Every year Hannah and Elkanah returned for their sacrifice at the temple, and every year Hannah brought Samuel a new robe to wear. For her faithfulness, God blessed Hannah with three more sons and two daughters (1 Samuel 2:21).

God was now training Samuel to take over as judge of Israel, as Eli's own sons had no regard for the Lord. As Samuel continued to grow "in favor both with the LORD and with men" (1 Samuel 2:26 NASB), the Lord declared, "Those who honor me I will honor, but those who despise me will be disdained" (1 Samuel 2:30 NIV).

Lord, if You should give me a child, guide me as You guided Hannah—to sincere faithfulness. Amen.

EVENING
Choose Life

"The thief comes only to steal and kill and destroy; I have come that they may have life, and have it to the full."

JOHN 10:10 NIV

God's Word shows us the lie—and the liar—behind defeating thoughts. We have an enemy who delights in our believing negative things, an enemy who wants only destruction for our souls. But Jesus came to give us life! We only have to choose it, as an act of the will blended with faith. When we rely on Him alone, He'll enable us to not only survive but *thrive* in our daily routine. Each day, let's make a conscious decision to take hold of what Christ offers us—life, to the full.

Loving Lord, help me daily to choose You and the life You want to give me. Give me the eyes of faith to trust that You will enable me to serve lovingly. Amen.

DAY 75

MORNING

What Riches Do You Possess?

Command those who are rich. . .not to be arrogant nor to put their hope in wealth, which is so uncertain, but to put their hope in God, who richly provides us with everything for our enjoyment.

1 TIMOTHY 6:17 NIV

God desires to bless us with possessions we can enjoy. But it displeases Him when His children strain to attain riches in a worldly manner out of pride or a compulsion to flaunt. Riches are uncertain, but faith in God to meet our provisions is indicative of the pure in heart. Pride diminishes the capacity for humility and trust in God. We are rich indeed when our hope and faith are not in what we have but in whom we trust.

Heavenly Father, my hope is in You for my needs and my desires. I surrender any compulsion to attain earthly wealth; rather, may I be rich in godliness and righteousness. Amen.

EVENING

Follow the Lord's Footsteps

Then He said to them, "Follow Me, and I will make you fishers of men."

MATTHEW 4:19 NKJV

Jesus asked His disciples to follow Him, and He asks us to do the same. Following Jesus requires staying right on His heels. We need to be close enough to hear His whisper. Stay close to His heart by opening the Bible daily. Allow His Word to speak to your heart and give you direction. Throughout the day, offer up prayers for guidance and wisdom. Keep in step with Him, and His close presence will bless you beyond measure.

Dear Lord, grant me the desire to follow You. Help me not to run ahead or lag behind. Amen.

DAY 76

MORNING

Annual or Perennial?

They are like trees planted along the riverbank, bearing fruit each season. Their leaves never wither, and they prosper in all they do.

Psalm 1:3 NLT

Annuals or perennials? Each has its advantages. Annuals are inexpensive, provide instant gratification, and keep boredom from setting in. Perennials require an initial investment but, when properly tended, faithfully provide beauty year after year—long after the annuals have dried up and withered away. Perennials are designed for the long haul—not just short-term enjoyment, but long-term beauty. The application to our lives is twofold. First, be a perennial—long lasting, enduring, slow growing, steady, and faithful. Second, don't be discouraged by your inevitable dormant seasons. Tend to your soul, and it will reward you with years of lush blossoms.

Father, be the gardener of my soul. Amen.

EVENING

Have You Looked Up?

The heavens proclaim the glory of God. The skies display his craftsmanship. Day after day they continue to speak; night after night they make him known.

Psalm 19:1–2 NLT

God has placed glimpses of creation's majesty—evidence of His love—throughout our world. Sunsets, seashells, flowers, snowflakes, changing seasons, moonlit shadows. Such glories are right in front of us, every single day! But we must develop eyes to see these reminders in our daily life and not let the cares and busyness of our lives keep our heads turned down. Have you looked up today?

Lord, open my eyes! Unstuff my ears! Teach me to see the wonders of Your creation every day and to point them out to others. Amen.

DAY 77

MORNING
Faultless

To him who is able to keep you from stumbling and to present you before his glorious presence without fault and with great joy.

JUDE 1:24 NIV

Jesus loves us so much despite our shortcomings. He is the One who can keep us from falling—who can present us faultless before the Father. Because of this, we can have our joy restored no matter what. Whether we have done wrong and denied it or have been falsely accused, we can come into His presence to be restored and lifted up. Let us keep our eyes on Him instead of on our need to justify ourselves to God or others.

Thank You, Jesus, for Your cleansing love and for the joy we can find in Your presence. Amen.

EVENING
Jesus, the Good Shepherd

"But he who enters by the door is a shepherd of the sheep. To him the doorkeeper opens, and the sheep hear his voice, and he calls his own sheep by name and leads them out."

JOHN 10:2–3 NASB

In our day we hear some who defend their heinous acts by saying, "Voices told me to do it." Certainly the one they chose to listen to was not the voice of Jesus Christ, for He cannot contradict Himself. True sheep listen only for the voice of their Shepherd.

God calls us by name, just as the shepherd has pet names for his sheep. Someday, when the King of kings, our Good Shepherd, calls us home to heaven, we'll hear the name He calls us.

Lord, guide me to safe pastures today. Never leave me. Amen

DAY 78

MORNING
Reality Check

Instead, you must worship Christ as Lord of your life. And if someone asks about your hope as a believer, always be ready to explain it. But do this in a gentle and respectful way. Keep your conscience clear. Then if people speak against you, they will be ashamed when they see what a good life you live because you belong to Christ.

1 PETER 3:15–16 NLT

Every day we are being watched—both by the Father and by the people around us. Our attitudes and speech often are weighed against beliefs we profess and the hope we claim. Take time to search your heart and your motivations. If your speech and attitude aren't Christ centered, re-aim your heart to hit the mark.

Lord, help me to be a good representative of You. Amen.

EVENING
Reflecting God in Our Work

Whatever you do, work at it with all your heart, as working for the Lord, not for human masters.

COLOSSIANS 3:23 NIV

As believers, we are God's children. No one is perfect, and for this there is grace. However, we may be the only reflection of our heavenly Father that some will ever see. Our attitudes and actions on the job speak volumes to those around us. Although it may be tempting to do just enough to get by, we put forth our best effort when we remember we represent God to the world. A Christian's character on the job should be a positive reflection of the Lord.

Father, help me today to represent You well through my work. I want to reflect Your love in all I do. Amen.

DAY 79

MORNING
Just Half a Cup

"I am coming to you now, but I say these things while I am still in the world, so that they may have the full measure of my joy within them."

JOHN 17:13 NIV

Our heavenly Father longs to bestow His richest blessings and wisdom on us. He loves us, so He desires to fill our cup to overflowing with the things that He knows will bring us pleasure and growth. Do you tell Him to stop pouring when your cup is only half-full? You may not even realize it, but perhaps your actions dictate that your cup remain half-empty. Seek a full cup, and enjoy the full measure of the joy of the Lord.

Dear Jesus, forgive me for not accepting the fullness of Your blessings and Your joy. Help me to see the ways that I prevent my cup from being filled to overflowing. Thank You for wanting me to have the fullness of Your joy. Amen.

EVENING
Hide and Seek

"And do you seek great things for yourself? Seek them not, for behold, I am bringing disaster upon all flesh, declares the LORD."

JEREMIAH 45:5 ESV

God warns us: *Don't seek great things.* The more we seek them, the more elusive they become. As soon as we think we have them in our grasp, they disappear. If we commit to more activities than we can realistically handle, the best result is that we can't follow through. Worse, we might make them our god. Jesus tells us what we should seek: the kingdom of God and His righteousness (Matthew 6:33). When we seek the right things, He'll give us every good and perfect gift (James 1:17). And that will be more than we can ask or dream.

Lord, please teach me to seek not greatness, but You. May You be the all in all of my life. Amen.

DAY 80

MORNING
Persevering through Adversity

"But if it is from God, you will not be able to stop these men; you will only find yourselves fighting against God." His speech persuaded them. They called the apostles in and had them flogged. Then they ordered them not to speak in the name of Jesus, and let them go. The apostles left the Sanhedrin, rejoicing because they had been counted worthy of suffering disgrace for the Name.

ACTS 5:39–41 NIV

Scripture overflows with stories of God's beloved children undergoing extreme hardships. Just because we have faith, hope, and trust in the Lord does not mean that life will be easy. Instead, God's love for us means that He will provide a way *through*, not around, adversity, resulting in His greater glory. Everyone experiences tough times. The goal, however, is not to find relief. It is to live in a way that shows how well we love and trust the Lord.

Father God, I know that no matter how troubled my life is, You can provide me a way to persevere. Help me to trust Your guidance and love. Amen.

EVENING
Where Is the Promise of His Coming?

Know this first of all, that in the last days mockers will come with their mocking, following after their own lusts, and saying, "Where is the promise of His coming? For ever since the fathers fell asleep, all continues just as it was from the beginning of creation." For when they maintain this, it escapes their notice that by the word of God the heavens existed long ago and the earth was formed out of water and by water, through which the world at that time was destroyed, being flooded with water.

2 PETER 3:3–6 NASB

How can a loving God destroy the very men and women and their world that He created? Look at how much time He provided for them to repent. From the time Noah received the order from God to build the ark until the rain began, a span of 120 years had elapsed. Certainly this was time enough for everyone to hear the prediction and take appropriate action.

Today I will repent of my sins. And, if I'm not entirely sure I've done so, today I will claim Jesus to be my Savior and Lord. Amen.

DAY 81

MORNING

Location, Location, Location

Those who live in the shelter of the Most High will find rest in the shadow of the Almighty. This I declare about the LORD: He alone is my refuge, my place of safety; he is my God, and I trust him.

PSALM 91:1–2 NLT

If something is getting you down in life, check your location. Where are your thoughts? Let what the world has conditioned you to think go in one ear and out the other. Stand on the truth, the promises of God's Word. Say of the Lord, "God is my Refuge! I am hidden in Christ! Nothing can harm me. In Him I trust!" Say it loud. Say it often. Say it over and over until it becomes your reality. And you will find yourself dwelling in that secret place every moment of the day.

God, You are my Refuge. When I abide in You, nothing can harm me. Your Word is the truth on which I rely. Fill me with Your light and the peace of Your love. It's You and me, Lord, all the way! Amen.

EVENING

Light My Path

Your word is a lamp for my feet,
a light on my path.

PSALM 119:105 NIV

God's Word is like a streetlamp. Often, we *think* we know where we're going and where the stumbling blocks are. We believe we can avoid pitfalls and maneuver the path successfully on our own. But the truth is that without God's Word, we are walking in darkness, stumbling and tripping. When we sincerely begin to search God's Word, we find the path becomes clear. God's light allows us to live our lives in the most fulfilling way possible, a way planned out from the very beginning by God Himself.

Jesus, shine Your light upon my path. I have spent too long wandering through the darkness, looking for my way. As I search Your Word, I ask You to make it a lamp for my feet so that I can avoid the pitfalls of the world and walk safely along the path You have created specifically for me. Amen.

DAY 82

MORNING
Daybreak

"As your days, so shall your strength be."
DEUTERONOMY 33:25 NKJV

There are times in life when we feel that the night season we're facing will last forever and a new morning will never come. For those particularly dark seasons of your life, you don't have to look to the east to find the morning star, but instead find that morning star in your heart. Allow the hope of God's goodness and love to rekindle faith. With the passing of the night, gather your strength and courage. A new day is dawning and with it new strength for the journey forward. All that God has promised will be fulfilled.

Heavenly Father, help me to hold tightly to faith, knowing in this situation that daybreak is on its way. Amen.

EVENING
Power Up

The Spirit of God, who raised Jesus from the dead, lives in you.
ROMANS 8:11 NLT

God is the same yesterday, today, and forever. His strength does not diminish over time. That same mountain-moving power you read about in the lives of people from the Old and New Testaments still exists today. We don't have to go it alone. Our heavenly Father wants to help. All we have to do is ask. He has already made His power available to His children. Whatever we face, wherever we go, whatever dreams we have for our lives, take courage and know that anything is possible when we draw on the power of God.

Father, help me to remember that You are always with me, ready to help me do all things. Amen.

DAY 83

MORNING

God Stands by His Word

"Behold, I am going to send My messenger, and he will clear the way before Me. And the Lord, whom you seek, will suddenly come to His temple; and the messenger of the covenant, in whom you delight, behold, He is coming," says the LORD of hosts.

MALACHI 3:1 NASB

God always keeps His promises. Through Moses, God had warned the nation of Israel that if they refused to obey, they would be taken into captivity. In 586 BC, this prophecy was fulfilled.

God spoke through the prophet Jeremiah, giving the exact duration of this captivity as seventy years. This is the number of years Israel remained in Babylon.

Today's scripture reveals two specific messages. First, a messenger will precede the Messiah, announcing Him to Israel. This would be John the Baptist (Luke 1:76).

Next, the Messiah will "come to His temple."

Jesus Christ, God's promise to the world, has come! Thank You for Your Word of Truth. Amen.

EVENING

Comfort Food

For whatever things were written before were written for our learning, that we through the patience and comfort of the Scriptures might have hope.

ROMANS 15:4 NKJV

Romans 15:4 tells us that the scriptures are comfort food for the soul. They were written and given so that, through our learning, we would be comforted with the truths of God. Worldly pleasures bring a temporary comfort, but the problem still remains when the pleasure or comfort fades. However, the words of God are soothing and provide permanent hope and peace. Through God's Word, you will be changed, and your troubles will dim in the bright light of Christ. So the next time you are sad, lonely, or disappointed, turn to the Word of God as your source of comfort.

Thank You, Father, for the rich comfort Your Word provides. Help me to remember to find my comfort in scripture rather than through earthly things that will ultimately fail me. Amen.

DAY 84

MORNING
Power of the Word

"The Spirit gives life; the flesh counts for nothing. The words I have spoken to you—they are full of the Spirit and life."

JOHN 6:63 NIV

Jesus told His followers that His words were Spirit and life. When we hear His Word, meditate on it, pray it, memorize it, and ask for faith to believe it, He comes to us in it and transforms our lives through it. Once the Word is in our mind or before our eyes and ears, the Holy Spirit can work it into our hearts and our consciences. Jesus told us to abide in His Word. . .putting ourselves in a place to hear and receive the Word. The rest is the beautiful and mysterious work of the Spirit.

Thank You, Jesus, the Living Word, who changes my heart and my mind through the power of Your Word. Amen.

EVENING
Can God Interrupt You?

In their hearts humans plan their course, but the LORD establishes their steps.

PROVERBS 16:9 NIV

Have you ever considered that perhaps God has ordained our interruptions? Perhaps, just perhaps, God may be trying to get your attention. There is nothing wrong with planning our day. However, we have such limited vision. God sees the big picture. Be open. Be flexible. Allow God to change your plans in order to accomplish His divine purposes. Instead of becoming frustrated, look for ways the Lord might be working. Be willing to join Him. When we do, interruptions become blessings.

Dear Lord, forgive me when I am so rigidly locked into my own agenda that I miss Yours. Give me Your eternal perspective so that I may be open to divine interruptions. Amen.

DAY 85

MORNING
A Step of Faith

Hope deferred makes the heart sick, but when the desire comes, it is a tree of life.

PROVERBS 13:12 NKJV

Jesus is your hope! He stands a short distance away, bidding you to take a walk on water—a step of faith toward Him. Let Him direct you over the rough waters of life, overcoming each obstacle one opportunity at a time. Don't look at the big picture in the midst of the storm, but focus on the one thing you can do at the moment to help your immediate situation—one step at a time.

Lord, help me not to concentrate on the distractions, but to keep my focus on which step to take next in order to reach You. Amen.

EVENING
Marvelous Thunder

"God's voice thunders in marvelous ways; he does great things beyond our understanding."

JOB 37:5 NIV

Have you ever reflected deeply on the power that God is? Not that He *has*, but that He is.

Consider this: The One who controls nature also holds every one of our tears in His hand. He is our Father, and He works on our behalf. He is more than enough to meet our needs; He does things far beyond what our human minds can understand. This One who is power loves you. He looks at you and says, *"I delight in you, My daughter."* Wow! His ways are marvelous and beyond understanding.

Lord God, You are power. You hold all things in Your hand and You chose to love me. You see my actions, hear my thoughts, watch my heartbreak. . .and You still love me. Please help me trust in Your power, never my own. Amen.

DAY 86

MORNING
Ruth, Faithful Daughter-in-Law

Then Elimelech, Naomi's husband, died; and she was left with her two sons. They took for themselves Moabite women as wives; the name of the one was Orpah and the name of the other Ruth. And they lived there about ten years.

RUTH 1:3–4 NASB

Ruth was a young woman when her husband died. In one of the greatest testaments of love in the Bible, she chose to remain with her widowed mother-in-law, Naomi, even choosing to believe in her God.

Few daughters-in-law would have persisted in devotion to a woman whose life held such abysmal tragedy and so little prospect for positive change. However, God had a glorious plan. "Now Naomi had a kinsman of her husband, a man of great wealth, of the family of Elimelech, whose name was Boaz" (Ruth 2:1 NASB).

Ruth gathered leftover grain from Boaz's fields so that she and Naomi might have food. And Boaz showed her favor. In time, Ruth would become Boaz's bride and mother to his son, a son whose lineage would include David and the Messiah, Jesus Christ.

Lord, may I learn from Ruth's example of abiding love. Amen.

EVENING
Eye Care

For thus says the LORD of hosts. . . "he who touches you touches the apple of His eye."

ZECHARIAH 2:8 NKJV

To think that we are the apple of God's eye is incredible. Consider the care He must take for us. He will go to great lengths to protect us from harm. When something or someone does attack us, God feels our pain. He is instantly aware of our discomfort, for it is His own. When the storms of life come, we must remember how God feels each twinge of suffering. Despite the adversity, we can praise God, for He is sheltering us.

Thank You, God, that You are so aware of what is happening to me. Thank You for Your protection. Amen.

DAY 87

MORNING

God's Mountain Sanctuary

And seeing the multitudes, he went up into a mountain. . .and. . .his disciples came unto him: and he opened his mouth, and taught them.

MATTHEW 5:1–2 KJV

Jesus often retreated to a mountain to pray. There He called His disciples to depart from the multitudes so that He could teach them valuable truths—the lessons we learn from nature. Do you yearn for a place where problems evaporate like the morning dew? Do you need a place of solace? God is wherever you are—behind a bedroom door, nestled alongside you in your favorite chair, or even standing at a sink full of dirty dishes. Come apart and enter God's mountain sanctuary.

Heavenly Father, I long to hear Your voice and to flow in the path You clear before me. Help me to find sanctuary in Your abiding presence. Amen.

EVENING

A Fresh New Harvest

Do not rejoice over me, my enemy; when I fall, I will arise; when I sit in darkness, the LORD will be a light to me.

MICAH 7:8 NKJV

The enemy of your soul wants you to consider each failure and dwell on the past, fully intending to rob you of your future. But God wants you to take that seed of hope that seems to have died and bury it in His garden of truth—trusting Him for a new harvest of goodness and mercy. Once you have buried that seed deep in the ground of God's love, it will grow and become a part of His destiny for your life.

Lord, help me not to focus on the past but to look to You every step of the way. Amen.

DAY 88

MORNING
Hold to God's Truth

For you have died and your life is hidden with Christ in God. When Christ, who is our life, is revealed, then you also will be revealed with Him in glory. Therefore consider the members of your earthly body as dead to immorality, impurity, passion, evil desire, and greed, which amounts to idolatry.

Colossians 3:3–5 NASB

Our churches are comprised of redeemed sinners. Some Christian testimonies really stir your heart. Some are from individuals who have turned from lives of debauchery and waste to become true seekers of God.

Paul's message is that Christ in us should cause a change in our lives, for we have been delivered from the "wrath of God." This metamorphosis should make a visible difference in how we are living our lives, for Christ has set up residence within us.

Let me be cautious of bypassing the Word of God and the Spirit of God to substitute visions of angels for the Gospel. Amen.

EVENING
A Fragrant Offering

Follow God's example, therefore, as dearly loved children and walk in the way of love, just as Christ loved us and gave himself up for us as a fragrant offering and sacrifice to God.

Ephesians 5:1–2 NIV

If we carry the scent of Christ in our daily walk, people will be drawn to us and want to "stay for a while." But how do we give off that amazing, inviting fragrance? There's really only one way—by imitating God. By loving others fully. By seeing them through His eyes. By looking with great compassion on those who are hurting, as Jesus did when He went about healing the sick and pouring out His life for those in need. As we live a life of love in front of those we care for, we exude the sweetest fragrance of all—Christ.

Dear Lord, I long to live a life that points people to You. As I care for those in need, may the sweet-smelling aroma of You and Your love be an invitation for people to draw near. Amen.

DAY 89

MORNING
Masterpiece

You made all the delicate, inner parts of my body and knit me together in my mother's womb.

PSALM 139:13 NLT

At the moment of your conception, roughly three million decisions were made about you. Everything from your eye color and the number of your wisdom teeth to the shape of your nose and the swirl of your fingerprints was determined in the blink of an eye. God is a big God. Unfathomable. Incomparable. Frankly, words just don't do Him justice. And He made *you*. You were knit together by a one-of-a-kind, amazing God who is absolutely, undeniably, head-over-heels crazy in love with you. Try to wrap your brain around that.

Heavenly Father and Creator, thank You for the amazing gift of life, for my uniqueness and individuality. Help me to use my life as a gift of praise to You. Amen.

EVENING
How about Some Fun?

A twinkle in the eye means joy in the heart, and good news makes you feel fit as a fiddle.

PROVERBS 15:30 MSG

God does not want His kids to be worn out and stressed out. A little relaxation, recreation, and—yes—*fun* are essential components of a balanced life. Even Jesus and His disciples found it necessary to get away from the crowds and pressures of ministry to rest. There's a lot of fun to be had out there—playing tennis or golf, jogging, swimming, painting, knitting, playing a musical instrument, visiting an art gallery, playing a board game, or going to a movie, a play, or a football game. Have you had any fun this week?

Lord, You are the One who gives balance to my life. Help me to find time today for a little relaxation, recreation, and even fun. Amen.

DAY 90

MORNING

Weary Days

Why art thou cast down, O my soul? and why art thou disquieted in me? hope thou in God: for I shall yet praise him for the help of his countenance. O my God, my soul is cast down within me: therefore will I remember thee from the land of Jordan, and of the Hermonites, from the hill Mizar.

Psalm 42:5–6 KJV

Our willingness to speak with God at the day's beginning shows our dependence on Him. We can't make it alone. It is a comforting truth that God never intended for us to trek through the hours unaccompanied. He promises to be with us. He also promises His guidance and direction as we meet people and receive opportunities to serve Him. Getting started is as simple as removing our head from the pillow and telling God good morning.

Lord, refresh my spirit and give me joy for today's activities. Amen.

EVENING

Ladies in Waiting

I will wait for the Lord. . . .
I will put my trust in him.

Isaiah 8:17 NIV

Do we want joy without accepting heartache? Peace without living through the stress? Patience without facing demands? God sees things differently. He's giving us the opportunity to learn through these delays, irritations, and struggles. Like Isaiah, we need to learn the art of waiting on God. He will come through every time—but in *His* time, not ours. The wait may be hours or days, or it could be years. But God is always faithful to provide for us. It is when we learn to wait on Him that we will find joy, peace, and patience through the struggle.

Father, You know what I need, so I will wait. Help me be patient, knowing that You control my situation and that all good things come in Your time. Amen.

DAY 91

MORNING
When I Think of the Heavens

When I consider your heavens, the work of your fingers, the moon and the stars, which you have set in place, what is mankind that you are mindful of them, human beings that you care for them?

PSALM 8:3–4 NIV

Daughter of God, you are important to your heavenly Father, more important than the sun, the moon, and the stars. You are created in the image of God, and He cares for you. In fact, He cares so much that He sent His Son, Jesus, to offer His life as a sacrifice for your sins. The next time you look up at the heavens, the next time you ooh and aah over a majestic mountain or emerald waves crashing against the shoreline, remember that those things, in all their splendor, don't even come close to you—God's greatest creation.

Oh Father, when I look at everything You have created, I'm so overwhelmed with who You are. Who am I that You would think twice about me? And yet You do. You love me, and for that I'm eternally grateful! Amen.

EVENING
The Days of Your Youth

Remember also your Creator in the days of your youth, before the evil days come and the years draw near when you will say, "I have no delight in them." . . . Fear God and keep His commandments, because this applies to every person. For God will bring every act to judgment, everything which is hidden, whether it is good or evil.

ECCLESIASTES 12:1, 13–14 NASB

Most of us have encountered women who freely share biblical truths "handed down to them" from their grandmothers or mothers. Is the faith being displayed in their lives?

The book of Ecclesiastes concludes with the admonition not only to remember our Creator when we are young, but to continue following His precepts throughout our time on earth.

Have you forgotten the God of your youth? Have His principles been compromised away by the pressures of a world that teaches that the Ten Commandments are optional? With the Lord's help, it's not too late to turn it all around.

Lord, if I look back and see a trail of regret, please give me the courage to change the view. Amen.

DAY 92

MORNING
The Dream Maker

"What no eye has seen, what no ear has heard, and what no human mind has conceived"—the things God has prepared for those who love him.

1 CORINTHIANS 2:9 NIV

Dreams, goals, and expectations are part of our daily lives. We have an idea of what we want and how we're going to achieve it. Disappointment can raise its ugly head when what we wanted—what we expected—doesn't happen like we thought it should or doesn't happen as fast as we planned. God knows the dreams He has placed inside of you. He created you and knows what you can do—even better than you know yourself. Maintain your focus—not on the dream but on the dream maker—and together you will achieve your dream.

God, thank You for putting dreams in my heart. I refuse to quit. I'm looking to You to show me how to reach my dreams. Amen.

EVENING
A Heavenly Party

"I tell you that in the same way there will be more rejoicing in heaven over one sinner who repents than over ninety-nine righteous persons who do not need to repent."

LUKE 15:7 NIV

The Father threw your very own party the moment you accepted His Son as your Savior. Did you experience a taste of that party from the response of your spiritual mentors here on earth? As Christians, we should celebrate with our new brothers and sisters in Christ every chance we get. If you haven't yet taken that step in your faith, don't wait! Heaven's party planners are eager to get your celebration started.

Father, I am so grateful that You rejoice in new Christians. Strengthen my desire to reach the lost while I am here on earth. Then, when I reach heaven, the heavenly parties will be all the sweeter! Amen.

DAY 93

MORNING
Follow Jesus

"Whoever serves me must follow me;
and where I am, my servant also will be.
My Father will honor the one who serves me."

JOHN 12:26 NIV

A disciple is someone who follows. That is the discipline we practice: We follow Jesus. Wherever He is, we go. In His presence we find the daily grace we need to live. As we serve Him, God honors us; He affirms our dignity and makes us all we were meant to be.

Jesus, I long to be Your disciple. Give me the grace to follow You, a heart to serve You, and a mind in tune with You every minute of every day. Amen.

EVENING
Choose to Laugh

Our mouths were filled with laughter.

PSALM 126:2 NIV

We women often plan perfect family events, only to find out how imperfectly things can turn out. The soufflé falls, the cat leaps onto the counter and licks the cheese ball, little Johnny drops Aunt Martha's crystal gravy dish (full of gravy, of course). The Bible says that Sarah laughed at the most unexpected, traumatic time of her life—when God announced that she would have a baby at the age of ninety (Genesis 18:12). At this unforeseen turn of events, she could either laugh, cry, or run away screaming. She chose to laugh.

Lord, give us an extra dollop of grace and peace to laugh about unexpected dilemmas that pop up—and to remember that our reaction is a choice. Amen.

DAY 94

MORNING
Anxiety Check!

Do not be anxious about anything, but in every situation, by prayer and petition, with thanksgiving, present your requests to God.

PHILIPPIANS 4:6 NIV

Checking to make sure we've locked the door, turned off the stove, and unplugged the curling iron just comes naturally. So why do we forget some of the bigger checks in life? Take anxiety, for instance. When was the last time you did an anxiety check? Days? Weeks? Months? Chances are, you're due for another. After all, we're instructed not to be anxious about anything. Instead, we're to present our requests to God with thanksgiving in our hearts. We're to turn to Him in prayer so that He can take our burdens. Once they've lifted, it's bye-bye anxiety!

Father, I get anxious sometimes. And I don't always remember to turn to You with my anxiety. In fact, I forget to check for anxiety at all. Today I hand my anxieties to You. Thank You that I can present my requests to You. Amen.

EVENING
Christ Eliminated All Ethnic Barriers

There is no distinction between Greek and Jew, circumcised and uncircumcised, barbarian, Scythian, slave and freeman, but Christ is all, and in all.

COLOSSIANS 3:11 NASB

To say we love Christ and yet maintain deeply rooted prejudices against others is inconsistent with everything He taught. For Christ came to reconcile all peoples to Himself, not separate us into factions.

Above all, God wants us to be harmonious in worship of Him and also in working with Him. "Now may the God who gives perseverance and encouragement grant you to be of the same mind with one another according to Christ Jesus, so that with one accord you may with one voice glorify the God and Father of our Lord Jesus Christ. Therefore, accept one another, just as Christ also accepted us to the glory of God" (Romans 15:5–7 NASB).

Lord, let true peace, which is Christ, be found in my heart as I am obedient to Your command to love one another, just as You have loved me (John 13:34). Amen.

DAY 95

MORNING

Difficult People

Do not turn your freedom into an opportunity for the flesh, but through love serve one another.

GALATIANS 5:13 NASB

Sometimes, like David, we need to turn our skirmishes with others over to the Lord. Then, by using our weapons—God's Word and a steadfast faith—we need to love and forgive others as God loves and forgives us. Although we may not like to admit it, we have all said and done some pretty awful things ourselves, making the lives of others difficult. Yet God has forgiven us *and* continues to love us. So do the right thing. Pull your feet out of the mire of unforgiveness, sidestep verbal retaliation, and stand tall in the freedom of love and forgiveness.

The words and deeds of others have left me wounded and bleeding. Forgiveness and love seem to be the last thing on my mind. Change my heart, Lord. Help me to love and forgive others as You love and forgive me. Amen.

EVENING

It's All Good

And we know that all things work together for good to them that love God, to them who are the called according to his purpose.

ROMANS 8:28 KJV

God can and does use all things in our lives for His good purpose. Remember Joseph in the cistern, Daniel in the lions' den, and Jesus on the cross? The Lord demonstrated His resurrection power in each of those cases. He does so in our lives as well. He brings forth beauty from ashes.

What are you facing that seems impossible? What situation appears hopeless? What circumstance is overwhelming you? Believe God's promise.

Dear Lord, thank You that You work all things together for Your good purpose. May I trust You to fulfill Your purpose in my life. Amen.

DAY 96

MORNING
A Strong Heart

Whom have I in heaven but you? And earth has nothing I desire besides you. My flesh and my heart may fail, but God is the strength of my heart and my portion forever.

Psalm 73:25–26 NIV

You don't have to be strong. In your weakness, God's strength shines through. And His strength surpasses anything you could produce, even on your best day. It's the same strength that spoke the heavens and the earth into existence. The same strength that parted the Red Sea. And it's the same strength that made the journey up the hill to the cross. So how do you tap into that strength? There's really only one way. Come into His presence. Spend some quiet time with Him. Allow His strong arms to encompass you. God is all you will ever need.

Father, I feel so weak at times. It's hard just to put one foot in front of the other. But I know You are my Strength. Invigorate me with that strength today, Lord. Amen.

EVENING
A Time to Mourn

There is an appointed time for everything. And there is a time for every event under heaven. . . .A time to weep and a time to laugh; a time to mourn and a time to dance.

Ecclesiastes 3:1, 4 NASB

Somehow we reach the faulty conclusion that if God loves us, all negative incidents are nixed. Do we doubt that the Father loved the Son and yet allowed the Son to suffer a cruel death on the cross? The penalty for sin was death, a penalty that had to be paid by someone absolutely sinless in order for us to be forgiven. Only Jesus Christ could fill that role.

If Christ Himself suffered, then why should we be immune from all maladies?

Occasionally a time of mourning enters our lives, sometimes stealing in almost silently, sometimes brashly breaking down the door to our well-constructed sense of security. Neither path reflects nor distorts the fact that God loves us. But tragedy and mourning are both part of the ebb and flow of the "rhythm of life."

Lord, through my veil of tears help me to view Your rescuing hand, that I might reach out to grasp You more firmly. Amen.

DAY 97

MORNING
King Forever

You, O God, are my king from ages past, bringing salvation to the earth.

Psalm 74:12 NLT

Sometimes it seems like every part of our lives is affected by change. Nothing ever seems to stay the same. These changes can leave us feeling unsteady in the present and uncertain about the future. It's different in God's kingdom. He's the King now, just as He was in the days of Abraham. His reign will continue until the day His Son returns to earth, and then on into eternity. We can rely—absolutely depend on—His unchanging nature. Take comfort in the stability of the King—He's our leader now and forever!

Almighty King, You are my Rock. When my world is in turmoil and changes swirl around me, You are my anchor and my center of balance. Thank You for never changing. Amen.

EVENING
Going Above and Beyond

Now to him who is able to do immeasurably more than all we ask or imagine, according to his power that is at work within us, to him be glory in the church and in Christ Jesus throughout all generations, for ever and ever!

Ephesians 3:20–21 NIV

Think for a moment. . . . What have you asked for? What have you imagined? It's amazing to think that God, in His infinite power and wisdom, can do immeasurably more than all that! How? According to the power that is at work within us. It's not our power, thankfully. We don't have enough power to scrape the surface of what we'd like to see done in our lives. But His power in us gets the job done. . .and more. Praise the Lord! Praise Him in the church and throughout all generations! He's an immeasurable God.

Heavenly Father, I feel pretty powerless at times. It's amazing to realize You have more power in Your little finger than all of mankind has put together. Today I praise You for being a God who goes above and beyond all I could ask or imagine. Amen.

DAY 98

MORNING
Put on Love

And over all these virtues put on love, which binds them all together in perfect unity.

Colossians 3:14 NIV

There is one accessory that always fits, always looks right, always is appropriate, and always makes us more attractive to others. When we wear it, we are beautiful. When we wear it, we become more popular, more sought after, more admired. What is that accessory, you ask, and where can you buy it? It's love, and you can't buy it anywhere. But it's free, and it's always available through the Holy Spirit. When we call on Him to help us love others, He cloaks us in a beautiful covering that draws people to us and makes us perfectly lovely in every way.

Dear Father, as I get dressed each day, help me to remember the most important accessory I can wear is Your love. Amen.

EVENING
Darkness into Light

We can rejoice, too, when we run into problems and trials, for we know that they help us develop endurance. And endurance develops strength of character, and character strengthens our confident hope of salvation.

Romans 5:3–4 NLT

Whether it's an illness, job loss, strained friendship, or even the everyday challenges that sneak up, we want to find the quickest way out. Fortunately, we have a loving God who promises to stay beside us through the darkness. Even though night does come, the quickest way to see the morning is to take God's hand and walk through the hard times. In the morning, the sun rises and the darkness fades, but God is still there. God never promised that our lives would be easy, but He did promise that He would always be with us—in the darkness and all through the night.

God, thank You for being a constant source of comfort and dependability in my life. Amen.

DAY 99

MORNING
Not Even His Brothers Believed

Therefore His brothers said to Him, "Leave here and go into Judea, so that Your disciples also may see Your works which You are doing. For no one does anything in secret when he himself seeks to be known publicly. If You do these things, show Yourself to the world." For not even His brothers were believing in Him.

JOHN 7:3–5 NASB

One of the most difficult challenges any believer faces is reaching family with Christ's message. Although Jesus' own brothers had daily viewed His sinless life, they were as blind as the Pharisees to who He really was.

Surely these siblings, Christ's earthly half brothers (Matthew 13:55–56; Mark 6:1–6), knew that the Jews were seeking to kill Him (John 7:1). But they were headed for Jerusalem to attend the Feast of Booths, as required by God. Jesus' brothers were embarking on a journey to a religious feast and yet rejecting their own Messiah.

Christ's half brothers were completely in tune with the world, and not with God.

Help me, Jesus, to set an example for my family of how to be in tune with You rather than with the world. Grant me the wisdom and guidance to help my loved ones become closer to You. Amen.

EVENING
Cartwheels of Joy

I'm singing joyful praise to GOD. I'm turning cartwheels of joy to my Savior God. Counting on GOD'S Rule to prevail, I take heart and gain strength. I run like a deer. I feel like I'm king of the mountain!

HABAKKUK 3:18–19 MSG

What would happen if we followed the advice of Habakkuk and turned a cartwheel of joy in our hearts—regardless of the circumstances—then leaned into and trusted His rule to prevail? Think of the happiness and peace that could be ours with a total surrender to God's care. Taking a giant step, armed with scriptures and praise and joy, we can surmount any obstacle put before us, running like a deer, climbing the tall mountains. With God at our side, it's possible to be king of the mountain.

Dear Lord, I need Your help. Gently guide me so I might learn to lean on You and become confident in Your care. Amen.

DAY 100

MORNING
Trials and Wisdom

Consider it pure joy, my brothers and sisters, whenever you face trials of many kinds, because you know that the testing of your faith produces perseverance. Let perseverance finish its work so that you may be mature and complete, not lacking anything. If any of you lacks wisdom, you should ask God, who gives generously to all without finding fault, and it will be given to you.

JAMES 1:2–5 NIV

Things won't be easy and simple until we get to heaven. So how can we lift our chins and head into tomorrow without succumbing to discouragement? We remember that God is good. We trust His faithfulness. We ask for His presence and peace during each moment. We pray for wisdom and believe that the God who holds the universe in His hands is working every single trial and triumph together for our good and for His glory. This passage in James tells us that when we lack wisdom we should simply ask God for it! Be encouraged that the Lord will give you wisdom generously without finding fault!

Lord Jesus, please give me wisdom. So many troubles are weighing me down. Help me give You all my burdens, and increase my faith and trust in You. Amen.

EVENING
Step by Step

For we walk by faith, not by sight [living our lives in a manner consistent with our confident belief in God's promises].

2 CORINTHIANS 5:7 AMP

The experiences and circumstances of our lives can often lead us to lose heart. The apostle Paul exhorts us to look away from this present world and rely on God by faith. *Webster's Dictionary* defines faith as a firm belief and complete trust. Trusting, even when our faith is small, is not an easy task. Today, grasp hold of God's Word and feel His presence. Hold tightly and don't let your steps falter. He is beside you and will lead you.

Dear heavenly Father, today I choose to clutch Your hand and feel Your presence as I trudge the pathways of my life. I trust You are by my side. Amen.

DAY 101

MORNING

Jonah's Prayer

"When my life was ebbing away,
I remembered you, LORD, *and my*
prayer rose to you, to your holy temple."

JONAH 2:7 NIV

In verse 6 of his great prayer from the belly of the fish, we read these words: "But you, LORD my God, brought my life up from the pit" (Jonah 2:6 NIV). When Jonah reached a point of desperation, he realized that God was his only hope. Have you been there? Not in the belly of a great fish, but in a place where you are made keenly aware that it is time to turn back to God? God loves His children and always stands ready to receive us when we need a second chance.

Father, like Jonah I sometimes think my own ways are better than Yours. Help me to be mindful that Your ways are always good and right. Amen.

EVENING

The Father Has Bestowed a Great Love

When He appears, we will be like Him,
because we will see Him just as He is.
And everyone who has this hope fixed on
Him purifies himself, just as He is pure.

1 JOHN 3:2–3 NASB

While we don't know when Jesus is coming again, we do know that our new bodies will coincide with this event. "When Christ, who is our life, is revealed, then you also will be revealed with Him in glory" (Colossians 3:4 NASB).

Yet the gift of our new bodies is only one aspect of the Father's incredible love for His children. His love prompts His children to purify themselves just as He is pure (1 John 3:3). They also abide in Him and practice righteousness (1 John 3:6–7), for they have been born of God (1 John 3:9; John 3:7).

Lord, the greatest gift I can lay before You is an act of my will that makes me Your child. Yes, I have been born again through You—mind, body, and spirit. Amen.

DAY 102

MORNING
Lord, Help!

"LORD, help!" they cried in their trouble, and he saved them from their distress. He calmed the storm to a whisper and stilled the waves. What a blessing was that stillness as he brought them safely into harbor!

PSALM 107:28–30 NLT

Samuel Morse, the father of modern communication, said, "The only gleam of hope—and I cannot underrate it—is from confidence in God. When I look upward, it calms my apprehensions for the future, and I seem to hear a voice saying: 'If I clothe the lilies of the field, shall I not also clothe you?' Here is my strong confidence, and I will wait patiently for the direction of Providence." The answer to your prayer does not depend on you. Your expressions of your heart spoken to your Father bring Him onto the scene for any reason you need Him.

Father, thank You for hearing my prayers. I know that You are always near to me and You answer my heart's cry. Help me to come to You first instead of trying to do things on my own. Amen.

EVENING
Raise the Roof

Come, let's shout praises to GOD, raise the roof for the Rock who saved us! Let's march into his presence singing praises, lifting the rafters with our hymns!

PSALM 95:1–2 MSG

Not many had it rougher than King David, who curled up in caves to hide from his enemies, or Paul in a dark dungeon cell, yet they still praised God despite the circumstances. And our God extended His grace to them as they acclaimed Him in their suffering. The Lord wants to hear our shouts of joy and see us march into the courtyard rejoicing. He hears our faltering songs and turns them into a symphony for His ears. So lift up your voice and join in the praise to our Creator and Lord.

Dear heavenly Father, I praise Your holy name. Bless You, Lord. Thank You for Your grace and mercy toward me. Amen.

DAY 103

MORNING

Be Still and Learn

His delight is in the law of the LORD,
and on His law [His precepts and teachings]
he [habitually] meditates day and night.

PSALM 1:2 AMP

It takes discipline to spend time with the Lord, but that simple discipline helps to keep our hope alive, providing light for our paths. When the schedule seems to loom large or the weariness of everyday living tempts you to neglect prayer and Bible study, remember they are your lifeline. They keep you growing in your relationship with the lover of your soul.

Heavenly Father, I want to know You more. I want to feel Your presence. Teach me Your ways that I may dwell in the house of the Lord forever. Amen.

EVENING

Biblical Encouragement for Your Heart

Don't be concerned about the outward beauty of fancy hairstyles, expensive jewelry, or beautiful clothes. You should clothe yourselves instead with the beauty that comes from within, the unfading beauty of a gentle and quiet spirit, which is so precious to God.

1 PETER 3:3–4 NLT

God is concerned with what is on the inside. He listens to how you respond to others and watches the facial expressions you choose to exhibit. He sees your heart. The Lord desires that you clothe yourself with a gentle and quiet spirit. He declares this as unfading beauty, the inner beauty of the heart. Focus on this and no one will even notice whether your jewelry shines. Your face will be radiant with the joy of the Lord, and your heart will overflow with grace and peace.

Lord, grant me a quiet and gentle spirit. I ask this in Jesus' name. Amen.

DAY 104

MORNING

The Gift of Prayer

First of all, then, I urge that petitions (specific requests), prayers, intercessions (prayers for others) and thanksgivings be offered on behalf of all people. . . . This [kind of praying] is good and acceptable and pleasing in the sight of God our Savior.

1 TIMOTHY 2:1, 3 AMP

There is such joy in giving gifts. Seeing the delight on someone's face to receive something unexpected is exciting. Perhaps the absolute greatest gift one person can give to another doesn't come in a box. It can't be wrapped or presented formally; instead, it is the words spoken to God for someone—the gift of prayer. When we pray for others, we ask God to intervene and to make Himself known to them. We can pray for God's plan and purpose in their lives. We can ask God to bless them or protect them. Who would God have you give the gift of prayer to today?

Lord, thank You for bringing people to my heart and mind who need prayer. Help me to pray the things that they need from You in their lives. Show me how to give the gift of prayer to those You would have me pray for. Amen.

EVENING

Jesus, Bread of Life

"As the living Father sent Me, and I live because of the Father, so he who eats Me, he also will live because of Me. This is the bread which came down out of heaven; not as the fathers ate and died; he who eats this bread will live forever."

JOHN 6:57–58 NASB

Some said that Jesus' teachings were too difficult to even bother with, while others stated that Christ was speaking about cannibalism. And the majority just walked away, refusing to follow Christ anymore. To continue following Him required faith and commitment.

To truly partake of Christ is to accept Him as He is, fully God and fully man, sent from God, recognizing our need for Him. He came first to the Jews, but they refused the message. What is your response?

Lord, when I don't understand the scriptures, Your Holy Spirit will provide me with comprehension. Amen.

DAY 105

MORNING

Encourage One Another

Therefore encourage one another and build each other up, just as in fact you are doing.

1 THESSALONIANS 5:11 NIV

Encouragement is more than words. It is also valuing, being tolerant of, serving, and praying for one another. It is looking for what is good and strong in a person and celebrating it. Encouragement means sincerely forgiving and asking for forgiveness, recognizing someone's weaknesses and holding out a helping hand, giving humbly while building someone up, helping others to hope in the Lord, and praying that God will encourage them in ways that you cannot. Whom will you encourage today? Get in the habit of encouraging others. It will bless them and you.

Heavenly Father, open my eyes to those who need encouragement. Show me how I can help. Amen.

EVENING

Because of Christ

All this comes from the God who settled the relationship between us and him, and then called us to settle our relationships with each other.

2 CORINTHIANS 5:18 MSG

God created a bridge to span the distance between ourselves and Him. That bridge is Christ, the best and fullest expression of divine grace. Because of Christ, we are in a relationship with the Creator of the entire world. And because of Christ, we are called to build bridges of our own, to span the distance between ourselves and others.

Jesus, there is no way I could bridge the chasm between God and myself. Your sacrifice draws me near to the Father. May my life be a reflection of my gratitude. Amen.

DAY 106

MORNING

Joyous Light

Whom having not seen, ye love; in whom, though now ye see him not, yet believing, ye rejoice with joy unspeakable and full of glory.

1 PETER 1:8 KJV

Jesus is the Light of the World. When we accept Him, the light is poured into us. The Holy Spirit comes to reside within, bringing His light—a glorious gift graciously given to us. When we realize the importance of the gift and the blessings that result from a life led by the Father, we can't contain our happiness. The joy and hope that fill our hearts wells up. Joy uncontained comes when Jesus becomes our Lord. Through Him, through faith, we have hope for the future. What joy! So let it spill forth in love.

Lord, help me to be a light unto the world, shining forth Your goodness. Amen.

EVENING

He Carries Us

In his love and mercy he redeemed them. He lifted them up and carried them through all the years.

ISAIAH 63:9 NLT

Are you feeling broken today? Depressed? Defeated? Run to Jesus and not away from Him.

He will carry us—no matter what pain we have to endure. No matter what happens to us. God sent Jesus to be our Redeemer. He knew the world would hate, malign, and kill Jesus. Yet He allowed His very flesh to writhe in agony on the cross—so that we could also become His sons and daughters. He loved me, and you, that much.

Lord Jesus, thank You for coming to us—for not abandoning us when we are broken. Thank You for Your work on the cross, for Your grace, mercy, and love. Help me to seek You even when I can't feel You, to love You even when I don't know all the answers. Amen.

DAY 107

MORNING
Walk a Mile in the Master's Shoes

For this very reason also, applying all diligence, in your faith supply moral excellence, and in your moral excellence, knowledge.

2 PETER 1:5 NASB

God, in His infinite grace and mercy, knows we'll stumble. We can place our hope in Him with confidence He'll understand. He's not there with a "giant thumb" to squash us as we toddle along, new in our spiritual walk. He doesn't look for opportunities to say, "Aha, you messed up!" Quite the contrary: He encourages us with His Word. As we grow and learn with the aid of the Spirit, our lives will also reflect more of Him. And as we grow ever more sure footed, we'll reach our destination—to be like our Father.

Gracious Lord, thank You for Your ever-present guidance. Amen.

EVENING
Linking Hearts with God

"You will receive power when the Holy Spirit comes on you; and you will be my witnesses. . .to the ends of the earth."

ACTS 1:8 NIV

God knows our hearts. He knows what we need to make it through a day. So in His kindness, He gave us a gift in the form of the Holy Spirit. As a Counselor, a Comforter, and a friend, the Holy Spirit acts as our inner compass. He upholds us when times are hard and helps us hear God's directions. When the path of obedience grows dark, the Spirit floods it with light. What revelation! He lives within us. Therefore, our prayers are lifted to the Father, to the very throne of God!

Father God, how blessed I am to come into Your presence. Help me, Father, when I am weak. Guide me this day. Amen.

DAY 108

MORNING
Unremarkable Lives

Then Jephthah the Gileadite died and was buried in one of the cities of Gilead. Now Ibzan of Bethlehem judged Israel after him.

JUDGES 12:7–8 NASB

What do you want etched into your own tombstone? Personally, I'd like to be remembered this way: "Studied the Word of God diligently and cared about bringing it to others."

But no such accolades are recorded for the four judges Jephthah, Ibzan, Elon, and Abdon. Jephthah is known mainly for his "rash vow," while Ibzan's claim to fame is a large family, whom he married off to the pagans dwelling in that area. Nothing is learned about Abdon except that "he had forty sons and thirty grandsons who rode on seventy donkeys" (Judges 12:14 NASB).

How can we discern the will of God for our lives? Daily prayer is definitely the main source. And this involves not only relating our needs to God, but also listening for His directions. For He never meant for us to traverse through this maze called life without the road maps He would supply.

Lord, remind me to linger in prayer, listening for Your voice. Amen.

EVENING
You Are a Woman of Worth

A wife of noble character who can find?
She is worth far more than rubies.
Her husband has full confidence in her and lacks nothing of value. She brings him good, not harm, all the days of her life.

PROVERBS 31:10–12 NIV

Are you the woman of worth that Jesus intends you to be? We often don't think we are. Between running a household, rushing to work, taking care of the children, volunteering for worthwhile activities, and still being a role model for our families, we think we've failed miserably. Sometimes we don't fully realize that learning to be a noble woman of character takes time. Our experiences can be offered to another generation seeking wisdom from others who have "been there." You are a woman of worth. God said so!

Father God, thank You for equipping me to be a woman of noble character. You tell me that I am more precious than jewels, and I claim and believe that wholeheartedly. I love You, Lord, and I will continue to put You first in my life. Help me to be the woman You intend me to be! Amen.

DAY 109

MORNING
By His Grace

A person is made right with God through faith, not through obeying the law.

ROMANS 3:28 NCV

Human laws can never make us into the people we are meant to be. No matter how scrupulous we try to be, we will always fall short. Our hands and hearts will come up empty. But as we fix our eyes on God, committing our lives and ourselves to Him, we are made right. We are healed and made whole by His grace, exactly as God meant us to be.

Father, rather than working to become righteous in Your sight, help me instead to focus on increasing my faith and trusting in Your grace. Amen.

EVENING
Like Little Children

Some people brought their little children to Jesus so he could touch them, but his followers told them to stop. When Jesus saw this, he was upset and said to them, "Let the little children come to me. Don't stop them, because the kingdom of God belongs to people who are like these children. I tell you the truth, you must accept the kingdom of God as if you were a little child, or you will never enter it."

MARK 10:13–15 NCV

This passage in Mark tells us that no matter how old we are, God wants us to come to Him with the faith of a child. He wants us to be open and honest about our feelings. He wants us to trust Him wholeheartedly, just like little kids do. As adults, we sometimes play games with God. We tell God what we think He wants to hear, forgetting that He already knows our hearts! God is big enough to handle your honesty. Tell Him how you really feel.

Father, help me come to You as a little child and be more open and honest with You in prayer. Amen.

DAY 110

MORNING
Loving Sisters

But Ruth replied, "Don't urge me to leave you or to turn back from you. Where you go I will go, and where you stay I will stay. Your people will be my people and your God my God."

RUTH 1:16 NIV

The story of Ruth and Naomi is inspiring on many levels. Both women realized that their commitment, friendship, and love for each other surpassed any of their differences. They were a blessing to each other. Do you have girlfriends who would do almost anything for you? A true friendship is a gift from God. Those relationships provide us with love, companionship, encouragement, loyalty, honesty, understanding, and more! Lasting friendships are essential to living a balanced life.

Father God, thank You for giving us the gift of friendship. May I be the blessing to my girlfriends that they are to me. Please help me to always encourage and love them and to be a loving support for them in both their trials and their happiness. I praise You for my loving sisters! Amen.

EVENING
Breath of Life

He heals the brokenhearted and binds up their wounds [healing their pain and comforting their sorrow].

PSALM 147:3 AMP

When your life brings disappointment, hurt, and pain that are almost unbearable, remember that you serve the One who heals hearts. He knows you best and loves you most. When the wind is knocked out of you and you feel like there is no oxygen left in the room, let God provide you with the air you need to breathe. Breathe out a prayer to Him and breathe in His peace and comfort today.

Lord, be my breath of life, today and always. Amen.

DAY 111

MORNING
Daily Miracles

"That is why I tell you not to worry about everyday life—whether you have enough food and drink, or enough clothes to wear. Isn't life more than food, and your body more than clothing?"

MATTHEW 6:25 NLT

With our eyes fixed on what we don't have, we often overlook the grace we have already received. God has blessed us in many ways. Our bodies function day after day in amazing ways we take for granted, and life is filled with an abundance of daily miracles. Why do we worry so much about the details when we live in such a vast sea of daily grace?

Father, You are my Provider. You have promised to give me everything I need. Help me to remember this truth and to lose myself in the vast sea of Your amazing grace. Amen.

EVENING
Healed Miraculously

Now there is in Jerusalem by the sheep gate a pool. . .having five porticoes. In these lay a multitude of those who were sick, blind, lame, and withered, [waiting for the moving of the waters; for an angel of the Lord went down at certain seasons into the pool and stirred up the water; whoever then first, after the stirring up of the water, stepped in was made well from whatever disease with which he was afflicted.]

JOHN 5:2–4 NASB

So many times when we cry out to the Lord for healing, He seems to be asking us the same question He posed to the man who had been sitting at this gate for thirty-eight years waiting for healing: "Do you wish to get well?" (John 5:6 NASB).

In other words, do you honestly desire to rid yourself of the things that debilitate you? For true healing of our souls requires a change of direction.

Lord, if sin is at the root of my infirmity, then bring me to swift repentance. But if my suffering is to point others toward Your glory, quench my thirst with Your living water. Amen.

DAY 112

MORNING

High Expectations

"They found grace out in the desert. . . .
Israel, out looking for a place to rest,
met God out looking for them!" God told
them, "I've never quit loving you and never
will. Expect love, love, and more love!"

JEREMIAH 31:2–3 MSG

Despite their transgressions, God told the Israelites He never quit loving them. That is true for you today. Look beyond any circumstances and you will discover God looking at you, His eyes filled with love. Scripture promises an overwhelming, unexpected river of love that will pour out when we trust the Lord our God. Rest today in His Word. Expect God's love, love, and more love to fill that empty place in your life.

Father, I read these words and choose this day to believe in Your unfailing love. Amen.

EVENING

A Continual Feast

The cheerful heart has a continual feast.

PROVERBS 15:15 NIV

Our choice of companions has much to do with our outlook. Negativity and positivity are both contagious. The writer of Proverbs says that a cheerful heart has a continual feast. So it's safe to assume that a grumpy heart will feel hungry and lacking, instead of full. While God calls us to minister to those who are hurting, we can do so with discernment. Next time someone complains, ask her to pray with you about her concerns. Tell her a story of how you overcame negativity or repaired a relationship. You might help turn her day around!

God, help me be a positive influence on my friends and family. Give me wisdom and the unwavering hope that comes from Christ, that I may share Your joy with others. Amen.

DAY 113

MORNING

Trust in the LORD with all your heart and lean not on your own understanding; in all your ways submit to him, and he will make your paths straight.

PROVERBS 3:5–6 NIV

Placing our trust in a loving heavenly Father can sometimes feel like stepping off a precipice. Perhaps it is because we can't see God. Trust is not easily attained. It comes once you have built a record with another over a period of time. It involves letting go and knowing you will be caught. In order to trust God, we must step out in faith. Challenge yourself to trust God with one detail in your life each day. Build that trust pattern and watch Him work. He will not let you down.

Father, I release my hold on my life and trust in You. Amen.

EVENING

A Good Morsel

Taste and see that the LORD is good; blessed is the one who takes refuge in him.

PSALM 34:8 NIV

The world gives the idea to nonbelievers that God isn't worth a taste. The world emphasizes a self-focus, while the Lord says to put others before self, and God before all. In reality, walking and talking with God is the best thing you can do for yourself. Like so many foods that are good for us, all it requires is that first taste, a tiny morsel, which whets the appetite for more of Him. Then you can be open to all the goodness, all the fullness of the Lord.

Lord, fill my cup to overflowing with Your love so that it pours out of me in a way that makes others want what I have. Amen.

DAY 114

MORNING
Be Happy!

Blessed are those who act justly,
who always do what is right.
PSALM 106:3 NIV

In the world that we live in today, some might think that a bank error or a mistake on a bill in their favor would be justification for keeping the money without a word. But a true Christ follower would not look at these kinds of situations as good or fortunate events. Our happiness is being honest, doing what is right, because that happiness is the promised spiritual reward. Because we want to be blessed by God, to be a happy follower of Him, we will seek to always do what is right.

Gracious and heavenly Father, thank You for Your blessings each and every day. I am thankful to be Your follower. When I am tempted to do something that would displease You, remind me that You will bless me if I act justly. My happiness will be a much better reward. In Your name, amen.

EVENING
All Is Vanity!

The words of the Preacher, the son of David, king in Jerusalem. "Vanity of vanities," says the Preacher, "Vanity of vanities! All is vanity."
ECCLESIASTES 1:1–2 NASB

At the end of his life, King Solomon, who is thought to be the writer of Ecclesiastes, concludes that the things of earth are but fleeting. Perhaps you, too, are prone to reflect on the tasks that occupy your days, concluding that nothing gets accomplished.

As we go through Ecclesiastes, Solomon repeatedly uses two key word pictures, "meaningless" and "under the sun." As king over Israel he had seen "all the works which have been done under the sun, and behold, all is vanity and striving after wind. . . . Because in much wisdom there is much grief, and increasing knowledge results in increasing pain" (Ecclesiastes 1:14, 18). Solomon had experienced the best the world has to offer. . .and it wasn't enough.

Lord, as I begin to learn the truths contained in this book, please help me view my priorities from Your perspective. Amen.

DAY 115

MORNING
Your Heavenly Father

The LORD's love never ends; his mercies never stop. They are new every morning; LORD, your loyalty is great.

LAMENTATIONS 3:22–23 NCV

Regardless of your relationship with your earthly father, your heavenly Father loves you with an *unfailing love*. He is faithful to walk with you through the ups and downs of life. Remember that every day is a day to honor your heavenly Father. Begin and end today praising Him for who He is. Express thanksgiving. Present your requests to Him. Tell Him how much you love Him. God longs to be your Abba Father, a loving Daddy to you, His daughter!

Father, thank You for being a loving God, my Abba Father, my Redeemer. Amen.

EVENING
The Gift of Encouragement

We have different gifts. . . . If it is to encourage, then give encouragement.

ROMANS 12:6, 8 NIV

Paul spoke of encouraging as a God-given desire to proclaim God's Word in such a way that it touches hearts to move them to receive the Gospel. Encouragement is a vital part to witnessing because encouragement is doused with God's love. For the believer, it stimulates our faith to produce a deeper commitment to Christ. It brings hope to the disheartened or defeated soul. It restores hope. How will you know your spiritual gift? Ask God and then follow the desires He places on your heart.

Father, help me tune in to the needs of those around me so that I might encourage them for the Gospel's sake for Your glory and their good. Amen.

DAY 116

MORNING

He Is Coming with the Clouds

Behold, He is coming with the clouds, and every eye will see Him, even those who pierced Him; and all the tribes of the earth will mourn over Him. So it is to be. Amen.

Revelation 1:7 NASB

Cecil B. DeMille was known for his extravagant movie productions. Who can forget his version of Moses parting the Red Sea? However, the appearance of Christ in the clouds will surpass every event that has ever taken place on earth. This future event will be a worldwide phenomenon in which every eye will see Him. And the hearts of those who refused to examine the evidence and refused to know Him will ache with the agonizing pain of conviction that it's simply too late. The purpose for His appearance this time will be to judge the world for its greatest sin, the rejection of His great gift of salvation.

Father, when humans have failed me I tend to blame You for their choices. Please break down the barriers in my heart that I might worship You. Amen.

EVENING

Start Your Day with God

In the morning, Lord, you hear my voice; in the morning I lay my requests before you and wait expectantly.

Psalm 5:3 NIV

As you wake up in the morning, thank the Lord for a new day. Ask Him to control your thoughts and attitude as you make the bed. Thank Him for providing for you as you toast your bagel. Ask that your self-image be based on your relationship with Christ as you get dressed and brush your teeth. Continue to pray as you drive to work or school. Spend time in His Word throughout the day. Then end your day by thanking Him for His love and faithfulness.

Dear Lord, thank You for the gift of a new day. Help me be aware of Your constant presence in my life. Amen.

DAY 117

MORNING

Listening Closely

I will listen to what God the LORD says.

PSALM 85:8 NIV

Listening is a learned art, too often forgotten in the busyness of a day. The alarm clock buzzes; we hit the floor running, toss out a prayer or maybe sing a song of praise, grab our car keys, and are out the door. If only we'd slow down and let the heavenly Father's words sink into our spirits, what a difference we might see in our prayer life. This day, stop. Listen. See what God has in store for you.

Lord, how I want to surrender and seek Your will. Please still my spirit and speak to me. Amen.

EVENING

Standing in the Light

Though I have fallen, I will rise. Though I sit in darkness, the LORD will be my light.

MICAH 7:8 NIV

With God, we know the low times aren't the end of our story. We may fall down, but He will lift us up. We may feel surrounded by darkness on every side, but He will be our light, guiding the way, showing us which step to take next. No matter where we are, what we've done, or what we're facing, God is our rescuer, our Savior, and our friend. God's children always have a future and a hope.

Dear Father, thank You for giving me confidence in a future filled with good things. When I'm down, remind me to trust in Your love. Thank You for lifting me out of darkness to stand in Your light. Amen.

DAY 118

MORNING

Encounter at the Well

There came a woman of Samaria to draw water. Jesus said to her, "Give Me a drink."

JOHN 4:7 NASB

Here lived a woman of ill repute. She was shunned by those who led wholesome lives. After all, she had had five husbands and now lived with a man, unmarried.

Although Jewish men didn't speak to women in public, Jesus asked this woman for a drink of water. Shocked, the woman responded, "How is it that You, being a Jew, ask me for a drink since I am a Samaritan woman?" (John 4:9 NASB).

Jesus Christ went right to the heart of her problem. "If you knew the gift of God, and who it is who says to you, 'Give Me a drink,' you would have asked Him, and He would have given you living water" (John 4:10 NASB). And when she asked where to get this living water, He explained the gift of eternal life to her.

Father, help me to seek out those who for whatever reason are shunned and despised. They need You so much. In Your name I pray, Amen.

EVENING

Pray about Everything

The LORD directs the steps of the godly. He delights in every detail of their lives.

PSALM 37:23 NLT

The Bible says that the Lord delights in every detail of His children's lives. Adult prayers don't have to be well ordered and formal. God loves hearing His children's voices, and no detail is too little or dull to pray about. Tell God that you hope the coffeehouse will have your favorite pumpkin-spice latte on their menu. Ask Him to give you patience as you wait in line. Thank Him for how wonderful that coffee tastes! Get into the habit of talking with Him all day long, because He loves you and delights in all of the facets of your life.

Dear God, teach me to pray about everything with childlike innocence and faith. Amen.

DAY 119

MORNING
A Joyful Heart

Sarah said, "God has brought me laughter, and everyone who hears about this will laugh with me."

GENESIS 21:6 NIV

In the Bible, King Solomon said, "Every day is hard for those who suffer, but a happy heart is like a continual feast" (Proverbs 15:15 NCV). Are you or someone you know unhappy? A little laughter might help. Begin with a smile. When you hear laughter, move toward it and try to join in. Seek the company of happy friends, and invite humor into your conversations. Most of all, praise God. Praise is the best way to heal a hurting soul. Praise God joyfully for His many blessings.

Lord, whenever my heart is heavy, encourage me to heal it with joy. Amen.

EVENING
God's Promises Bring Hope

"For I know the plans I have for you. . . plans to prosper you and not to harm you, plans to give you hope and a future."

JEREMIAH 29:11 NIV

The writer of the well-known hymn "It Is Well with My Soul" penned those words at the most grief-stricken time of his life after his wife and three children were tragically killed at sea. His undaunted faith remained because he believed in a God who was bigger than the tragedy he faced. God's promises gave him hope and encouragement. Despite your circumstances, God has a plan for you, one that will give you encouragement and hope and a brighter future.

Father, may I always say, "It is well with my soul," knowing Your promises are true and I can trust You no matter what. Amen.

MORNING

And now, dear brothers and sisters, one final thing. Fix your thoughts on what is true, and honorable, and right, and pure, and lovely, and admirable. Think about things that are excellent and worthy of praise.

PHILIPPIANS 4:8 NLT

Dig through the scriptures and find truths from God's Word to combat any false message that you may be struggling with. Write them down and memorize them. Here are a few to get started:

God looks at my heart, not my outward appearance. (1 Samuel 16:7)

I am free in Christ. (1 Corinthians 1:30)

I am a new creation. My old self is gone! (2 Corinthians 5:17)

The next time you feel negativity and false messages slip into your thinking, fix your thoughts on what you know to be true. Pray for the Lord to replace the doubts and negativity with His words of truth.

Lord God, please control my thoughts and help me set my mind and heart on You alone. Amen.

EVENING

The Lord Attends to the Righteous

The eyes of the LORD are toward the righteous and His ears are open to their cry.

PSALM 34:15 NASB

This morning I read the following scripture: "FOR THE EYES OF THE LORD ARE TOWARD THE RIGHTEOUS, AND HIS EARS ATTEND TO THEIR PRAYER, BUT THE FACE OF THE LORD IS AGAINST THOSE WHO DO EVIL" (1 Peter 3:12 NASB). The Spirit of God heard my cry and took my petition before the Father who answers my prayer, for I have confessed belief in Him.

If you have discarded the commands of God, then you are not God's child. "You are from God, little children, and have overcome them; because greater is He who is in you than he who is in the world. They are from the world; therefore they speak as from the world, and the world listens to them" (1 John 4:4–5 NASB).

Lord, guide me in this last hour so that I will continue to spread the Gospel and not walk away. Amen.

DAY 121

MORNING

The Simple Things

In him our hearts rejoice,
for we trust in his holy name.

PSALM 33:21 NIV

God knows all the simple pleasures you enjoy—and He created them for your delight. When the simple things that can come only by His hand fill you with contentment, He is pleased. He takes pleasure in you. You are His delight. Giving you peace, comfort, and a sense of knowing that you belong to Him is a simple thing for Him. Take a moment today and step away from the busyness of life. Take notice and fully experience some of those things you enjoy most. Then share that special joy with Him.

Lord, thank You for the simple things that bring pleasure to my day. I enjoy each gift You've given me. I invite You to share those moments with me today. Amen.

EVENING

Encourage Others

Worry weighs a person down;
an encouraging word cheers a person up.

PROVERBS 12:25 NLT

There is so much sorrow in this world. At any given time, there are many people within your sphere of influence who are hurting. Worry weighs them down as they face disappointment, loss, and other trials. Think about how much it means to you when someone takes the time to encourage you. Do the same for others. Be the voice of encouragement. There is blessing to be found in lifting up those around you.

Father, as I go through this week, make me an encourager. Provide opportunities for me to encourage those around me. I truly desire to cheer up the hearts of those who are worried. Amen.

DAY 122

MORNING
Whispers in the Wind

Then Jesus told him, "Because you have seen me, you have believed; blessed are those who have not seen and yet have believed."

JOHN 20:29 NIV

We can't see God. We can't take Him by the hand or even converse with Him face-to-face like we do a friend. But we still know He is present in our lives because we can experience the effects. God moves among His people, and we can see it. God speaks to His people, and we can hear the still, small voice. And, just like we can feel the wind across our cheeks, we can feel God's presence. We don't need to physically see God to know that He exists and that He's working.

You are like the wind, Lord. Powerful and fast moving, soft and gentle. We may not see You, but we can sense You. Help us to believe, even when we can't see. Amen.

EVENING
The End of Your Rope

Do not be far from me, for trouble is near and there is no one to help.

PSALM 22:11 NIV

The late youth evangelist Dave Busby said, "The end of your rope is God's permanent address." Jesus reaches down and wraps you in His loving arms when you call to Him for help. The Bible tells us that He is close to the brokenhearted (Psalm 34:18). We may not have the answers we are looking for here in this life, but we can be sure of this: God sees your pain and loves you desperately. Call to Him in times of trouble. If you feel that you're at the end of your rope, look up! His mighty hand is reaching toward you.

Heavenly Father, I feel alone and afraid. Surround me with Your love and give me peace. Amen.

DAY 123

MORNING
Absolute Assurance of Eternal Life

"He who believes in the Son has eternal life; but he who does not obey the Son will not see life, but the wrath of God abides on him."

JOHN 3:36 NASB

Rigo Lopez sought assurance alone in a motel room as he surveyed the shattered pieces of his life. He'd just left his second wife and his children. Tears rolled down his cheeks and he had no answers.

He turned on the TV, and by the grace of God, Billy Graham's voice carried a message of hope. "You can have absolute assurance today of your salvation," Graham preached. Those words went directly to the source of pain in Rigo's heart. Rigo then prayed, "God, give me that assurance. Help me to know that You can forgive me and salvage the ruins of my life."

Rigo returned to his family and began again. He studied and eventually taught the Bible to others. The Word of God says that we can have absolute assurance of eternal life today. Rigo grasped God's truth and his life was transformed.

Lord, I am assured of my salvation. Help me share this absolute truth with those in despair. Amen.

EVENING
Loving the Unlovable

"You have heard the law that says, 'Love your neighbor' and hate your enemy. But I say, love your enemies! Pray for those who persecute you! In that way, you will be acting as true children of your Father in heaven."

MATTHEW 5:43–45 NLT

Sometimes running into difficult people can actually be a "divine appointment"! Maybe you're the only person they'll see all week who wears a smile on her face. When you happen upon others whom you'd rather not talk to, take the time to pray for your attitude and then pray for them. Greet them with a smile and look them in the eye. There is no reason to fear difficult people if you trust in God. He will show you what to do and say as you listen to His promptings (Luke 12:12).

Heavenly Father, I pray that You would help me not to shy away from the people You have allowed to cross my path. Help me speak Your truth and share Your love boldly. Amen.

DAY 124

MORNING

Satisfied

Satisfy us in the morning with your unfailing love, that we may sing for joy and be glad all our days.

PSALM 90:14 NIV

God wants to fulfill you. He wants you to feel satisfied with life so that you will catch yourself humming or singing His praises all day long. Even when life is hard, He is waiting to comfort you with His unfailing love so that gladness will creep over your heart once more.

Father, You are the Author of joy. Thank You so much for Your unfailing love that fills me to the brim. Give me grace and gladness every minute of every day. Amen.

EVENING

Praying the Mind of Christ

We demolish arguments and every pretension that sets itself up against the knowledge of God, and we take captive every thought to make it obedient to Christ.

2 CORINTHIANS 10:5 NIV

By reading and praying scripture and using positive statements in our prayers that claim what God has already said He will do for us, the mind of Christ is being activated in us. By taking captive every thought, we learn to know what thought is of God, what belongs to us, and what is of the enemy. Recognize, take captive, and bind up the thoughts that are of the enemy and throw them out! The more we commune with God, fellowship with Him, and learn from Him, the more we cultivate the mind of Christ.

Lord, help me identify the thoughts that are not Your thoughts and purge them. I know that soon Your thoughts will be the ones that I hear, and not the enemy's. In this way, I will hear You more clearly so I may be an obedient disciple. Amen!

DAY 125

MORNING

But those who wait for the LORD [who expect, look for, and hope in Him] will gain new strength and renew their power; they will lift up their wings [and rise up close to God] like eagles [rising toward the sun]; they will run and not become weary, they will walk and not grow tired.

ISAIAH 40:31 AMP

As long as we are warring inside, we will not find rest. We must find out what Jesus wants for our lives and then obey. Feasting on His Word and learning more about Him will give us the direction we need and the ability to trust. It is only when we understand our salvation and surrender that we can come to Him, unencumbered by guilt or fear, and lay our head on His chest. Safe within His embrace, we can rest.

Father, I am weary and need Your refreshing Spirit to guide me. I trust in You. Amen.

EVENING

Refreshment in Dry Times

"The grass withers and the flowers fall, but the word of our God endures forever."

ISAIAH 40:8 NIV

Sometimes our lives feel just like the grass—dry and listless. Maybe we're in a season where things seem to stand still, and we've tried everything to change our circumstances for the better to no avail. It is during those times that we need to remember the faithfulness of God and the permanence of His Word. His promises to us are many and true! God will never leave us or forsake us; and He will provide for, love, and protect us. And, just like the drought, eventually our personal dry times will give way to a time of growth, refreshment, and beauty.

Dear Lord, help me to remember Your love during difficult times of dryness. Even though it's sometimes hard to hear Your voice or be patient during hard times, please remind me of Your many promises, and remind me to stand firmly on them. You are everything I need and the refreshment I seek. Praises to my Living Water! Amen.

DAY 126

MORNING

Fearfully and Wonderfully Made

For You formed my inward parts; You wove me in my mother's womb. I will give thanks to You, for I am fearfully and wonderfully made; wonderful are Your works, and my soul knows it very well. My frame was not hidden from You, when I was made in secret, and skillfully wrought in the depths of the earth; Your eyes have seen my unformed substance; and in Your book were all written the days that were ordained for me, when as yet there was not one of them.

PSALM 139:13–16 NASB

Each of us has not only an inborn sense that there is a God but also an understanding that we possess a designed intent. Your parents aren't responsible for your creation—God is. Had He not willed your very existence, you would not have happened. God wants to use your life to further His kingdom.

Lord, please renew my understanding that You created me in Your own image and likeness with a body, mind, and spirit. Amen.

EVENING

Whole and Healthy

When Jesus heard this, he told them, "Healthy people don't need a doctor—sick people do. I have come to call not those who think they are righteous, but those who know they are sinners."

MARK 2:17 NLT

With Jesus, we never need to pretend to be something we aren't. We don't need to impress Him with our spiritual maturity and mental acuity. Instead, we can come to Him honestly, with all our neediness, admitting just how weak we are. When we do, we let down the barriers that keep Him out of our hearts. We allow His grace to make us whole and healthy.

Jesus, help me to resist the temptation to be something I'm not. Instead, give me a spirit of vulnerability so that I can receive Your healing grace. Amen.

DAY 127

MORNING

Jungle of Life

God's word is alive and working and is sharper than a double-edged sword. It cuts all the way into us, where the soul and the spirit are joined, to the center of our joints and bones. And it judges the thoughts and feelings in our hearts.

HEBREWS 4:12 NCV

When you take the Bible and live according to God's plans, obeying Him, God's Word cuts like a machete through the entanglements of life. When you choose to use the Sword of Truth, it clears a path and can free you from the weights of the world that try to entrap and ensnare you. No matter what the challenges of life are saying to you today, take His Word and speak His plans into your life. Choose His words of encouragement and peace instead of the negative things life's circumstances are telling you.

God, I want to live in Your truth. I want to believe what You say about me in the Bible. Help me to speak Your words today instead of the problem. Help me believe. Amen.

EVENING

Everlasting Light

In Him was life and that life was the light of all mankind. The light shines in the darkness, and the darkness has not overcome it.

JOHN 1:4–5 NIV

Jesus is the Light of the World who holds out wonderful hope for us. Set your prayer life to start with praise and adoration of the King of kings. Lift your voice in song, or read out loud from the Word. The light will eliminate the darkness every time. Keep your heart and mind set on Him as you walk through the day. Praise for every little thing; nothing is too small for God. A grateful heart and constant praise will bring the light into your day.

Dear Lord, how we love You. We trust in You this day to lead us on the right path lit with Your light. Amen.

DAY 128

MORNING
Strength Is Not in Numbers

The LORD said to Gideon, "The people who are with you are too many for Me to give Midian into their hands, for Israel would become boastful, saying, 'My own power has delivered me.' Now therefore come, proclaim in the hearing of the people, saying, 'Whoever is afraid and trembling, let him return and depart from Mount Gilead.' "

JUDGES 7:2–3 NASB

Why can't we get it through our heads that if God is on our side, we don't need anyone else? Perhaps because we can't see Him.

Gideon had the same challenge. His own "battle strategy" included amassing a multitude that would obliterate the Midianites. And God told him no. God did not desire to perform a miracle that might be misconstrued as an act accomplished by human hands.

Instead, God had Gideon keep whittling down that number of troops. Finally, with a mere three hundred men, Gideon crossed the Jordan and won the battle. But the people who followed him still hadn't understood.

Lord, have I watched Your hand of deliverance in my own life only to become complacent? Help me repent! Amen.

EVENING
O the Deep, Deep Love of Jesus

I pray that out of his glorious riches he may strengthen you with power through his Spirit in your inner being, so that Christ may dwell in your hearts through faith. And I pray that you, being rooted and established in love, may have power, together with all the Lord's holy people, to grasp how wide and long and high and deep is the love of Christ.

EPHESIANS 3:16–18 NIV

What an amazing picture. That He should care for us in such a way is almost incomprehensible. Despite our shortcomings, our sin, He loves us. It takes a measure of faith to believe in His love. When we feel a nagging thought of unworthiness, of being unlovable, trust in the Word and sing a new song. For His love is deep and wide.

Lord, thank You for loving me, even when I'm unlovable. Amen.

DAY 129

MORNING

His Steady Hand

The Lord makes firm the steps of the one who delights in him; though he may stumble, he will not fall, for the Lord upholds him with his hand.

Psalm 37:23–24 niv

The Lord knows there are times when we will stumble. We may even backslide into the very activity that caused us to call on the Lord for salvation in the first place. But His Word assures us His love is eternal and when we cry out to Him, He will hear. Do not be discouraged with those stumbling blocks in your path, because the Lord is with you always. Scripture tells us we are in the palm of His hand. Hope is found in the Lord. He delights in us and wants the very best for us because of His perfect love.

Lord God, the cross was necessary for sinners like me. I thank You that You loved me enough to choose me, and I accepted Your free gift of salvation and perfect love. Amen.

EVENING

The Ultimate Act of Love

Bring joy to your servant, Lord, for I put my trust in you. You, Lord, are forgiving and good, abounding in love to all who call to you.

Psalm 86:4–5 niv

Forgiveness doesn't require that the person who did the hurting apologize or acknowledge what he or she has done. It's not about making the score even. It doesn't even require forgetting about the incident. But it is about admitting that the one who hurt us is human, just like we are. We surrender our right for revenge and, like God, let go and give the wrongdoer mercy, therefore blessing and ultimately choosing to love that person.

Gracious and loving Father, thank You that You love me and have forgiven me of my sins. May I be more like You in forgiving others. Although I may not be able to forgive as easily as You do, please encourage me to take those small steps. In forgiving others, Father, I am that much closer to being like You. Amen.

DAY 130

MORNING
What God Shows Us

The Lord is righteous in everything he does; he is filled with kindness.

Psalm 145:17 NLT

Did you know that the word kind comes from the same root as kin? Both words originally had to do with intimate shared relationships like the ones that exist between members of the same family. This is what God shows us: the kindness of a good father, the gentleness of a good mother, the understanding of a brother or sister.

Good Father, thank You for Your kindness and for creating me with a longing to be close to You. May I find rest in Your nearness. Amen.

EVENING
Reap in Joy!

Remember this: Whoever sows sparingly will also reap sparingly, and whoever sows generously will also reap generously.

2 Corinthians 9:6 NIV

Each of us wants to feel appreciated, and we like to deal with a friendly person. Have you ever worked with a person who seemed to have a perpetually bad attitude? You probably didn't feel particularly encouraged after an encounter with this coworker. Yes, sometimes things go wrong, but your attitude in the thick of it is determined by your expectations. If you expect things to turn out well, you'll generally have a positive mental attitude. Treat everyone with genuine kindness, courtesy, and respect, and that is what will be reflected back to you.

Heavenly Father, help me plant the seeds of patience, love, compassion, and courtesy in all those I come in contact with. Please let me make an eternal difference in these people's lives. I want to joyfully reap a rich harvest for Your kingdom. Amen!

DAY 131

MORNING

I Give Up

God so loved the world that he gave his one and only Son, that whoever believes in him shall not perish but have eternal life.

JOHN 3:16 NIV

Our Creator God cares enough about us to delve into our everyday lives and help us. Through the Holy Spirit within, God's gentle hand of direction will sustain each of us, enabling us to grow closer to our Father. The closer we grow, the more like Him we desire to be. Then His influence spreads through us to others. When we surrender, He is able to use our lives and enrich others. What a powerful message: Give up and give more!

Lord, thank You for loving us despite our frailties. What an encouragement to me today. Amen.

EVENING

Why Praise God?

Though he slay me, yet will I trust in him.

JOB 13:15 KJV

It's difficult to praise God when problems press in harder than a crowd exiting a burning building. But that's the time to praise Him the most. We wait for our circumstances to change, while God desires to change us despite them. Praise coupled with prayer in our darkest moments is what moves the mighty hand of God to work in our hearts and lives. How can we pray and praise God when everything goes wrong? The bigger question might be: How can we not?

Jesus, help me to pray and praise You despite my circumstances. Amen.

DAY 132

MORNING
Born Again

"Truly, truly, I say to you, unless one is born again he cannot see the kingdom of God."

JOHN 3:3 NASB

Nicodemus came to Christ under cover, by night. Although the Pharisees, the group of religious leaders to which he belonged, had reached the conclusion that Christ was sent from God, they hadn't bridged the gap to full understanding.

Nicodemus obviously heard what Christ said and couldn't shake it loose from his thoughts. He sought the truth, so Christ made it as clear as a starlit night.

Later in the scriptures, we see Nicodemus as the one who boldly risks his life to help Joseph of Arimathea take Christ's body from the cross. And Nicodemus brought an expensive "mixture of myrrh and aloes, about a hundred pounds weight. So they took the body of Jesus and bound it in linen wrappings with the spices, as is the burial custom of the Jews" (John 19:39–40 NASB).

Lord, You told Nicodemus he must be born again. I praise You that You are the God of second chances, the God of truth! Amen.

EVENING
Thrive!

Those who trust in their riches will fall, but the righteous will thrive like a green leaf.

PROVERBS 11:28 NIV

Money seems so important in our world. Many things we want depend on money—that remodeling project we're hoping to do, the Christmas gifts we want to give, the vacation we hope to take, and the new car we want to drive. There's nothing wrong with any of those things, but our enjoyment of them will always be fleeting. Only God's daily grace makes us truly grow and thrive.

Father, remind me that while caring for my family, making money, and preparing for my future are good things, they are not my identity. Help me to find my purpose, my worth, in You. Amen.

DAY 133

MORNING

As for God, his way is perfect;
the word of the LORD is tried: he is a
buckler to all them that trust in him.

2 SAMUEL 22:31 KJV

God's Word is such an incredible gift—one that goes hand in hand with prayer. It's amazing, really, that the Creator of the universe gave us the scriptures as His personal Word to us. When we're faithful to pick up the Word, He is faithful to use it to encourage us. Reading and praying through scripture is one of the keys to finding and keeping our sanity, peace, and joy.

God, thank You for Your gift of the
holy scriptures and sweet communion
with You through prayer. Amen.

EVENING

Knowing God's Precepts

Teach me Your statutes. Make me understand the way of Your precepts, so I will meditate on Your wonders. My soul weeps because of grief; strengthen me according to Your word. Remove the false way from me, and graciously grant me Your law.

PSALM 119:26–29 NASB

Martin Luther, an Augustinian monk, recognized that the precepts he learned from studying the scriptures didn't mesh with the teachings of the Roman Catholic Church. Therefore, in 1517, he openly stated his objections to the Catholic Church by nailing his Ninety-Five "Theses" to the door of the church at Wittenberg. This began the revival that led to the formation of the Protestant Church.

Confession of sin is the beginning of true hope. For when we acknowledge that we've failed, God can use our broken and contrite heart, through the Holy Spirit, to mold us anew.

Understand and walk in the way of His precepts by meditating on God's Word. If you're not participating in an in-depth Bible study, consider finding or starting one.

Lord, teach me Your ways, that I might live
out Your precepts before my family
and loved ones. Amen.

DAY 134

MORNING

The Right Focus

Turning your ear to wisdom and applying your heart to understanding—indeed, if you call out for insight and cry aloud for understanding, and if you look for it as for silver and search for it as for hidden treasure, then you will understand the fear of the LORD and find the knowledge of God.

PROVERBS 2:2–5 NIV

Frustration and stress can keep us from clearly seeing the things that God puts before us. Time spent in prayer and meditation on God's Word can often wash away the dirt and grime of the day-to-day and provide a clear picture of God's intentions for our lives. Step outside the pressure and into His presence, and get the right focus for whatever you're facing today.

Lord, help me to avoid distractions and keep my eyes on You. Amen.

EVENING

Pass It On!

After the usual readings from the books of Moses and the prophets, those in charge of the service sent them this message: "Brothers, if you have any word of encouragement for the people, come and give it."

ACTS 13:15 NLT

Encouragement brings hope. Have you ever received a word from someone that instantly lifted your spirit? Did you receive a bit of good news or something that diminished your negative outlook? Perhaps a particular conversation helped to bring your problems into perspective. Paul passed on encouragement and many benefited. So the next time you're encouraged, pass it on! You may never know how your words or actions benefited someone else.

Lord, thank You for the wellspring of encouragement through Your holy Word. Amen.

DAY 135

MORNING
Seek God

"I love all who love me.
Those who search will surely find me."
PROVERBS 8:17 NLT

Scripture tells us that God loves those who love Him and that if we search for Him, we will surely find Him. One translation of the Bible says it this way: "Those who seek me early and diligently will find me" (Proverbs 8:17 AMP). Seek God in all things and in all ways. Search for Him in each moment of every day you are blessed to walk on this earth. He is found easily in His creation and in His Word. He is with you. Just look for Him. He wants to be found!

Father in heaven, thank You for Your unfailing love for me. Help me to search for You diligently. I know that when I seek, I will find You. Amen.

EVENING
Open the Book

For everything that was written in the past was written to teach us, so that through endurance taught in the Scriptures and the encouragement they provide we might have hope.
ROMANS 15:4 NIV

Life is tough. We get discouraged and, at times, disheartened to the point of such despair it's hard to recover. Reading *all* of God's Word is paramount. It is the source of hope, peace, encouragement, salvation, and so much more. It moves people to take action while diminishing depression and discouragement. As the writer of Hebrews put it, "For the word of God is alive and active. Sharper than any double-edged sword" (Hebrews 4:12 NIV). Need some encouragement? Open the Book.

Lord, help me read Your Word consistently to empower me with the hope and encouragement I need. Amen.

DAY 136

MORNING

Which of you, intending to build a tower, sitteth not down first, and counteth the cost, whether he have sufficient to finish it?

LUKE 14:28 KJV

Every person has the same amount of life each day. What matters is how you spend it. It's easy to waste your day doing insignificant things, leaving little time for God. The most important things in life are eternal endeavors. Spending time in prayer to God for others. Giving your life to building a relationship with God by reading His Word and growing in faith. Sharing Christ with others and giving them the opportunity to know Him. These are things that will last. What are you spending your life on? What are you getting out of what you give yourself to each day?

Heavenly Father, my life is full. I ask that You give me wisdom and instruction to give my life to the things that matter most. The time I have is precious and valuable. Help me to invest it wisely in eternal things. Amen.

EVENING

God's Message to the Churches

"But I have this against you, that you have left your first love."

REVELATION 2:4 NASB

One of my favorite questions to ask couples over dinner is "How did you meet?" Each story invariably presents a set of impossible circumstances that had to be orchestrated in order to bring this man and woman together. As these details are relayed, a glow begins to come back into the eyes of those remembering. There is nothing to compare with that "first bloom of love."

This is the kind of love that God desires from us. That on-fire, totally consuming, single focus of our attention. His call to the church at Ephesus then was that they remember their first love—and rekindle their purpose to seek Him first.

Oh Lord, may Your light be the fire in my soul! Amen.

DAY 137

MORNING

Paul's Prayer for the Jews

Brethren, my heart's desire and my prayer to God for them is for their salvation.

ROMANS 10:1 NASB

Is the deepest concern of your heart that those whom you love will share heaven with Christ? The deepest longing of Paul's soul was that the Jews might know their Messiah.

Paul longed for the Israelites, "to whom belongs the adoption as sons, and the glory and the covenants and the giving of the Law and the temple service and the promises," to understand that Christ had come to save them (Romans 9:4 NASB).

The Jews couldn't truly be God's children until they partook of the light of truth. "For the Scripture says, 'WHOEVER BELIEVES IN HIM WILL NOT BE DISAPPOINTED.' For there is no distinction between Jew and Greek; for the same Lord is Lord of all, abounding in riches for all who call on Him; for 'WHOEVER WILL CALL UPON THE NAME OF THE LORD WILL BE SAVED' " (Romans 10:11–13 NASB).

Lord, clarify Your Word, that women may yield in faith. Amen.

EVENING

Thankful, Thankful Heart

I will praise you, LORD, with all my heart. I will tell all the miracles you have done.

PSALM 9:1 NCV

When you choose to approach life from the positive side, you can find thankfulness in most of life's circumstances. It completely changes your outlook, your attitude, and your countenance. When you are tempted to feel sorry for yourself or to blame others or God for difficulties, push PAUSE. Take a moment and rewind your life. Look back and count the blessings God has given you. As you remind yourself of all He has done for you and in you, it will bring change to your attitude and give you hope in the situation you're facing. Count your blessings today.

Lord, I am thankful for my life and all You have done for me. When life happens, help me to respond to it in a healthy, positive way. Remind me to look to You and trust You to carry me through life's challenges. Amen.

DAY 138

MORNING
Love Your Enemies

"Love your enemies, do good to them, and lend to them without expecting to get anything back. Then your reward will be great."

LUKE 6:35 NIV

God calls us to a love so brave, so intense that it defies logic and turns the world on its side. He calls us to love like He loves. That means we must show patience where others have been short. We must show kindness where others have been cruel. We must look for ways to bless, when others have cursed. God promises great rewards for those who do this. Oh, the rewards may not be immediate. But when God promises great rewards, we can know without doubt that any present struggle will be repaid with goodness and blessing, many times over.

Dear Father, help me to love those who hate me, bless those who curse me, and show kindness to those who have been cruel. Help me to love like You love. Amen.

EVENING
An Angel Visits Ophrah

Then the angel of the LORD came and sat under the oak that was in Ophrah. . . Gideon was beating out wheat in the wine press in order to save it from the Midianites. The angel of the LORD appeared to him and said to him, "The LORD is with you, O valiant warrior."

JUDGES 6:11–12 NASB

The Lord was about to sell a very surprised man named Gideon on the idea of becoming Israel's next judge. God knew Gideon longed for deliverance for Israel. Once again Israel had turned to their age-old sin of idolatry.

Have you ever felt like the weight of the world rested on your shoulders? Well, that's Gideon for you. "O Lord, how shall I deliver Israel? Behold, my family is the least in Manasseh, and I am the youngest in my father's house" (Judges 6:15). The Lord answered Gideon with the same resounding message of assurance that He always gives to His servants: "Surely I will be with you" (Judges 6:16). God is with us in the fight and that's enough!

Father, hold my hand today and every day. Amen.

DAY 139

MORNING
Nehemiah and the Walls of Jerusalem

"The remnant there in the province who survived the captivity are in great distress and reproach, and the wall of Jerusalem is broken down and its gates are burned with fire."

NEHEMIAH 1:3 NASB

Nehemiah records the events that took place as Jerusalem's walls were repaired. Fortified walls were necessary not only to guard the perimeter of the great city, but also to demonstrate the renewed pride and unity of its citizens.

Nehemiah requested that King Artaxerxes send him to Judah that he might rebuild the walls. And all of Nehemiah's time of fasting and prayer was answered as the king wrote letters of safe passage for him to all "the governors of the provinces beyond the River" (Nehemiah 2:7 NASB). In God's timing Nehemiah shared his plan with the remnant of Israel.

Lord, let me learn from Nehemiah's example. Let me seek Your will through prayer and study, never losing sight of Your Son. Amen.

EVENING
Rejoice!

Rejoice in the Lord always. I will say it again: Rejoice!

PHILIPPIANS 4:4 NIV

When God is the source of our joy, we will never lose that joy. Circumstances may frustrate us and break our hearts. But God is able to supply all our needs. He is able to restore broken relationships. He can give us a new job or help us to succeed at our current job. Through it all, despite it all, we can rejoice in knowing that we are God's, and He loves us.

Dear Father, thank You for loving me. Help me to make You the source of my joy. Amen.

MORNING

"For even if the mountains walk away and the hills fall to pieces, my love won't walk away from you, my covenant commitment of peace won't fall apart." The God who has compassion on you says so.

Isaiah 54:10 MSG

We must rest in God's wild, unbending love for us. He promises in Isaiah that no matter what happens, He will never remove Himself from us. When we believe Him wholeheartedly and rest in His love, we will be filled with fear-busting peace and adventurous faith. That faith allows us to dream big dreams and conquer the worries that keep us chained.

Lord, thank You for Your love, which never leaves me. Help me to rest in Your love above all else. Amen.

EVENING

God's Protection for Widows

The Lord will tear down the house of the proud, but He will establish the boundary of the widow.

Proverbs 15:25 NASB

Christmas shopping preoccupied my father's thoughts as he picked out one special gift for each child, something he or she had wanted all year. But just after the last gift had been purchased, a severe heart attack overtook my dad.

My mother's first concern was how she might continue caring for her children, all ten of whom lived at home. No matter what her hardships, Mom has honored God, in whom she placed her faith and the care of her life. She's now been widowed far longer than the years she was married. She's raised her children, paid off her mortgage, and passed down her love of art to all her grandchildren.

Father, let me share Your Word with those women who now find themselves alone—"Now she who is a widow indeed and who has been left alone, has fixed her hope on God and continues in entreaties and prayers night and day" (1 Timothy 5:5 NASB). Amen.

DAY 141

MORNING
Full Redemption and Love

Israel, put your hope in the LORD,
for with the LORD is unfailing love
and with him is full redemption.

PSALM 130:7 NIV

The Bible tells us that God removes our sins as far as the east is from the west (Psalm 103:12) and that He remembers our sin no more (Isaiah 43:25; Hebrews 8:12). It's so important to confess your sins to the Lord as soon as you feel convicted and then turn from them and move in a right direction. There is no reason to hang your head in shame over sins of the past. Don't allow the devil to speak lies into your life. You have full redemption through Jesus Christ!

Dear Jesus, I confess my sin to You.
Thank You for blotting out each mistake
and not holding anything against me.
Help me to make right choices through
the power of Your Spirit inside me. Amen.

EVENING
Unfailing Love

I will instruct you and teach you in the way you should go; I will counsel you with my loving eye on you. . . . Many are the woes of the wicked, but the LORD's unfailing love surrounds the one who trusts in him.

PSALM 32:8, 10 NIV

God's love surrounds us always—if we trust in Him. Have you put your complete trust in the Lord? If not, open your heart to Him and ask Him to become the Lord of your life. Jesus is standing at the door of your heart, ready to come in when you respond (Revelation 3:20). Or maybe you've already accepted Christ as your Savior, but you're not really sure if He can be trusted. Know that He has been faithful to His children through all generations and that He is working out every circumstance in your life for your own good (Romans 8:28).

Father God, I praise You for Your unfailing
love. Continue to counsel me and lead me
in the way I should go. Thank You for
watching over me. Help me trust
You completely. Amen.

DAY 142

MORNING

Joel Prophesies a Final Judgment

Hasten and come, all you surrounding nations, and gather yourselves there. Bring down, O LORD, Your mighty ones. Let the nations be aroused and come up to the valley of Jehoshaphat, for there I will sit to judge all the surrounding nations.

JOEL 3:11–12 NASB

Jerusalem will be the site of the world's last and greatest battle as all the surrounding nations rage against the Holy City. However, the powerful, almighty God of the universe will intervene on Israel's behalf.

"The LORD roars from Zion and utters His voice from Jerusalem, and the heavens and the earth tremble. But the LORD is a refuge for His people and a stronghold to the sons of Israel. Then you will know that I am the LORD your God, dwelling in Zion, My holy mountain. So Jerusalem will be holy, and strangers will pass through it no more" (Joel 3:16–17 NASB).

Lord, I don't like to consider the brutality of this final judgment. However, I know that You are fair and just and have given men and women ample time and warning to repent. Amen.

EVENING

The Stone the Builders Rejected

The stone which the builders rejected has become the chief corner stone.

PSALM 118:22 NASB

When a building is started, a cornerstone must be placed precisely because the rest of the structure is lined up with it. Likewise, Jesus Christ is the Cornerstone of the Church. And His Church is composed of both Jews and Gentiles, united as the body of Christ and dependent upon Him for guidance.

Before the world began, God envisioned His Church. Jesus Christ, the Son, would come and die for its members so that they would be cleansed from sin. And Christ would be the very foundation upon which this Church would stand.

Is Jesus Christ the true Cornerstone of your church? If you're looking for a church home, make sure you check the "foundation" first.

Lord Jesus Christ, You alone are to be the Cornerstone of my life. Please help me to discard those concerns that block my view of You. Amen.

DAY 143

MORNING
Peaceful Hearts

You will keep in perfect peace all who trust in you, all whose thoughts are fixed on you!

Isaiah 26:3 NLT

Peace seems very far away sometimes. But it's not! Peace isn't an emotion we can work up in our own strength. It's one of the gifts of grace God longs to give us. All we need to do is focus on Him. As we give Him all our worries, one by one, every day, He will do His part: He will keep our hearts at peace.

Jesus, I am incredibly grateful for Your peace. It is a gift I need every moment of every day. When my heart gets anxious, comfort me with the peace only You can provide. Amen.

EVENING
Look Up!

Your love, Lord, reaches to the heavens, your faithfulness to the skies.

Psalm 36:5 NIV

In Bible times, people often studied the sky. Looking up at the heavens reminded them of God and His mighty wonders. A rainbow was God's sign to Noah that a flood would never again destroy the earth. God used a myriad of stars to foretell Abraham's abundant family, and a single star heralded Christ's birth. This immense space that we call "sky" is a reflection of God's infinite love and faithfulness. So take time today. Look up at the heavens, and thank God for His endless love.

Heavenly Father, remind me to stop and appreciate Your wonderful creations. And as I look upward, fill me with Your infinite love. Amen.

DAY 144

MORNING
Thou Shalt Not Worry!

"Do not worry about tomorrow,
for tomorrow will worry about itself.
Each day has enough trouble of its own."

MATTHEW 6:34 NIV

What if the Lord had written an eleventh commandment: "Thou shalt not worry." In a sense, He did! He commands us in various scriptures not to fret. So, cast your anxieties on the Lord. Give them up! Let them go! Don't let worries zap your strength and your joy. Today is a gift from the Lord. Don't sacrifice it to fears and frustrations! Let them go. . .and watch God work!

Father God, lift all anxiety from my heart and make my spirit light again. I know that I can't do it on my own. But with You, I can let go. . .and watch You work! I praise You, God! Amen.

EVENING
Joy. . .Minute by Minute

Keep your eyes focused on what is right,
and look straight ahead to what is good.

PROVERBS 4:25 NCV

Ever wonder how you can be perfectly happy one minute and upset the next? If joy is a choice, then it's one you have to make. . .continually. We are often ruled by our emotions, which is why it's so important to stay focused, especially when you're having a tough day. Don't let frustration steal even sixty seconds from you. Instead, choose joy!

Dear heavenly Father, please help me to keep my emotions in check today—and every day. If I keep my focus on You—and because of Your goodness, God—I can always choose joy. Amen.

DAY 145

MORNING
Finding the Messiah

He found first his own brother Simon and said to him, "We have found the Messiah" (which translated means Christ).

John 1:41 NASB

I'll never forget the day that I accepted Jesus Christ as my Savior. I'd been drawn to church twice that day, aware that my soul ached for peace. So many Christians had told me that all I needed to do was "pray and ask Christ into my life." But that seemed overly simplistic. How could this action change my life?

A short time before, while recovering from a compression fracture in my back, I began attending a Bible study. Now those scriptures I'd heard there began to come back to me. It wasn't a matter of reciting words. Instead, asking Christ into my life meant being willing to trade all the emptiness and estrangement within my soul for the completeness that He alone could provide.

Lord, I pray for strength to share Your love with unbelieving family members. Amen.

EVENING
An Offering of Joy

Then my head will be exalted above the enemies who surround me; at his sacred tent I will sacrifice with shouts of joy; I will sing and make music to the Lord.

Psalm 27:6 NIV

It's one thing to offer a sacrifice of joy when things are going your way and people are treating you fairly. But when you've been through a terrible betrayal, it's often hard to recapture that feeling of joy. As you face hurts and betrayals, remember that God is the lifter of your head. Sing praises and continue to offer a sacrifice of joy!

Lord, lift my head. Wrap me in Your warm embrace. Help me to remember that even though I've experienced betrayal, I can still praise You and offer a sacrifice of joy. I love You, Father! Amen.

DAY 146

MORNING

Renewing Our Minds

Present your bodies a living and holy sacrifice, acceptable to God, which is your spiritual service of worship. And do not be conformed to this world, but be transformed by the renewing of your mind, so that you may prove what the will of God is, that which is good and acceptable and perfect.

ROMANS 12:1–2 NASB

Mary had lived an exemplary life and was betrothed to Joseph. Then an angel came with an announcement that would cast a shadow of doubt on her impeccable character. God had told Mary to bear His Son.

Leaving the results of this decision in the hands of her powerful God, Mary accepted her role as the mother of the Messiah. And during the difficult days that followed, she allowed the Word of God to renew her mind.

Lord, I am grateful for Mary's example. Amen.

EVENING

A Joyous Treasure

"The kingdom of heaven is like treasure hidden in a field. When a man found it, he hid it again, and then in his joy went and sold all he had and bought that field."

MATTHEW 13:44 NIV

Have you ever stumbled across a rare treasure—one so priceless that you would be willing to trade everything you own to have it? If you've given your heart to Christ, if you've accepted His work on Calvary, then you have already obtained the greatest treasure of all. . .new life in Him. Oh, what immeasurable joy comes from knowing He's placed that treasure in your heart for all eternity!

Father, thank You for the gift of Your Son. Because of Your loving sacrifice, I can forever have joy in my heart. . .knowing that I will spend eternity in heaven with You. Amen.

DAY 147

MORNING
Those Born of God Obey Him

Whoever believes that Jesus is the Christ is born of God, and whoever loves the Father loves the child born of Him. By this we know that we love the children of God, when we love God and observe His commandments.

1 JOHN 5:1–2 NASB

When our children disobey, we feel not only extreme disappointment but a sense that they don't love us. For if they did, they would understand that our instructions are meant to guide them over the rough terrain of life. This is exactly how God feels when we fail to follow Him, for He equates love with obedience.

Lord, if I'm wandering without purpose, please bring me close to You. Amen.

EVENING
Joy in the Battle

Then they returned, every man of Judah and Jerusalem, and Jehoshaphat in the forefront of them, to go again to Jerusalem with joy; for the LORD had made them to rejoice over their enemies.

2 CHRONICLES 20:27 KJV

Enemy forces were just around the bend. Jehoshaphat, king of Judah, called his people together. After much prayer, he sent the worshippers (the Levites) to the front lines, where they began singing joyful praises as they went. The battle was won! When you face your next battle, praise your way through it! Strength and joy will rise up within you! Prepare for victory!

No matter what kind of hardship I face, Father God, I want to praise my way through it and come through even stronger than I was before. Thank You for helping me to win life's battles, both large and small. Amen.

DAY 148

MORNING
Eternal Joy!

And the ransomed of the L*ORD shall return, and come to Zion with songs and everlasting joy upon their heads: they shall obtain joy and gladness, and sorrow and sighing shall flee away.*

ISAIAH 35:10 KJV

Have you ever pondered eternity? Forever and ever and ever. . . ? Our finite minds can't grasp the concept, and yet one thing we understand from scripture—we will enter eternity in a state of everlasting joy and gladness. No more tears! No sorrow! An eternal joy fest awaits us! Now that's something to celebrate!

When life becomes difficult, help me to keep things in perspective, Father. The hardships I face in the day-to-day are but blips in time compared to the eternal joy I will experience in heaven. Thank You for joy that lasts forever. Amen.

EVENING
Joyous Freedom

Blessed is he whose transgression is forgiven, whose sin is covered.

PSALM 32:1 KJV

What if you were locked up in a prison cell for years on end? You waited for the day when the jailer would turn that key in the lock—releasing you once and for all. In a sense, experiencing God's forgiveness is like being set free from prison. Can you fathom the joy? Walking into the sunshine for the first time in years? Oh, praise Him for His forgiveness today!

Sweet freedom, Lord. . . It's a beautiful feeling to have experienced the joy of Your complete and utter forgiveness. Thank You for setting my spirit free! Amen.

DAY 149

MORNING
The Gathering at the Water Gate

And all the people gathered. . .at the square. . . in front of the Water Gate, and they asked Ezra the scribe to bring the book of the law of Moses which the LORD had given to Israel. Then Ezra the priest brought the law before the assembly . . .on the first day of the seventh month. He read from it before the square. . .and all the people were attentive to the book of the law.

NEHEMIAH 8:1–3 NASB

Through inspired teamwork, Nehemiah and the remnant of Israel finished rebuilding the wall in only fifty-two days (Nehemiah 6:15). Even their enemies lost the will to fight, recognizing this accomplishment as coming from the hand of Israel's God. Four times Sanballat and Geshem sent messages to Nehemiah, hoping to drag him away from finishing his task. And each time Nehemiah responded by saying, "I am doing a great work and I cannot come down" (Nehemiah 6:3 NASB). Sanballat accused Nehemiah of appointing prophets to proclaim that a king was in Judah (Nehemiah 6:7).

Still, Nehemiah refused to become agitated or frightened. Instead, he relied on God's strength.

Lord, let Nehemiah be an example of trust for me. Amen.

EVENING
Focusing on the Eternal Future

The LORD has made everything for its own purpose, even the wicked for the day of evil.

PROVERBS 16:4 NASB

Horoscopes in newspapers and psychic telephone hotlines exist because people have a natural curiosity to know the future. Despite the phenomenal success of recent Hollywood blockbusters, I can assure you an attack by aliens is not on the horizon. No, our real threat will come from within the very real but unseen spiritual realm, not the extraterrestrial.

Surrounding us are beings from another world, but they belong to Satan. And their sole purpose is to seduce us into wavering from the truth. They dangle and then entangle us from the scaffolding of unbelief. *Did God mean what He said? Doesn't He want us to have any fun? Do we really need Him telling us what to do?* Absolutely! Only God can give us a secure, peaceful, and perfect future. An eternal future in heaven with Him.

Lord, there have been times when I compromised the truth of Your Word. Please help me get back on track. Place my feet firmly on the pavement of Your Word. Amen.

DAY 150

MORNING
Pressed Down, Running Over

Give, and it shall be given unto you; good measure, pressed down, and shaken together, and running over, shall men give into your bosom.

Luke 6:38 KJV

"Give, and it shall be given unto you." Likely, if you've been walking with the Lord for any length of time, you've heard this dozens of times. Do we give so that we can get? No, we give out of a grateful heart, and the Lord—in His generosity—meets our needs. Today, pause and thank Him for the many gifts He has given you. Do you feel the joy running over?

Lord, help me to always give from a grateful heart and never because I plan to get something in return. You have given me abundant blessings, Father. Thank You for always meeting my needs. Amen.

EVENING
Who Exalts?

No one from the east or the west or from the desert can exalt themselves. It is God who judges: He brings one down, he exalts another.

Psalm 75:6–7 NIV

Sometimes we grumble when others are exalted. We feel left out. Why do others prosper when everything around us seems to be falling apart? We can't celebrate their victories. We aren't joyful for them. Shame on us! God chooses whom to exalt. . .and when. We can't pretend to know His thoughts. But we can submit to His will and celebrate with those who are walking through seasons of great favor.

God, it's so hard to be happy for others when I feel like I haven't been blessed in the same way. Please help me to rejoice when others experience Your favor, while I continue to trust that You have a plan for my life—and that Your plan is good! Amen.

DAY 151

MORNING
A Sacrifice of Praise

Is any among you afflicted? let him pray.
Is any merry? let him sing psalms.

JAMES 5:13 KJV

It's tough to praise when you're not feeling well, isn't it? But that's exactly what God calls us to do. If you're struggling today, reach way down deep. . . . Out of your pain, your weakness, offer God a sacrifice of praise. Spend serious time in prayer. Lift up a song of joy—even if it's a weak song! You'll be surprised how He energizes you with His great joy!

I'm struggling today, God. But that's no surprise to You, is it? You know just how I feel. Please energize my sluggish spirit. I want to sing praises to You! Amen.

EVENING
When Will Christ Rapture the Faithful?

Now we request you, brethren, with regard to the coming of our Lord Jesus Christ and our gathering together to Him, that you not be quickly shaken from your composure or be disturbed either by a spirit or a message or a letter as if from us, to the effect that the day of the Lord has come. Let no one in any way deceive you.

2 THESSALONIANS 2:1–3 NASB

Paul and Timothy had founded the church at Thessalonica. For a time these Thessalonians remained strong. But then came persecution so severe that they were shaken to their roots. If these trial-filled days comprised their last moments on earth, where was the hope of being "caught up in Christ"? Paul wanted to dispel their misconceptions and correct several weaknesses in this church.

Before the antichrist bursts onto the world scene, there will be a great falling away from the truth (1 Timothy 4:1–3).

Even so, come Lord Jesus!
In Your name I pray, amen.

MORNING

Thus says the Lord, *"For three transgressions of Damascus and for four I will not revoke its punishment."*

Amos 1:3 NASB

Throughout the Old Testament we've read accounts of God's wrath and fury directed toward those whom He loved who were flagrantly disobedient. But God also extended His loving hand of protection to those who walked in obedience.

Amos was a simple sheepherder from a small city about ten miles south of Jerusalem. He was called by God to deliver a warning to these stiff-necked, idol-worshipping people of the northern kingdom of Israel.

Contained within the nine chapters of this book is a list of the cities and peoples whom God considered ripe for judgment, along with the specific warnings. As angry as God already was, He still gave these people two years to repent before the great earthquake came. Still, the people refused to listen.

Lord, thank You for Amos's prophecy: "Also I will restore the captivity of My people Israel, and they will rebuild the ruined cities and live in them" (Amos 9:14 NASB*). Amen.*

EVENING

Joyful in Glory

Let the saints be joyful in glory: let them sing aloud upon their beds.

Psalm 149:5 KJV

When do you like to spend time alone with the Lord? In the morning, as the stillness of the day sweeps over you? At night, when you rest your head upon the pillow? Start your conversation with praise. Let your favorite worship song or hymn pour forth! Tell Him how blessed you are to be His child. This private praise time will strengthen you and will fill your heart with joy!

As I enter into this conversation with You, Father, I praise You. Thank You for being Lord—and leader—of my life. Amen.

DAY 153

MORNING

Finishing with Joy

But none of these things move me, neither count I my life dear unto myself, so that I might finish my course with joy.

Acts 20:24 KJV

The Christian life is a journey, isn't it? We move from point A to point B, and then on from there—all the while growing in our faith. Instead of focusing on the ups and downs of the journey, we should be looking ahead, to the finish line. We want to be people who finish well. Today, set your sights on that unseen line that lies ahead. What joy will come when you cross it!

Father God, help me to keep my eyes on the finish line so I can finish my journey with joy. Amen.

EVENING

Everyday Joy

For in him we live, and move, and have our being.

Acts 17:28 KJV

Every breath we breathe comes from God. Every step we take is a gift from our Creator. We can do nothing apart from Him. In the same sense, every joy, every sorrow. . .God goes through each one with us. His heart is for us. We can experience joy in our everyday lives, even when things aren't going our way. We simply have to remember that He is in control. We have our being. . .in Him!

Thank You for being in control of all things, God. I would rather have You by my side than anyone else in the world—through every up, down, and in between, You are there! Amen.

DAY 154

MORNING

The Apple of God's Eye

"For the day of the LORD draws near on all the nations. As you have done, it will be done to you. Your dealings will return on your own head."

OBADIAH 1:15 NASB

Obadiah is such a tiny Old Testament book that you've probably overlooked it. Yet there are prophecies and promises for Israel here that can't be missed.

Israel, the people God had chosen, began to feel so overconfident that they considered themselves invincible. But it wasn't God choosing them that made them special. Instead, it was the protection of God that rendered them unique as a people. But now their arrogance and lack of true worship rendered them vulnerable to attack. Obadiah calls Israel back to worship their God, but also issues a warning to Edom, the nation intent on wiping them out.

Lord, let me remember that it is Christ who is the head of His Church and I am but a member of the body. Amen.

EVENING

Mercy Multiplied

Mercy unto you, and peace, and love, be multiplied.

JUDE 1:2 KJV

Have you ever done the math on God's mercy? If so, you've probably figured out that it just keeps multiplying itself out, over and over again. We mess up; He extends mercy. We mess up again; He pours out mercy once again. In the same way, peace, love, and joy are multiplied back to us. Praise the Lord! God's mathematics work in our favor.

Father God, I am so thankful that Your math works differently than mine! Amen.

DAY 155

MORNING

A Discerning Woman

Wisdom reposes in the heart of the discerning and even among fools she lets herself be known.

PROVERBS 14:33 NIV

Dorothy, a precious older woman, faithfully attended my Bible study group each week despite the fact that she suffered from congestive heart failure. She was the kind of person one treasured as a gift, knowing the time with her would be all too brief. She shared the contents of her heart freely, no longer restricted behind the confining walls of decorum. From her perspective, the word *cherish* didn't exist in her husband's vocabulary.

We would pray and cry together over the grief her marriage had caused her soul. And then she'd sit and play a beautiful hymn on the piano. This is the way the Lord ministered to her pain. Confident of her eternal destination, she exuded serenity, wisdom, peace, and love. Today's proverb says that "wisdom reposes in the heart of the discerning." How well Dorothy understood this.

Lord, everyone has a cross to bear. But because You bore Calvary's cross for me, I have the hope of eternal life. Amen.

EVENING

Go Out with Joy

For ye shall go out with joy, and be led forth with peace: the mountains and the hills shall break forth before you into singing, and all the trees of the field shall clap their hands.

ISAIAH 55:12 KJV

God reveals Himself in a million different ways, but perhaps the most breathtaking is through nature. The next time you're in a mountainous spot, pause and listen. Can you hear the sound of God's eternal song? Does joy radiate through your being? Aren't you filled with wonder and with peace? The Lord has, through the beauty of nature, given us a rare and glorious gift.

When I view the wonders of Your marvelous creation, Lord, my heart fills with absolute joy! Amen.

DAY 156

MORNING
Second Chances

For his anger lasts only a moment, but his favor lasts a lifetime; weeping may stay for the night, but rejoicing comes in the morning.

PSALM 30:5 NIV

Don't you love second chances? New beginnings? If only we could go back and redo some of our past mistakes. . .what better choices we'd make the second time around. Life in Jesus is all about the rebirth experience—the opportunity to start over. Each day is a new day, in fact. And praise God! The sorrows and trials of yesterday are behind us. With each new morning, joy dawns!

I am so glad you allow second chances, Father. Thank You for each new morning that is an opportunity to start over! Amen.

EVENING
Esther Is Chosen

Then the king's attendants, who served him, said, "Let beautiful young virgins be sought for the king."

ESTHER 2:2 NASB

The book of Esther is a beautiful story of a woman's absolute faith and trust in her God. God placed Esther in a position of authority—in order to save the people of Israel.

Mordecai, a Jew in Susa, had returned from the Babylonian exile and was raising his orphaned niece, Esther. And she was "beautiful of form and face. . . . Esther was taken to the king's palace" (Esther 2:7–8 NASB).

Wisely, "Esther did not make known her people or her kindred" (Esther 2:10 NASB). Esther lived in the ultimate spa resort where, for over twelve months, she received beauty treatments and perfume baths.

Finally, "Esther was taken to King Ahasuerus. . . . The king loved Esther more than all the women, and she found favor and kindness with him. . .so that he set the royal crown on her head and made her queen instead of Vashti" (Esther 2:16–17 NASB).

In the beginning, Esther was unaware of how God would use her life. Lord, let me be as available and obedient to You. Amen.

DAY 157

MORNING
Joyous Tomorrow

But if we hope for that we see not,
then do we with patience wait for it.
ROMANS 8:25 KJV

Are you in a "waiting" season? Is your patience being tested to the breaking point? Take heart! You are not alone. Every godly man and woman from biblical times till now went through seasons of waiting on the Lord. Their secret? They hoped for what they could not see. (They never lost their hope!) And they waited patiently. So, as you're waiting, reflect on the biblical giants and realize. . .you're not alone!

Father, thank You for Your Word that gives examples of others who have walked the same path before me. Because of You, I know that I am not alone—today, tomorrow, or any day after that! Amen.

EVENING
Israel Breaks the Covenant

"I said, 'I will never break My covenant
with you, and as for you, you shall make no
covenant with the inhabitants of this land;
you shall tear down their altars.'
But you have not obeyed Me."
JUDGES 2:1–2 NASB

No sooner had the Israelites taken possession of their land than that they forgot all the Lord's admonitions.

God's hand was now against them for choosing to worship idols instead of honoring Him. But God never stopped loving these people He'd chosen. "When the LORD raised up judges for them, the LORD was with the judge and delivered them from the hand of their enemies all the days of the judge; for the LORD was moved to pity by their groaning because of those who oppressed and afflicted them" (Judges 2:18 NASB).

For a while the people followed the judges, but as soon as one of these leaders died, the Israelites sought out their idols again. So God left five enemy nations as strongholds within the region to test Israel's obedience to His commandments (Judges 3:3).

Lord, fill me with Your strength that I might not backslide into the pit of disobedience again. Amen.

DAY 158

MORNING

Enjoying Life

Let all who seek You rejoice and be glad in You; and let those who love Your salvation say continually, "Let God be magnified." . . . You are my help and my deliverer.

PSALM 70:4–5 NASB

Sometimes we approach God robotically: "Lord, please do this for me. Lord, please do that." We're convinced we'll be happy, if only God grants our wishes, like a genie in a bottle. We're going about this backward! We should start by praising God. Thank Him for life, health, and the many answered prayers. Our joyous praise will remind us just how blessed we already are! Then—out of genuine relationship—we make our requests known.

Father God, my joy comes from You—and only You. Without You I could never experience all of the joys that life has to offer. Thank You! Amen.

EVENING

Jonah Flees God's Call

The word of the LORD came to Jonah the son of Amittai saying, "Arise, go to Nineveh the great city and cry against it, for their wickedness has come up before Me." But Jonah rose up to flee to Tarshish from the presence of the LORD.

JONAH 1:1–3 NASB

Jonah flat out didn't want this job, no way, no how! Therefore, he decided to "get out of Dodge." And the quickest route happened to be on the next boat sailing.

God had solicited Jonah's help in bringing a message to Nineveh. However, Jonah's fear of these Ninevites loomed far greater than his fear of the Lord.

But God always gives men and women a chance to change, and so He set about the task of getting Jonah's attention in a way he'd never forget.

Lord, I know that finally Jonah responded in faith. Please help me take responsibility for the areas You're ready to work on in my life. Amen.

DAY 159

MORNING

A Royal Vision

Yes, joyful are those who live like this! Joyful indeed are those whose God is the LORD.

PSALM 144:15 NLT

How wonderful to realize you're God's child. He loves you and wants nothing but good for you. Doesn't knowing you're His daughter send waves of joy through your soul? How happy we are when we recognize that we are princesses. . .children of the most high God! Listen closely as He whispers royal secrets in your ear. Your heavenly Father offers you keys to the kingdom. . .and vision for the road ahead.

Joy floods my soul when I think about how much You love me, Lord. Thank You for making me Your child. Amen.

EVENING

The Key to Happiness

He who heeds the word wisely will find good, and whoever trusts in the LORD, happy is he.

PROVERBS 16:20 NKJV

Want the key to true happiness? Try wisdom. When others around you are losing their heads, losing their cool, and losing sleep over their decisions, choose to react differently. Step up to the plate. Handle matters wisely. Wise choices always lead to joyous outcomes. And along the way, you will be setting an example for others around you to follow. So, c'mon. . .get happy! Get wisdom!

Father, thank You for the wisdom of Your Word, which will always point me in the right direction when I have a choice to make. Amen.

DAY 160

MORNING
He Dwelt among Us

And the Word became flesh, and dwelt among us, and we saw His glory, glory as of the only begotten from the Father, full of grace and truth.

JOHN 1:14 NASB

That phrase "dwelt among us" means God took on the form of a human body, leaving the peace, security, and hope of heaven, and came to earth to become a model for men and women.

How do you teach children not to lie, cheat, or steal? By being an example before them of proper behavior. Jesus showed us by example what it means to lead a perfect life, despite the evil surrounding Him. "For we do not have a high priest who cannot sympathize with our weaknesses, but One who has been tempted in all things as we are, yet without sin" (Hebrews 4:15 NASB).

When Satan bombarded Christ during an intense time of temptation in the wilderness, Christ showed us how to repel such attacks successfully—through liberal use of the Word of God, prayer, and obedience.

Lord, strengthen my faith today. Help me to overcome the evil one's daily temptations. Amen

EVENING
A Net of Love

No one has ever seen God; but if we love one another, God lives in us and his love is made complete in us.

1 JOHN 4:12 NIV

It's hard to be a good witness if you've got a sour expression on your face. People aren't usually won to the Lord by grumpy friends and coworkers. If you hope to persuade people that life in Jesus is the ultimate, then you've got to let your enthusiasm shine through. Before you reach for the net, spend some time on your knees, asking for an infusion of joy. Then, go catch some fish!

Dear heavenly Father, I want to be a good witness for You. Help me remember to exude joy and love. . .so others will be drawn to You. Amen.

DAY 161

MORNING
Not Withholding

Anything I wanted, I would take.
I denied myself no pleasure. I even found
great pleasure in hard work,
a reward for all my labors.
ECCLESIASTES 2:10 NLT

Work beckons. Deadlines loom. You're trying to balance your home life against your work life, and it's overwhelming. Take heart! It is possible to rejoice in your labors—to find pleasure in the day-to-day tasks. At work or at play. . .let the Lord cause a song of joy to rise up in your heart.

Help me to slow down—every day—and enjoy the moments as they come, Father God. May I not become so busy that I miss out on life's simple pleasures. Amen.

EVENING
Hearing God's Spirit Speak

For to us God revealed them through the Spirit; for the Spirit searches all things, even the depths of God. . . . Now we have received, not the spirit of the world, but the Spirit who is from God, so that we may know the things freely given to us by God.
1 CORINTHIANS 2:10, 12 NASB

To understand the things of God, you can't totally rely on what you received in your early education.

If you came to Christ as an adult, it's probably necessary to start from the beginning—using the Bible, not your memory. Find out what you believe and know why you believe it. If you never arrive at this understanding, how on earth can you share your faith with others?

Here's an excuse heard often: "We can't try to interpret the Bible ourselves because we'll get confused." But to refuse the Holy Spirit the opportunity to instruct you, as He promised He would, is to refuse true understanding.

Lord, fill my mind and heart with true understanding. Amen.

DAY 162

MORNING
Joy in Your Work

Go, eat your food with gladness, and drink your wine with a joyful heart, for God has already approved what you do.

ECCLESIASTES 9:7 NIV

Ever feel like nothing you do is good enough? Your boss is frustrated over something you've done wrong. The kids are complaining. Your neighbors are even upset at you. How wonderful to read that God accepts our works, even when we feel lacking. He encourages us to go our way with a merry heart, completely confident that we are accepted in the Beloved.

When it feels like I'm a complete failure—and that I am letting others down, Lord—please infuse my soul with confidence. No matter what, I am Yours. I am accepted. I am loved. Amen.

EVENING
The Wise Woman Builds Her House

The wise woman builds her house, but the foolish tears it down with her own hands. He who walks in his uprightness fears the LORD, but he who is devious in his ways despises Him.

PROVERBS 14:1–2 NASB

Every woman must understand God's "building codes" in order to strengthen her own household. The blueprints must be followed. From these, a concrete foundation is laid. Likewise, how can a woman provide guidance within her home unless she first seeks wisdom from the Lord?

Next comes the framing. This skeletal structure furnishes the undergirding and strength to support the home. Prayer is just such sustenance to the family.

Now the insulation is added within the walls. This corresponds to godly friends and church members who provide a cushion to bolster us during the storms of life.

Finally, color-coated stucco and trim put the finishing touches on the exterior of the house. Our family portrays a unique image within our neighborhood. And the love we have for each other reflects the love and worship given to God.

Lord, You are the Master Builder. To stay upright I must follow Your blueprints. Amen.

DAY 163

MORNING
He First Loved Us

This is how God showed his love among us: He sent his one and only Son into the world that we might live through him.

1 JOHN 4:9 NIV

Many things about God are quite a mystery. If there is anything at all that we can understand for sure, though, we can know He loves us. There is nothing we could ever do to make God *stop* loving us, because certainly we did nothing to make Him start. God is concerned about everything we do. He celebrates our victories and cries with us during our difficult times. God proved His love for us long before we were ever born! How could we not love such a God who first loved us so much?

You have always loved me, God, and You will love me forever. I am so grateful! Compared to Yours, my love is small, but I love You with all my heart. Amen.

EVENING
Esther Thwarts a Royal Plot

In those days, while Mordecai was sitting at the king's gate, Bigthan and Teresh, two of the king's officials from those who guarded the door, became angry and sought to lay hands on King Ahasuerus. But the plot became known to Mordecai and he told Queen Esther, and Esther informed the king in Mordecai's name.

ESTHER 2:21–22 NASB

Overhearing a private conversation in which a murder plot was discussed, Esther's uncle, Mordecai, a Jew, channeled this information back to his niece, whom the king trusted.

An official, Haman, had been promoted shortly after this incident had taken place. The king had commanded that all who were at the king's gate bow down and pay homage to Haman. However, Mordecai refused and "Haman was filled with rage" (Esther 3:5 NASB).

Therefore, Haman set an evil plan in motion. Then Haman talked the king into issuing a decree that his people, the Jews, be destroyed.

Lord, what a dark hour this was for Your people, but You had already put a plan into action. Amen.

DAY 164

MORNING

In the multitude of my anxieties within me,
Your comforts delight my soul.

PSALM 94:19 NKJV

We don't know for sure who wrote Psalm 94, but we can be certain that the psalmist was annoyed and anxious when he wrote it. He cries out to God, asking Him to "pay back to the proud what they deserve" (v. 2 NIV). Then, he goes on with a list of accusations about the evil ones. . . . "In the multitude of my anxieties within me." Does that phrase describe you? When anxiety overwhelms us, we find relief in the words of Psalm 94:19. When we turn our anxious thoughts over to God, He brings contentment to our souls.

Dear God, on those days when frustration and anxiety overwhelm me, please come to me, comfort my soul, and remind me to praise You. Amen.

EVENING

Shine On!

Let the message about Christ, in all its richness, fill your lives. Teach and counsel each other with all the wisdom he gives. Sing psalms and hymns and spiritual songs to God with thankful hearts.

COLOSSIANS 3:16 NLT

We need to live the Word of God every day. It will shine through us! The old song says, "They will know we are Christians by our love." This means reflecting the love of God in everything we do. When we spend time in God's Word, we find peace, wisdom, and contentment that we get from no other place. This is a peace we love to have. This is happiness! Imagine being anything but thankful to God for filling us with His love, peace, and wisdom!

Oh Lord, my Rock and my Redeemer, may my words and my actions be a reflection of Your Word and pleasing in Your sight. Amen.

DAY 165

MORNING
Jonah Is Swallowed by a Great Fish

"Pick me up and throw me into the sea. Then the sea will become calm for you, for I know that on account of me this great storm has come upon you."

JONAH 1:12 NASB

The storm-tossed sailors have two options and neither one sounds like the right one.

Although these men were mad at Jonah for involving them in his duel with God, they were also aware that tossing him overboard like unwanted cargo would almost certainly spell his death. It wasn't until they had no other option that they finally complied with his request.

As soon as they threw Jonah into the water, the sea stopped raging. "Then the men feared the LORD greatly, and they offered a sacrifice to the LORD and made vows. And the LORD appointed a great fish to swallow Jonah, and Jonah was in the stomach of the fish three days and three nights" (Jonah 1:16–17 NASB).

Lord, You alone have the ability to deliver a great fish to swallow a man whole and not harm him. Help me trust You for creative solutions to all my problems. Amen.

EVENING
In the Beginning, Christ

In the beginning was the Word, and the Word was with God, and the Word was God. He was in the beginning with God.

JOHN 1:1–2 NASB

An elderly woman once lived next door to us whom everyone came to call "Aunt Esther." At ninety-one, Esther's spunky, conquer-any-obstacle attitude drew people to her.

But the church she attended was nothing more than a cult of false teachers. These teachers presented a new spin on an old lie, saying Jesus Christ did not exist in the flesh but was instead spirit.

Aunt Esther would sit and take a dose of the Bible, but she followed the truth with a soul-poisoning gulp from her cult's own book. Over and over I recited the first three verses of John's Gospel to her. At the age of ninety-three she suffered a stroke. Knowing her death was imminent, I lay on the floor next to her bed, praying all through the night. When she died a day later, she knew Christ as her Savior.

Lord, I am so grateful to You for taking all those who profess Your name to be with You! Amen.

DAY 166

MORNING
Visible Reminders

Let the morning bring me word of your unfailing love, for I have put my trust in you.

Psalm 143:8 NIV

We don't know if David was a morning person or a night owl, but he chose to start his day looking for visible reminders of God's unfailing love. It might have been easy to remember God's love for him if he had witnessed a glorious morning sunrise, but if the night had been stormy and he was dealing with spooked sheep in the midst of a downpour, God's unfailing love may have felt a little distant. Whether or not conditions were favorable for faith, David believed in God's unfailing love—even if he couldn't see it in the world around him.

I awake in the morning, and You are there. You are with me all day long and throughout the night. Thank You, heavenly Father, for Your ever-present love. Amen.

EVENING
Loyal Hearts

"For the eyes of the Lord *range throughout the earth to strengthen those whose hearts are fully committed to him."*

2 Chronicles 16:9 NIV

God seeks a relationship with those who have open and receiving hearts. He is not looking to condemn or judge but to find hearts committed to knowing Him and learning His way. He desires people who want to talk and listen to Him and who have a deep thirst to serve and please Him. God looks for us, and the only requirement is for each of us to have a fully devoted heart. We open our hearts and hands to receive Him, and He will find us.

Find me, Lord; draw me near to You. Open up my heart so that I may fully receive all that You want to pour into it. Amen.

DAY 167

MORNING

God's Command

So He said, "Come." And when Peter had come down out of the boat, he walked on the water to go to Jesus.

MATTHEW 14:29 NKJV

Jesus stayed behind to send the crowds away—and then to pray. Later that evening, the disciples, wrestling their boat against a contrary wind, saw a ghostly figure approaching. Jesus assured them it was He, and Peter asked the Lord to command him to come. Jesus did—and Peter, briefly, walked on water. What does it take for an ordinary person to walk on water? A command of God. By the power of God, ordinary men and women, responding to God's call, have successfully accomplished difficult, even impossible, tasks.

You are my Strength, oh Lord. Whenever I feel like giving up, I will turn to You believing that You will give me the power to carry on. Amen.

EVENING

Our Bodies, God's Temple

Do you not know that you are a temple of God and that the Spirit of God dwells in you?

1 CORINTHIANS 3:16 NASB

As we go about the business of life, perhaps it's hard to remember that God indwells us. The apostle Paul constantly wrestled with desiring to do the right thing but having his flesh at war with his spirit. "For I know that nothing good dwells in me, that is, in my flesh; for the willing is present in me, but the doing of the good is not. For the good that I want, I do not do, but I practice the very evil that I do not want" (Romans 7:18–19 NASB).

"However, you are not in the flesh but in the Spirit, if indeed the Spirit of God dwells in you. . . . If Christ is in you, though the body is dead because of sin, yet the spirit is alive because of righteousness" (Romans 8:9–10 NASB).

Lord, let me live as though I believe You are permeating my very being. Amen.

DAY 168

MORNING
Hold His Hand

"For I am the Lord your God who takes hold of your right hand and says to you, Do not fear; I will help you."

Isaiah 41:13 NIV

God desires to help us. When we walk through life hand in hand with God, we can face anything. His love covers us. His presence is our guard. We can do all things through Christ because we are given His strength. Do you feel as though you're walking through life alone? Do not fear. Are you in need of love, protection, courage, and strength? Reach out your hand. Allow Jesus to take hold of it. Receive His love and protection. Bask in His courage and strength. Take hold of His hand!

Dear Lord, thank You that I do not have to fear. You will help me by taking my hand. Amen.

EVENING
God of Possible

Jesus looked at them and said, "With man this is impossible, but with God all things are possible."

Matthew 19:26 NIV

No one can be saved by their own efforts! Man's greatest efforts pale in comparison to the requirements of a holy God. But grace, freely offered by God and accepted by individuals, will admit us to heaven. With God, all things *are* possible—especially enabling forgiven sinners to live eternally. Realizing we can do nothing is the key to gaining everything.

Dear Father, I appreciate Your grace—Your loving-kindness that I don't deserve. There is nothing I have done to earn it. Grace is Your gift to me, and I thank You. Amen.

DAY 169

MORNING

"Go into the village ahead of you; there, as you enter, you will find a colt tied on which no one yet has ever sat; untie it, and bring it here. If anyone asks you, 'Why are you untying it?' you shall say, 'The Lord has need of it.' "

LUKE 19:30–31 NASB

Jesus came to them riding on a donkey, just as it had been prophesied. But why a donkey? The reason was that He might present Himself to them as their humble servant and King. If He had ridden into Jerusalem on a horse, He would have presented Himself as a warrior, ready for battle. That horse has already been prophesied for the end times (Revelation 19:11).

Lord, thank You for all the "absolutes" of scripture. I believe You are exactly who You claim to be, God Incarnate. Amen.

EVENING

Truth

"You will know the truth, and the truth will set you free."

JOHN 8:32 NLT

What lies do you believe about yourself? How might those lies be preventing you from experiencing God's plan for *your* life? The next time you're tempted to believe a lie, write it down. Then find a scripture passage that speaks truth over the situation. Write that scripture verse across the lie. Commit the truth to memory. Over time God's Word will transform your thinking and you'll begin to believe the truth. Then something amazing will happen—you'll be set free.

Father, thank You for the truth Your Word speaks about my life. Open my eyes to the truth and help me to believe it. Amen.

DAY 170

MORNING

The Need for Godly Judges

Does any one of you, when he has a case against his neighbor, dare to go to law before the unrighteous and not before the saints? Or do you not know that the saints will judge the world? If the world is judged by you, are you not competent to constitute the smallest law courts?

1 CORINTHIANS 6:1–2 NASB

God meant for His Church to govern themselves so that true justice would be served. But He also intended that the believers work out their differences in love. Today men and women have quit counting on the power of God to rule in their lives and have turned instead to the "courts of the unbelievers," where they have not found justice.

The verses above are meant to give you hope. For the saints of God will one day judge those who operate within this world's system of injustice. As God brings down His own pair of legal scales to weigh and measure, they will be held accountable to Him.

Lord, help me remember the meaning of justice. May my court of law be governed by Your Holy Spirit in my heart. Amen.

EVENING

Never Lost for Long

For "whoever calls on the name of the LORD shall be saved."

ROMANS 10:13 NKJV

You call out to God, but maybe for a little while you don't hear anything. You may have to listen intently for a while, but eventually you are reassured by His voice. When He calls your name you know you are safe. You may have to take a few steps in the dark, but by moving toward Him you eventually see clearly. A light comes on in your heart, and you recognize where you are and what you need to do to get back on the path God has set before you.

Heavenly Father, help me to stay focused on You. Show me how to remove distractions from my life so I can stay close to You. Amen.

DAY 171

MORNING
The First to View the Resurrection

Mary Magdalene came early to the tomb, while it was still dark.

JOHN 20:1 NASB

Peter and John ran to the tomb, viewed the linen wrappings, and then left again (John 20:6–10). They left too soon, missing the miracle. "But Mary was standing outside the tomb weeping; and so, as she wept, she stooped and looked into the tomb; and she saw two angels. . . . And they said to her, 'Woman, why are you weeping?' She said to them, 'Because they have taken away my Lord, and I do not know where they have laid Him.' When she had said this, she turned around and saw Jesus standing there, and did not know that it was Jesus" (John 20:11–14 NASB).

She said to him, "Sir, if you have carried Him away, tell me where you have laid Him, and I will take Him away" (John 20:15 NASB).

But then He said, "Mary!" (John 20:16 NASB). And the sound of His voice calmed her frantic fears, dried her tears, and warmed her heart.

Lord, many times I miss the miracle You have already prepared. Open my eyes! Amen.

EVENING
Every Step of the Way

Never stop praying.

1 THESSALONIANS 5:17 NLT

God wants to be involved in our daily routines. He wants to hear from us and waits for us. God never promised an easy life to Christians. If we will allow Him, though, God will be there with us every step of the way. All we need to do is come to Him in prayer. With these three simple words from 1 Thessalonians 5:17, our lives can be fulfilling as we live to communicate with our Lord.

Father, when I pray, remind me that prayer is not only about talking to You, but also about listening to You. Open my heart to Your words. Amen.

DAY 172

MORNING
A Valuable Deposit

He anointed us, set his seal of ownership on us, and put his Spirit in our hearts as a deposit, guaranteeing what is to come.

2 CORINTHIANS 1:21–22 NIV

When we commit our lives to Christ, He doesn't let us flail around in this mixed-up world without any help. We have the deposit of the Holy Spirit with us all the time, and He also gives us His Word and the help of other Christians to keep us strong in the Lord. So whenever you feel alone or overwhelmed with life, remember that God has anointed you, set His seal upon you, and deposited the Holy Spirit right inside your heart. That is the most valuable deposit of all!

Dear Lord, thank You for depositing Your Holy Spirit in my heart to lead and guide me. Help me to listen. Amen.

EVENING
Idols of Their Own Making

Among the gods there is none like you, Lord; no deeds can compare with yours. . . . For you are great and do marvelous deeds; you alone are God.

PSALM 86:8, 10 NIV

When men and women refuse to worship the true God, they invariably end up trying to fashion one on their own. The reason is natural: We were all created with a "God-shaped void" inside our souls. The purpose of this void is to draw us to the Lord in commitment.

Satan applies every subversive tactic in his arsenal in order to dim our understanding of God's attributes. Therefore, it's up to us to find the truth to combat the evil one's lies. Fortunately, God is constantly guiding us in our search for knowledge and understanding.

Lord, You've given me an entire Bible to read so that I might learn of Your love, concern, and compassion. Develop in me that sensitivity to "hear the prompting of Your Spirit" while You guide me toward the truth. Amen.

DAY 173

MORNING
Esther Requests a New Law

On that day King Ahasuerus gave the house of Haman, the enemy of the Jews, to Queen Esther; and Mordecai came before the king, for Esther had disclosed what he was to her. . . . And Esther set Mordecai over the house of Haman. Then Esther spoke again to the king, fell at his feet, wept and implored him to avert the evil scheme of Haman the Agagite and his plot which he had devised against the Jews. The king extended the golden scepter to Esther. So Esther arose and stood before the king.

ESTHER 8:1–4 NASB

Esther and Mordecai were among the few in the king's palace who had acted in the king's behalf. Everyone else desired personal gain. Esther had risked her life not only for her people but also for the king. Had it not been for God's intervention, Haman undoubtedly would have hanged Esther on that gallows right along with Mordecai.

Lord, I thank You for this account of Esther's obedience, loyalty, and trust. Amen.

EVENING
Fear and Dread

"What I feared has come upon me; what I dreaded has happened to me."

JOB 3:25 NIV

Do we have a secret fear or dread? God knew Job's secret fears, but still called him "blameless and upright" (Job 1:8 NIV). God doesn't withhold His love if we harbor unspoken dread. He doesn't love us any less because of secret anxieties. The Lord "is like a father to his children. . .he remembers we are only dust" (Psalm 103:13–14 NLT). God never condemned Job (and He'll never condemn us) for private fears. He encourages us, as He did Job, to trust Him. He alone retains control over all creation and all circumstances (Job 38–41).

Father, please stay beside me when what I dread most comes to me. Amen.

DAY 174

MORNING

Planted Deep

Fix these words of mine in your hearts and minds; tie them as symbols on your hands and bind them on your foreheads.

DEUTERONOMY 11:18 NIV

Memorizing Bible verses isn't a fashionable trend in today's world, but learning key verses plants the Word of God deeply in our hearts. We draw strength and nourishment in dark times from remembering what God told us in the Bible. In times of crisis we recall God's promises of hope and comfort. In our everyday moments, repeating well-known verses reminds us that God is always with us—whether it feels like it or not.

What an awesome gift You have given me, God—the Bible! I will fix Your words in my mind and heart and carry them with me wherever I go. Amen.

EVENING

Light in the Dark

The light shines in the darkness, and the darkness has not overcome it.

JOHN 1:5 NIV

Jesus said in John 12:46 (NIV), "I have come into the world as a light, so that no one who believes in me should stay in darkness." He also promised that He is always with us. Because we have Him, we have light. If we fail to perceive it, if we seem to be living in darkness, perhaps we have turned our backs to the light of His countenance. Maybe we are covering our eyes with the cares of this world. Clouds of sin may be darkening our lives, but He has not left us. He promises us that in following Him we will not walk in darkness but have the light of life.

Lord Jesus, show me my blind spots. Where am I covering my own eyes or walking away from You? Turn me back to You, the light of life. Amen.

DAY 175

MORNING

True and Lasting Justice

"In a certain city there was a judge who did not fear God and did not respect man. There was a widow in that city, and she kept coming to him, saying, 'Give me legal protection from my opponent.' For a while he was unwilling; but afterward he said to himself, 'Even though I do not fear God nor respect man, yet because this widow bothers me, I will give her legal protection, otherwise by continually coming she will wear me out.' "

LUKE 18:2–5 NASB

In New Testament times, whether a case was considered depended upon the plaintiffs' ability to "gain the attention of the judges' attendants." This widow already had three strikes against her. As a woman, she had no priority standing in the court. As a widow, she didn't have a husband to fight for her in these legal proceedings. And finally, without the funds to pay for assistance, she was without hope.

If you've been denied justice here on earth, you have a God who sees all and knows all. Justice will be served!

Lord, You judge rightly. You will administer to the guilty the punishment they truly deserve. Amen.

EVENING

Revel in the Beauty

He has made everything beautiful in its time. He has also set eternity in the human heart; yet no one can fathom what God has done from beginning to end.

ECCLESIASTES 3:11 NIV

No one can completely "fathom what God has done." That's what makes Him God. And yet, still we try. Thankfully, our hearts don't need to understand; neither do they need earthly "fixes." They just need to be set free, to find God and revel in the beauty of His never-ending creation. Believers, stop letting unanswerable questions prevent you from loving Him more completely. And unbelievers, ask yourself, if you had every material thing you could want, wouldn't your heart still be reaching out for eternity?

I have questions, God—so many unanswered questions about life and about You. Increase my trust in You. Help me to set aside my uncertainty and to delight in Your never-ending love. Amen.

DAY 176

MORNING
Jumping Hurdles

God's way is perfect.
All the LORD's promises prove true.
PSALM 18:30 NLT

Maybe there are times when you just don't think you can take one more disappointment or hurt. That's the perfect time to draw strength from God and His Word. Meditate on encouraging scriptures, or play a song that you know strengthens your heart and mind. Ask God to infuse you with His strength, and you'll find the power to take another step, and another—until you find yourself on the other side of that challenge you're facing today.

God, give me strength each day to face the obstacles I am to overcome. I am thankful that I don't have to face them alone. Amen.

EVENING
Micah Knew His God

Hear, O peoples, all of you; listen, O earth and all it contains, and let the Lord GOD be a witness against you, the Lord from His holy temple. For behold, the LORD is coming forth from His place. He will come down and tread on the high places of the earth.
MICAH 1:2–3 NASB

The events recorded in Micah would be fulfilled in the near and far-distant future.

"The mountains will melt under Him and the valleys will be split, like wax before the fire, like water poured down a steep place. All this is for the rebellion of Jacob and for the sins of the house of Israel. . . . For I will make Samaria a heap of ruins in the open country, planting places for a vineyard. I will pour her stones down into the valley and will lay bare her foundations" (Micah 1:4–6 NASB).

Why was God doing this to His people? Both Judah and Israel had forsaken their God, becoming steeped in idolatry.

Lord, keep me from following in the footsteps of the rebellious so that I might not require bitter lessons of truth. Amen.

DAY 177

MORNING
My Future Is in Your Hands

The LORD says, "I will guide you along the best pathway for your life. I will advise you and watch over you."

PSALM 32:8 NLT

Are plans running wild in your head? Remember that the Lord is watching over you, and He is there to guide you. He wants you to seek Him out. Don't try to make your dreams happen all by yourself. Get on your knees and ask Him to direct your plans each morning. Don't be afraid to put your future in His hands!

Father, thank You for always being faithful to me. Continue to watch over me and direct my path. Amen.

EVENING
Living with a View of Heaven

How lovely are Your dwelling places, O LORD of hosts! My soul longed and even yearned for the courts of the LORD; my heart and my flesh sing for joy to the living God.

PSALM 84:1–2 NASB

King David had an eternal perspective. Israel constantly battled their enemies. How he must have longed for a lasting peace. But he had to settle for that little niche of peace he carved out for himself while pondering what heaven was like, anticipating the day he'd dwell with God. For the God of perfection created for Himself a place of eternal security.

What wonderful knowledge we have that God desires to share this incredible place with His imperfect creatures! Despite our sinful nature, God truly loves us with an eternal affection.

David accepted Your love for him, Lord. Help me to live in Your will so that my life is a blessing to You. Amen.

DAY 178

MORNING

The Preacher's Livelihood

Who at any time serves as a soldier at his own expense? Who plants a vineyard and does not eat the fruit of it? Or who tends a flock and does not use the milk of the flock?

1 CORINTHIANS 9:7 NASB

Those who bring us the Word of God deserve a living wage. This is the point Paul is making. After all, the apostles had given up their homes and any semblance of normal family life in order to travel and present the Gospel. "Do we not have a right to eat and drink? Do we not have a right to take along a believing wife, even as the rest of the apostles and the brothers of the Lord and Cephas? Or do only Barnabas and I not have a right to refrain from working?" (1 Corinthians 9:4–6 NASB).

The word *apostle* means "one sent under commission." And if they had been called into service by God, weren't they entitled to financial support from the body of believers?

Lord, let me remember in my prayers, tithes, and offerings all those who labor to bring the Word of God to me and others. Amen.

EVENING

Keep Smiling

"When they were discouraged, I smiled at them. My look of approval was precious to them."

JOB 29:24 TLB

Our most authentic forms of communication occur without a word. Rather, they flow from an understanding smile, a compassionate touch, a loving gesture, a gentle presence, or an unspoken prayer. God used Job, an ordinary man with an extraordinary amount of love and wisdom—a man whose only adornment was righteous living and a warm smile. And He wants to use us, too. So keep smiling. Someone may just need it.

Remind me, Jesus, to bless others through my actions. A warm smile, a simple act of kindness, a loving touch might be just what someone needs today. Remind me, please. Amen.

DAY 179

MORNING

Learn Contentment

I am not saying this because I am in need,
for I have learned to be content
whatever the circumstances.

PHILIPPIANS 4:11 NIV

Contentment is learned and cultivated. It is an attitude of the heart. It has nothing to do with material possessions or life's circumstances. It has everything to do with being in the center of God's will and knowing it. Contentment means finding rest and peace in God's presence—nothing more, nothing less. It is trusting that God will meet all of your needs. May we learn to say confidently, *The Lord is my Shepherd, I shall not want*. That is the secret of contentment.

Dear Lord, teach me how to be content
in You, knowing that You will provide
all that I need. Amen.

EVENING

The Father Has Commanded Us to Love

Grace, mercy and peace will be with us,
from God the Father and from Jesus Christ,
the Son of the Father, in truth and love.

2 JOHN 1:3 NASB

A foundation of any small-group or home Bible study should be the love its members display toward one another. It was just such a group that John addressed in this letter.

As a church elder, John reminded these believers that God didn't consider loving one another an option (2 John 1:6).

John shows us the process by which the Word of the Lord can penetrate our hearts. First, we are to know the truth (2 John 1:1–3), for it is by God's grace that we can love others.

Next, John admonishes us to walk according to His commandments (2 John 1:4–6).

Lastly, we must abide in the truth, who is Christ (2 John 1:7–11).

Jesus Christ. . .heralded by a star, proclaimed
by angels, announced by the shepherds,
and given by the Father to a world in need of
a Savior. Oh come let us adore Him! Amen.

DAY 180

MORNING
The Reason for Job's Suffering

Job. . .was blameless, upright, fearing God and turning away from evil. Seven sons and three daughters were born to him. His possessions also were 7,000 sheep, 3,000 camels, 500 yoke of oxen, 500 female donkeys, and very many servants.

JOB 1:1–3 NASB

Satan intimated to God that Job only loved Him because of all the blessings Job had received. "Then the LORD said to Satan, 'Behold, all that he has is in your power, only do not put forth your hand on him' " (Job 1:12).

Job's life became an unwelcome ride on a trolley called tragedy. In one day he lost all his children and his house, servants, and livestock. And through all of this, Job refused to blame God or sin.

Lord, as a Christian, lead me so that I do not expect You to be my "celestial Santa Claus." Lead me so I continue to follow, no matter the circumstances. Amen.

EVENING
Love Is. . .

And now these three remain: faith, hope and love. But the greatest of these is love.

1 CORINTHIANS 13:13 NIV

Who can deny the power of faith? Throughout history, faith has closed the mouths of lions, opened blind eyes, and saved countless lost souls. And the scriptures note that without it we cannot please God (Hebrews 11:6). Yet as wonderful as these qualities are, it is love that God deems the greatest. Love lasts and never fails. It is patient, kind, unselfish, and honest; it never keeps a record of wrongs or delights in evil. In a word, love is God. And there is no *One* greater.

Father, I strive to love patiently, kindly, unselfishly, and honestly because in doing so I become more perfect in love and more like You! Amen.

DAY 181

MORNING
He Is Faithful

If we are unfaithful, he remains faithful, for he cannot deny who he is.

2 TIMOTHY 2:13 NLT

Sometimes we treat our relationship with God the same as we do with other people. We promise Him we'll start spending more time with Him in prayer and Bible study. Soon the daily distractions of life get in the way, and we're back in our same routine, minus prayer and Bible study. Even when we fail to live up to our expectations, our heavenly Father doesn't pick up His judge's gavel and condemn us for unfaithfulness. Instead, He remains a faithful supporter, encouraging us to keep trying to hold up our end of the bargain. Take comfort in His faithfulness, and let that encourage you toward a deeper relationship with Him.

Father, thank You for Your unending faithfulness. Every day I fall short of Your standards, but You're always there, encouraging me and lifting me up. Please help me to be more faithful to You—in the big things and in the little things. Amen.

EVENING
The Content of Our Thoughts

Woe to those who scheme iniquity, who work out evil on their beds!

MICAH 2:1 NASB

Micah acknowledges that the source of evil thoughts is the human mind. Other portions of scripture also bear out this truth.

"Transgression speaks to the ungodly within his heart; there is no fear of God before his eyes. For it flatters him in his own eyes concerning the discovery of his iniquity and the hatred of it. The words of his mouth are wickedness and deceit; he has ceased to be wise and to do good. He plans wickedness upon his bed; he sets himself on a path that is not good; he does not despise evil" (Psalm 36:1–4 NASB).

Therein lies the problem, that we at some point begin to accept wickedness as good. And the things we devise in our minds then become the vehicle for our actions.

Lord, guard my mind from evil that I might not ruminate on such things and be propelled into ungodly actions. Amen.

DAY 182

MORNING
Jesus Alone Is Worthy

"Stop weeping; behold, the Lion that is from the tribe of Judah, the Root of David, has overcome so as to open the book and its seven seals."

REVELATION 5:5 NASB

As the Lamb stood to receive "the book," an awed hush fell over His celestial audience. He alone was worthy because He had met God's requirements to redeem the earth. The prize was His.

The judgments of God comprise the book. These are a series of progressively worsening catastrophes, deserved by those who have consistently rejected God, salvation in Christ, and His Word.

Lord, I know that Jesus Christ is God in the flesh, born to die on the cross for my sins. Because of His sacrifice, I will be able to celebrate forever with Him in heaven. Amen.

EVENING
Heavenly Appreciation

God is not unjust; he will not forget your work and the love you have shown him as you have helped his people and continue to help them.

HEBREWS 6:10 NIV

Sometimes it seems our hard work is ignored. When our work for Christ seems to go unnoticed by our church family, we can be assured that God sees our hard work and appreciates it. We may not receive the "church member of the month" award, but our love for our brothers and sisters in Christ and our work on their behalf is not overlooked by God. The author of Hebrews assures us that God is not unjust—our reward is in heaven.

Dear Lord, You are a God of love and justice. Even when I do not receive the notice of those around me, help me to serve You out of my love for You. Amen.

DAY 183

MORNING
God's Heart

"I will give them an undivided heart and put a new spirit in them; I will remove from them their heart of stone and give them a heart of flesh."

EZEKIEL 11:19 NIV

God is willing to give us an undivided heart—a heart that is open and ready to see, hear, and love God. This heart has a single focus: loving God and others with a tenderness that we know comes from Someone beyond us. The good news is we have already had successful surgery, and our donor heart is within us. We received our heart transplant when Jesus died for us, creating new spirits within us. God's heart changes everything and creates us as new people with living hearts.

Thank You, Lord, for giving me a new heart, a heart so perfect in love that it will last me forever. Amen.

EVENING
God, Judge of Immorality Past and Present

Now these things happened as examples for us, so that we would not crave evil things as they also craved. . . . Nor let us act immorally, as some of them did, and twenty-three thousand fell in one day.

1 CORINTHIANS 10:6, 8 NASB

By reading the entire Bible we have the privilege of learning from God's dealings with men and women throughout recorded history so we will not fall into the same traps. Twenty-three thousand people fell by the sword in one day because they joined themselves with pagan gods in sexual rituals, refusing to obey the true God.

How can we stop ourselves from falling into sin? By remembering: "No temptation has overtaken you but such as is common to man; and God is faithful, who will not allow you to be tempted beyond what you are able, but with the temptation will provide the way of escape also, so that you will be able to endure it" (1 Corinthians 10:13 NASB).

Father, help me avoid temptation by taking one step closer to You. Amen.

DAY 184

MORNING

Twelve Stones

"When you come to the edge of the waters of the Jordan, you shall stand still in the Jordan."

JOSHUA 3:8 NASB

Joshua had gathered the people together, revealing the Lord's words. Then the people left their tents and followed the priests who carried the ark of the covenant. When they reached the banks of the Jordan, the water stopped flowing. . .and the nation of Israel crossed over!

The men of Israel now followed God's command: "Take up for yourselves twelve stones from here out of the middle of the Jordan" (Joshua 4:3 NASB). These stones represented each of the tribes of Israel. Piled up high, they produced a visible monument to the miracle God performed.

The forty-thousand-man liberation force, fully equipped for battle, then proceeded to cross the desert plains of Jericho.

As the news spread of God's miracle, so had the level of terror. Jericho was "locked down and secured" behind its gates. But God instructed Israel's warriors to march around the city for six days. No obstacle can prevent God's plan from being realized!

Lord, please pave my way with stones from You, stones of dedication, perseverance, and compassion. Amen.

EVENING

Spirit and Truth

"But the time is coming—indeed it's here now—when true worshipers will worship the Father in spirit and in truth."

JOHN 4:23 NLT

God is everywhere all the time, and He doesn't just want to be worshipped at church. You can worship God on your way to work, during class, as you clean your house and pay your bills. Worship is about living your life in a way that is pleasing to the Lord and seeking Him first in all things. Paying your bills? Ask God how He wants you to spend your money. That is pleasing to Him, and that is worship. In the middle of class? Be respectful of your professors, and use the brain God gave you to complete your studies. If you are living your everyday life to please God, that is worship!

Father, help me to live my life in ways that please You. Let my focus be on worshipping You in everything I do. Amen.

DAY 185

MORNING

Never Alone

"But the Advocate, the Holy Spirit, whom the Father will send in my name, will teach you all things and will remind you of everything I have said to you."

JOHN 14:26 NIV

Jesus called the Holy Spirit "the Advocate," a translation of the Greek word *parakletos*: "one called alongside to help." It can also indicate Strengthener, Comforter, Helper, Adviser, Counselor, Intercessor, Ally, and Friend. The Holy Spirit walks with us to help, instruct, comfort, and accomplish God's work on earth. Through His presence inside us, we know the Father. In our deepest time of need, He is there. He comforts and reveals to us the truth of God's Word. Jesus is always with us because His Spirit lives in our hearts. No Christian ever walks alone!

Strengthener, Comforter, Helper, Adviser, Counselor, Intercessor, Ally, Friend—oh Holy Spirit of God! Thank You for dwelling within my heart, guiding me, and drawing me near to the Father. Amen.

EVENING

The Holy Spirit, Our Great Gift

Therefore I make known to you that no one speaking by the Spirit of God says, "Jesus is accursed"; and no one can say, "Jesus is Lord," except by the Holy Spirit.

1 CORINTHIANS 12:3 NASB

For twenty-nine years I waded through the motions of life, wondering whether the Creator really cared for me at all.

It's no accident that despair caused me to succumb to messages of doubt concerning God's nature and character. The evil one is, after all, the author of confusion and lies. However, as I tested the spirits the truth became clear. "By this you know the Spirit of God: every spirit that confesses that Jesus Christ has come in the flesh is from God; and every spirit that does not confess Jesus is not from God; this is the spirit of the antichrist, of which you have heard that it is coming, and now it is already in the world" (1 John 4:2–3 NASB).

Lord, I know if I'm listening to a message that makes me depressed and defeated that it's from Satan. I know the one that says I'm worth dying for is from Christ. Amen.

DAY 186

MORNING
Changing Our Perspective

Turn my eyes away from worthless things; preserve my life according to your word.

Psalm 119:37 NIV

The book of Psalms offers hundreds of verses that can easily become sentence prayers. "Turn my eyes from worthless things" whispered before heading out to shop, turning on the television, or picking up a magazine can turn those experiences into opportunities to see God's hand at work in our lives. He can change our perspective. He will show us what has value for us. He can even change our appetites, causing us to desire the very things He wants for us. When we pray this prayer, we are asking God to show us what He wants for us. He knows us and loves us more than we know and love ourselves. We can trust His love and goodness to provide for our needs.

Father, imprint this scripture in my mind today. In moments of need, help me remember to pray this prayer and to relinquish my desires to You. Amen.

EVENING
God Breathed

All Scripture is inspired by God and is useful to teach us what is true and to make us realize what is wrong in our lives. It corrects us when we are wrong and teaches us to do what is right.

2 Timothy 3:16 NLT

God's Word continues to be God breathed! It is as relevant today as it ever was! Scripture speaks to us in our current situations just as it did to people a few thousand years ago. . .just as it will for eternity. Situations and cultures and languages and technologies have changed all throughout history, but God has been able to speak to people exactly where they are through His living Word. There is certainly no other book, collection of books, or any other thing in the world that can do that. Only the living Word, which continues to be God breathed.

Dear God, all things pass into history except for You and Your Word. How wonderful it is that Your Word transcends time, is relevant in the present, and will live forever! Amen.

DAY 187

MORNING
Emulating Christ

To Timothy, my true child in the faith: Grace, mercy and peace from God the Father and Christ Jesus our Lord. As I urged you upon my departure for Macedonia, remain on at Ephesus so that you may instruct certain men not to teach strange doctrines. . . . But the goal of our instruction is love from a pure heart and a good conscience and a sincere faith.

1 TIMOTHY 1:2–3, 5 NASB

Paul wrote this letter to encourage Timothy in his own leadership role, knowing that the worst thing this young believer could do was to try and emulate Paul instead of Christ. For Paul held no doubt in his mind concerning Timothy's call from God. "This command I entrust to you, Timothy, my son, in accordance with the prophecies previously made concerning you, that by them you fight the good fight, keeping faith and a good conscience, which some have rejected and suffered shipwreck in regard to their faith" (1 Timothy 1:18–19 NASB).

Lord, help me to emulate Your pure heart and sincere faith. I want to follow Your commands. Amen.

EVENING
God as He Really Is

The LORD is compassionate and gracious, slow to anger, abounding in love. . . . He does not treat us as our sins deserve or repay us according to our iniquities.

PSALM 103:8, 10 NIV

Our attitude toward God can influence the way we handle what He has given us. Some people perceive God as a harsh and angry judge, impatiently tapping His foot, saying, *"When will you ever get it right?"* People who see God this way can become paralyzed by an unhealthy fear of Him. However, the Bible paints a very different picture of God. Psalm 103 says He is gracious and compassionate, that He does not treat us as our sins deserve. What difference can it make in your life to know that you serve a loving God who is longing to be gracious to you?

Lord, thank You for Your compassion, Your grace, and Your mercy. Help me to see You as You really are. Amen.

DAY 188

MORNING

Joyful Service

Wherefore I put thee in remembrance that thou stir up the gift of God, which is in thee.

2 TIMOTHY 1:6 KJV

This passage is a reminder to every believer. It demonstrates that our God-given gifts remain strong only through active use and fostering. Gifts left unattended or unused become stagnant and, like an unattended fire, die. Just as wood or coal fuels a fire, faith, prayer, and obedience are the fresh fuels of God's grace that keep our fires burning. But this takes action on our part. Are you using the gifts God has given you? Can He entrust you with more? Perhaps today is the day to gather the spiritual tinder necessary to stoke the fire of God within.

God, You have given me special talents and inspiring gifts. I pray, open my eyes to sharing those gifts. Through faith and obedience I will joyfully use them to serve You. Amen.

EVENING

Living a Complete Life

It is a good thing to receive wealth from God and the good health to enjoy it.

ECCLESIASTES 5:19 NLT

God has promised to supply all your needs, but it takes action on your part. Seeking wisdom for your situation and asking God to direct you in the right decisions will help you find a well-balanced life that will produce success, coupled with the health to enjoy it. It may be as simple as realizing a vacation is exactly what you need, instead of working throughout the year and taking your vacation in cash to pay for new bedroom furniture. Know when to press forward and when to stop and enjoy the life God has given you for His good pleasure—and yours!

Lord, I ask for Your wisdom to help me balance my life so I can be complete in every area of my life. Amen.

DAY 189

MORNING

God Has Been There, Done That

"It is God who removes the mountains. . . who alone stretches out the heavens and tramples down the waves of the sea."

JOB 9:5, 8 NASB

In one theology class I took, the teacher asked us to examine the ways in which we attempt to stuff God into a box. As A.W. Tozer said, "We tend immediately to reduce God to manageable terms."

As our human nature cries out to control what we don't understand, this feat becomes impossible. For the God who has created all that we see, hear, touch, taste, and smell has been there and done that. When we accept this, our own importance seems diminished.

Even as Job screamed for relief from his pain, he recognized that both blessings and testing through trials flowed from the same loving hands (Job 10:8–9, 12).

I await the balm of good news from You, Lord. "O may Your lovingkindness comfort me, according to Your word to Your servant. May Your compassion come to me that I may live, for Your law is my delight" (Psalm 119:76–77 NASB). Amen.

EVENING

Faith and Action

And I keep praying that this faith we hold in common keeps showing up in the good things we do, and that people recognize Christ in all of it.

PHILEMON 1:6 MSG

Our actions and reactions are a powerful gauge of how serious we are about our faith. When others wrong us, do we refuse to forgive, and risk misrepresenting Christ, or do we freely offer forgiveness as an expression of our faith? God calls us to faith and forgiveness in Christ Jesus so that Christians and non-Christians alike will see our good deeds and praise God.

Dear Lord, please let me remember that people look to me for a glimpse of You. Let my actions always reflect my faith in You. Amen.

DAY 190

MORNING

Jesus Christ Came in the Flesh

Anyone who goes too far and does not abide in the teaching of Christ, does not have God; the one who abides in the teaching, he has both the Father and the Son. If anyone comes to you and does not bring this teaching, do not receive him into your house, and do not give him a greeting; for the one who gives him a greeting participates in his evil deeds.

2 John 1:9–11 NASB

There is no greater evil than to fail to recognize who Jesus Christ is, God in the flesh. God has tried from the beginning of time to build a bridge to humankind. He gave men and women His laws and yet they failed to obey. Then the Lord sent His prophets. But the people refused to listen. And finally, He sent Jesus, to show us how to live upon the earth. And instead of responding to His offer of salvation, men nailed Him to a cross.

Lord, strengthen my faith so that I can love those who don't know You, so that I can reveal the true identity of Your Son. Amen.

EVENING

Holding the Line

When I said, "My foot is slipping,"
your unfailing love, Lord, supported me.
When anxiety was great within me,
your consolation brought me joy.

Psalm 94:18–19 NIV

Often we may feel that our feet are slipping in life. We lose our grip. Anxiety becomes a sleep robber, headache giver, and joy squelcher. Fear takes over our hearts. All we can think is, *Just get me out of here!* But we must remember who is anchoring our life. God's powerful grip secures us—even in the most difficult times. He comforts us with His loving presence that defies understanding. He provides wisdom to guide our steps through life's toughest challenges. We can rest assured that His support is steady, reliable, and motivated by His love for us.

Jesus, my Rock and Fortress, thank You that Your strength is made available to me. Steady me with the surety of Your love. Replace my anxiety with peace and joy, reflecting a life that's secured by the Almighty. Amen.

DAY 191

MORNING
Standing Firm

I. . .didn't dodge their insults, faced them as they spit in my face. And the Master, GOD, stays right there and helps me, so I'm not disgraced. Therefore I set my face like flint, confident that I'll never regret this. My champion is right here. Let's take our stand together!

ISAIAH 50:6–8 MSG

Isaiah reminds us that we are not alone in our battles—even when everyone is against us and we feel outnumbered and outmaneuvered. But remember, your champion, God, is right there, saying, "*I am not leaving you! We are sticking this out together. You can put your chin up confidently, knowing that I, the Sustainer, am on your side. Let's take our stand together!*"

Lord, boldly stand beside me. May the strength of Your arms gird me as I take a stand for You. Lift my chin today; give me confidence to face opposition, knowing You are right there with me. Amen.

EVENING
The God of Our Salvation

Help us, O God of our salvation, for the glory of Your name; and deliver us and forgive our sins for Your name's sake. Why should the nations say, "Where is their God?" Let there be known among the nations in our sight, vengeance for the blood of Your servants which has been shed.

PSALM 79:9–10 NASB

God swore to Israel that He loved them. Now David calls upon the Lord to forgive the people, knowing full well that their present troubles directly correspond to their disobedience.

Have you ever cried out to God for deliverance, recognizing that your own circumstances were a direct result of leaving the Lord out of the decision making? We've all been there at one time or another. But God's not surprised. He watched us make this awful choice and then witnessed the harm we did to ourselves and others.

However, David recognized that if he didn't "own his sin" and ask forgiveness from his Lord, there was absolutely no hope for new beginnings.

We thank You that we can come to You as Lord and Messiah. You are truly a God of forgiveness. Amen.

DAY 192

MORNING
He Hears Me

I love the LORD because he hears my voice and my prayer for mercy.

PSALM 116:1 NLT

Isn't that mind blowing? The almighty God of the universe who created and assembled every particle in existence hears us when we come before Him. Maybe we go to the Lord in song, praising. Maybe we spend some time reading and thinking about God's Word. Maybe we are praying to Him as we reach out for His comfort. Whatever we do, God hears us and is interested in what we have to say. Isn't that a great reason to love the Lord? May we never forget to give thanks to God daily for the opportunity that He provides us simply to be heard.

I have so many reasons to love You, Lord, so many reasons to worship and praise You. How grateful I am that You hear my voice! I love You, Lord. Amen.

EVENING
Secure in Truth

Throw off your old sinful nature and your former way of life, which is corrupted by lust and deception. Instead, let the Spirit renew your thoughts and attitudes. Put on your new nature, created to be like God—truly righteous and holy.

EPHESIANS 4:22–24 NLT

In Christ, we have a new mind-set—fresh thinking. We know we are loved and treasured. The very God who spoke the universe into existence loved us enough to leave heaven and live in this imperfect world so He could save us from eternity in the hell we so deserved. Talk about significance! The delusions of this world fall away in light of who He is and what He has done for love of us. Our daily intake of His Word secures us in those truths. The lies of the evil one become ineffective.

Christ, rid me of my old way of thinking. Put the new mind-set within me to see daily the lies I fall for. Help me to walk in rightness and holiness, reflecting You in all I am. Amen.

DAY 193

MORNING
What Response Does God Require?

With what shall I come to the LORD and bow myself before the God on high? . . .
He has told you, O man, what is good;
and what does the LORD require of you
but to do justice, to love kindness,
and to walk humbly with your God?

MICAH 6:6, 8 NASB

Christ has already paid the price that needed to be exacted for our sins. He took the whips, the lashes, the nailing to the cross, the verbal rebukes, and also the physical agony on our behalf. The God of this universe looked upon our futility and became a man, and then He sacrificed His life so that we who did not and could not ever deserve His mercy might obtain it. Jesus Christ did all this because He is both just and kind.

Though I expend every effort, I can never rid myself of sin. You've already provided the only way in which I can be cleansed. Amen.

EVENING
Object of Faith

"And as Moses lifted up the serpent in the wilderness, even so must the Son of Man be lifted up, that whoever believes in Him should not perish but have eternal life."

JOHN 3:14–15 NKJV

When Nicodemus inquires of Jesus how a man receives eternal life, Jesus recalls this Old Testament image. Knowing He would be lifted up on a cross, the Lord Jesus points Nicodemus and us to faith in Him alone. We must repent of our sin and believe in the Son of God who died on the cross. Sin and its consequences are around us like serpents, but into the midst of our fallen world God has sent Jesus to save us. He is the object of our faith. The crucified and resurrected Christ is the answer. He is the Way, the Truth, and the Life.

Father, fix my gaze on Your Son lifted up for me. Amen.

DAY 194

MORNING
Order in Our Prayers

First of all, then, I urge that entreaties and prayers, petitions and thanksgivings, be made on behalf of all men, for kings and all who are in authority, so that we may lead a tranquil and quiet life in all godliness and dignity. This is good and acceptable in the sight of God our Savior, who desires all men to be saved and to come to the knowledge of the truth.

1 TIMOTHY 2:1–4 NASB

The demands of this world, and the pace at which our technology is racing, can sometimes overwhelm us, causing feelings of panic, powerlessness, and even paranoia. Is there a solution that brings life back into perspective? Yes. And God calls it prayer.

Prayer isn't some mystical entity to be attained by a few saintly little ladies in the church. Instead, it is an act of worship on the part of the created toward the Creator. Prayer is simply "talking to God" about everything that affects our lives.

Spirit of God, fall afresh on me that I might lift my voice in petition to You. Amen.

EVENING
Three in One

I am Alpha and Omega, the beginning and the end, the first and the last.

REVELATION 22:13 KJV

What makes our God unique among the religions of the world? No other religion has a God whose Son is equal to the Father. The Jews and Muslims reject the idea of God having a Son. Only Christianity has a triune God—three persons in one God. The Bible is unique because in it God fully reveals who He is. Since Jesus is fully God, let it renew our hope and faith in our Savior. He who created all things out of nothing will re-create this world into a paradise without sin.

Jesus, I learn how to live by Your human example, and I trust in You as my God—Father, Son, and Holy Spirit—three persons, one God, one perfect You! Amen.

DAY 195

MORNING
His Fortunes Restored

The LORD restored the fortunes of Job when he prayed for his friends, and the LORD increased all that Job had twofold. . . . The LORD blessed the latter days of Job more than his beginning; and he had 14,000 sheep and 6,000 camels and 1,000 yoke of oxen and 1,000 female donkeys. He had seven sons and three daughters.

JOB 42:10, 12–13 NASB

Don't you just love stories with happy endings? Reading through the book of Job makes anyone cry out for a great finish.

In today's scripture, we join up again with Job's three friends. Well, the long arm of God's justice finally caught up with them and the Lord called them to accountability (Job 42:8).

Finally, Job received the Lord's public vindication. Revenge doesn't get any sweeter than that! And don't you know that Eliphaz, Bildad, and Zophar were "sweatin' it big time" as they awaited Job's eloquent prayer that would restrain God's hand of wrath!

Lord, through Job's pain, agony, and loss You placed "wisdom in his innermost being" concerning deep and marvelous truths about Your character (Job 38:36). When I am afflicted, remind me to turn toward You. Amen.

EVENING
Chosen

"I have chosen you and have not rejected you."

ISAIAH 41:9 NIV

The Lord doesn't dump us when we don't measure up. And He doesn't choose us one minute only to reject us a week later. We need not fear being deserted by our loving Father. He doesn't accept or reject us based on any arbitrary standards. He loves us with an everlasting love (Jeremiah 31:3). By His own mercy and design, "he hath made us accepted in the beloved" (Ephesians 1:6 KJV).

Father, thank You that I don't need to fear Your rejection of me. Amen.

The LORD *will keep you from all harm—*
he will watch over your life; the LORD
will watch over your coming and
going both now and forevermore.

PSALM 121:7–8 NIV

Our lives are like an ancient city contained within walls. In an ancient city, the gatekeeper's job was to make decisions about what went in and out of the city. God is the gatekeeper of our lives. He is always watching, always guarding, and ever vigilant in His care of us, even when we are least aware that He is doing so. Proverbs 2:8 (NKJV) says, "He guards the paths of justice, and preserves the way of His saints." By sending His Son to save us and His Spirit to dwell in us, He has assured us that we are never forgotten and never alone.

Forgive me, Father, for how often I forget about You. Help me remember that You are guarding and preserving me and that nothing comes into my life without Your permission. Amen.

EVENING

Endless Supply of Love

We love because he first loved us.

1 JOHN 4:19 NIV

The power of God's love within us fuels our love when human love is running on empty. He plants His love within our hearts so we can share Him with others. We draw from His endless supply. Love starts with God. God continues to provide His love to nourish us. God surrounds us with His love. We live in hope and draw from His strength, all because He first loved us.

Oh God, the human love I know on earth cannot compare with Your love. When I feel empty, Your love fills me up. Your love is perfect. It never fails. Amen.

DAY 197

MORNING

Welcoming Other Believers

The elder to the beloved Gaius, whom I love in truth. . . Beloved, you are acting faithfully in whatever you accomplish for the brethren, and especially when they are strangers.

3 John 1:1, 5 NASB

Gaius, a strong and cordial believer, was dearly loved by the apostle John. We see in today's scripture that John refers to him as "beloved." Gaius extended a hand of loving fellowship to all who came to worship.

But it was the truth to which Gaius was a witness that had molded this extraordinary life—one centered on obedience to God. Gaius provided genuine hospitality. And evidently this included opening his own home, heart, and pocketbook to others so that the Word of God might go forth.

If only we all might have such pure motives for assisting others—that they might receive God's Word and see His love flowing all around them.

Father, my church will likely be filled with people who may only "press the flesh with the faithful" once or twice a year. May I give these inquiring minds a warm reception. Amen.

EVENING

Never Settle

For in him dwelleth all the fulness of the Godhead bodily. And ye are complete in him.

Colossians 2:9–10 KJV

Paul stated clearly that the fullness of deity lives in bodily form in Christ. He is God the Son, and when you have God in your heart, you are complete. You don't need anything added—whether ceremonies or so-called secret knowledge—to make you *more* complete. If the Spirit of Jesus Christ dwells in your heart and you are connected to God, you've got it all! Don't let anyone persuade you otherwise (Colossians 2:8). Don't settle for substitutes.

Jesus, You complete me. Since You dwell in my heart, I am forever connected with God and heaven. I have all that I need—salvation and Your perfect, eternal love. Amen.

DAY 198

MORNING
Promises of God

"For the LORD your God is living among you. He is a mighty savior. He will take delight in you with gladness. With his love, he will calm all your fears. He will rejoice over you with joyful songs."

ZEPHANIAH 3:17 NLT

Look at all the promises packed into this one verse of scripture! God is with you. He is your mighty Savior. He delights in you with gladness. He calms your fears with His love. He rejoices over you with joyful songs. Wow! What a bundle of hope is found here for the believer. Like a mother attuned to her newborn baby's cries, so is your heavenly Father's heart for you. He delights in being your Father. You are blessed to be a daughter of the King.

Father, thank You for loving me the way You do. You are all I need. Amen.

EVENING
Nahum Proclaims Israel's Restoration

Behold, on the mountains the feet of him who brings good news, who announces peace! Celebrate your feasts, O Judah; pay your vows. For never again will the wicked one pass through you; he is cut off completely.

NAHUM 1:15 NASB

No news could be sweeter than the confirmation that a mighty enemy army was about to suffer a great demise. God gave Nahum, the prophet, just such a vision concerning the great Assyrian invaders who had devastated Judah. It had been such a long time that these pagans began boasting that no god would be able to deliver the Israelites. However, the true God of power and might was now ready to act against them for enslaving His people. And they never saw it coming!

Lord, You are a mighty foe indeed! Why do people devise plots against You? Amen.

DAY 199

MORNING

Get Above It All

Set your minds and keep focused habitually on the things above [the heavenly things], not on things that are on the earth [which have only temporal value].

COLOSSIANS 3:2 AMP

Sometimes the most difficult challenges you face play out in your head—where a struggle to control the outcome and work out the details of life can consume you. Once removed—far away from the details—you can see things from a higher perspective. Close your eyes and push out the thoughts that try to grab you and keep you tied to the things of the world. Reach out to God and let your spirit soar. Give your concerns to Him and let Him work out the details. Rest in Him and He'll carry you above it all, every step of the way.

God, You are far above any detail of life that concerns me. Help me to trust You today for answers to those things that seem to bring me down. I purposefully set my heart and mind on You today. Amen.

EVENING

Extend Hospitality

Do not forget to show hospitality to strangers, for by so doing some people have shown hospitality to angels without knowing it.

HEBREWS 13:2 NIV

The author of Hebrews 13:2, most likely Paul, reminded Christians to extend hospitality to strangers. He suggested that some strangers might even be angels sent from God. Today, most strangers to whom we extend generosity and hospitality are probably not angels, but we can't know if someday God will allow us to entertain an angel without us knowing it. When you practice hospitality, God might be using you to minister to others. What are some ways that you can extend hospitality to strangers?

Lord, teach me to be wise when extending hospitality to strangers. Enlighten me. Teach me new ways to minister to others and show them Your amazing love. Amen.

DAY 200

MORNING

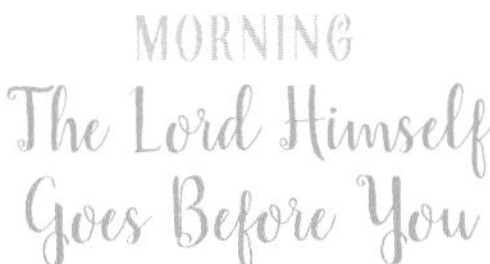

"The Lord himself goes before you and will be with you; he will never leave you nor forsake you. Do not be afraid; do not be discouraged."

Deuteronomy 31:8 niv

Joshua 1:9 (niv) tells us to "be strong and courageous. Do not be afraid; do not be discouraged, for the Lord your God will be with you wherever you go." Be encouraged! Even when it feels like it, you are truly never alone. And never without access to God's power. If you've trusted Christ as your Savior, the Spirit of God Himself is alive and well and working inside you at all times. What an astounding miracle! The Creator of the universe dwells within you and is available to encourage you and help you make right choices on a moment-by-moment basis.

Thank You, Lord, for the incredible gift of Your presence in each and every situation I face. Allow me to remember this and to call upon Your name as I go about each day. Amen.

EVENING

Joshua Is Chosen

"Be strong and courageous, for you shall go with this people into the land which the Lord has sworn to their fathers to give them, and you shall give it to them as an inheritance."

Deuteronomy 31:7 nasb

God did not allow those who taunted Moses to challenge the authority of his successor. Moses, who is preparing to die, names Joshua as his successor. Right there, in the presence of all Israel, Moses admonishes Joshua to "be strong and courageous." God chose Joshua because he had faithfully served Moses throughout all their years in the wilderness.

Near the end of his life, Moses recited the words of the song God had given to him (Deuteronomy 32:1–2 niv): "Listen, you heavens, and I will speak; hear, you earth, the words of my mouth. Let my teaching fall like rain and my words descend like dew, like showers on new grass, like abundant rain on tender plants"—and then it continues for forty-one more verses. Please take time to read it all.

Lord, I forget sometimes that those in leadership are chosen by You. And with responsibility comes accountability. Amen.

DAY 201

MORNING

Joy in the Morning

All who seek the LORD will praise him. Their hearts will rejoice with everlasting joy.

PSALM 22:26 NLT

Every day, God provides us with beauty all around to cheer and help us. It may come through the beauty of flowers or the bright blue sky in the morning—or maybe the white snow covering the trees of a glorious winter wonderland. It may be through the smile of a child or the grateful face of the one we care for. Each and every day, the Lord has a special gift to remind us of whose we are and to generate the joy we need to succeed.

Lord God, I thank You for Your joy; I thank You for providing it every day to sustain me. I will be joyful in You. Amen.

EVENING

Never Forgotten

"See, I have engraved you on the palms of my hands."

ISAIAH 49:16 NIV

In the middle of tumultuous times, it's tempting to proclaim that God has forgotten us. Both Israel and Judah struggled with the idea that God had abandoned them. But God took steps to contradict this notion. In an image that prefigures Jesus' crucifixion, God boldly proclaimed that His children were engraved on the palms of His hands. The nail-scarred hands that His Son would endure bear the engraved names of all of us who call upon Him as Savior and Lord. God does not forget us in the midst of our troubles! It is His nail-scarred hand that reaches down and holds our own.

Jesus, the scars on Your hands are because of me—a testament to my salvation. My name is engraved on Your hand as a child of God. Oh, thank You, dear Jesus! Amen.

DAY 202

MORNING
When Will Our Suffering Cease?

Blessed be the God and Father of our Lord Jesus Christ, the Father of mercies and God of all comfort, who comforts us in all our affliction so that we will be able to comfort those who are in any affliction with the comfort with which we ourselves are comforted by God. . . . But if we are afflicted, it is for your comfort and salvation.

2 Corinthians 1:3–4, 6 NASB

My son, an experienced mountain biker and triathlete, hit some debris in the street when he was riding recently and was thrown from his bike and onto a pile of bricks. His knee required surgery to repair the breaks.

He and his fiancée have learned to depend upon each other in a new way: she is providing the medical expertise, while he has learned to allow her to intervene. And both of them depend entirely on the Lord's sufficiency.

This is the purpose of our trials, that we might comfort one another and lean on the Lord's strength.

Thank You, God, that in heaven all suffering will cease. Amen.

EVENING
God Knows

Your eyes saw my unformed body; all the days ordained for me were written in your book before one of them came to be.

Psalm 139:16 NIV

God knows the days of all people. Job said, "A person's days are determined; you have decreed the number of his months" (Job 14:5 NIV). The same knowledge applies to our new birth. He created us anew in Christ Jesus for good works "which God prepared in advance for us to do" (Ephesians 2:10 NIV). The God who knows everything about us still loves us. With the psalmist, let us declare, "Such knowledge is too wonderful for me, too lofty for me to attain" (Psalm 139:6 NIV).

God, how can You know all about everyone who has lived or ever will live? Your ways are so far beyond my understanding, and yet You love me. You are so wonderful! Amen.

DAY 203

He will not let your foot slip—he who watches over you will not slumber.

PSALM 121:3 NIV

The Psalms tell us that God does *not* sleep. He watches over us, never once averting His eyes even for a few quick moments of rest. God guards our every moment. The Lord stays up all night, looking after us as we sleep. He patiently keeps His eyes on us even when we roam. He constantly comforts when fear or illness make us toss and turn. Like a caring parent who tiptoes into a sleeping child's room, God surrounds us even when we don't realize it. We can sleep because God never slumbers.

Oh God, how grateful I am that You never sleep. When weariness overtakes me, You guard me like a mother who watches over her child. I love You, Father! Amen.

EVENING
The Lord of Parables

Listen, O my people, to my instruction; incline your ears to the words of my mouth. I will open my mouth in a parable; I will utter dark sayings of old, which we have heard and known, and our fathers have told us.

PSALM 78:1–3 NASB

Christ did not dabble in nonsense. But sometimes Jesus offered His perfect insight in parables, or through stories with hidden meanings. "To you it has been granted to know the mysteries of the kingdom of God, but to the rest it is in parables, so that SEEING THEY MAY NOT SEE, AND HEARING THEY MAY NOT UNDERSTAND" (Luke 8:10 NASB).

Jesus had just shared with them the parable about the sower and the seed. He knew that those whose hearts were open and receptive to Him would understand its meaning. On the other hand, those whose hearts held only antagonism, jealousy, and self-righteousness would not understand even if He spoke plainly.

Is your heart ready to listen to Jesus?

When you examine the content of my heart, Lord, which type of soil have I prepared for Your Word? Amen.

DAY 204

Don't let anyone look down on you because you are young, but set an example for the believers in speech, in conduct, in love, in faith and in purity.

1 TIMOTHY 4:12 NIV

Much of the wisdom we gain comes through experiences we try to shed in an effort to get back to a purer, more innocent state. Young believers can be a reminder to the older generation of the joy and enthusiasm a pure faith can generate. And they have another important task; after all, "peer pressure" doesn't always have to be negative. The young are best positioned to bring other young folk to God, and that is work fully deserving of respect.

Dear God, help me to rediscover childlike innocence, the simplicity of faith without doubt. It is in that purest form of belief that I am nearest to You. Amen.

EVENING

What Is Your Foundation?

"Woe to him who builds a city with bloodshed and founds a town with violence!"

HABAKKUK 2:12 NASB

Martin Luther was pierced by a verse in Habakkuk, and his reaction changed the course of church history. "The righteous will live by his faith" (Habakkuk 2:4 NASB). But in whom is this faith placed? If our faith is in Christ, we are established upon firm ground. But if it's in systems, programs, or even religion, it's doomed to fail.

The people of Judah were entering their darkest hour. The Babylonians had invaded this southern kingdom three times. During the final siege, both Jerusalem and the temple were destroyed. Habakkuk is seeking assurance from the Lord that He will save them from extinction.

Thank You, God, for Your promise to Habakkuk: "For the vision is yet for the appointed time; it hastens toward the goal and it will not fail. Though it tarries, wait for it; for it will certainly come, it will not delay" (Habakkuk 2:3 NASB). Amen.

DAY 205

MORNING
Martha and Mary

A woman named Martha welcomed Him into her home. She had a sister called Mary, who was seated at the Lord's feet, listening to His word. But Martha was distracted with all her preparations; and she came up to Him and said, "Lord, do You not care that my sister has left me to do all the serving alone? Then tell her to help me."

Luke 10:38–40 NASB

Martha, ever the perfect hostess, was left to do all the work. It didn't seem fair. However, what Martha really desired was a release from her compulsive neatness. And that's when the Lord presented her with a process for "chilling out."

Who knew better than Christ how to put the pressures of life into perspective? He had only three years in which to establish His ministry, train up His disciples, and present the Gospel. Yet we see no record of Him hurrying others or running at a frantic pace.

Have you taken time to get to know your Lord? Perhaps your life, like Martha's, is missing the best part.

Lord, I pray for peace today from my busy schedule so I may learn at Your knee. Amen.

EVENING
His Love Endures Forever

God, God, save me! I'm in over my head, quicksand under me, swamp water over me; I'm going down for the third time. I'm hoarse from calling for help, bleary-eyed from searching the sky for God.

Psalm 69:1–3 MSG

The psalm writers had a very real, genuine relationship with God. They sang praises to God, they got angry with God, they felt abandoned by God, they didn't understand God's slow response. . .and yet they continued to live by faith, deeply convinced that God would overcome. These ancient prayers remind us that nothing can shock God's ears. We can tell Him anything and everything. He won't forsake us—His love endures forever.

Oh Lord, You know the secrets of my heart. Teach me to talk to You through every emotion and every circumstance. My focus belongs on You. Amen.

DAY 206

MORNING

Paul's Trip to Paradise

I know a man in Christ who fourteen years ago. . .was caught up into Paradise and heard inexpressible words, which a man is not permitted to speak. On behalf of such a man I will boast; but on my own behalf I will not boast, except in regard to my weaknesses.

2 CORINTHIANS 12:2, 4–5 NASB

God propelled Paul up to heaven for a glimpse of what was ahead for him and all believers.

But why does Paul present this vision as though it happened to someone else? Remember that he had been trained as a rabbi and had received a thorough knowledge of the law. Rabbis often refer to themselves in the third person to refrain from sounding unduly prideful.

Lord, Your magnificent presence is all I need to provide me with the momentum to continue spreading Your Word. Amen.

EVENING

A Strong Spring

My voice shalt thou hear in the morning, O LORD; in the morning will I direct my prayer unto thee, and will look up.

PSALM 5:3 KJV

We need to begin our busy days on a strong spring, too. Not with just a good cup of coffee, but some time spent with our source of strength. Taking five minutes or an hour—or more if we're really disciplined—in prayer and Bible reading can make the difference in our day. No matter if we're facing wresting kids out of bed or fighting traffic all the way to work, that special time can give us a "spring in our step" today.

Thank You, Lord, for another day. Be my source of strength today. In Jesus' blessed name. Amen.

DAY 207

MORNING

For You are my rock and my fortress.

Psalm 71:3 NASB

For several months before I attended my first writers' conference in Southern California, I worked feverishly compiling a manuscript for a book. However, when an editor at the conference looked it over, he told me that it needed work. Being new to the field of writing, I was devestated by his remarks.

I sought solace upon a large rock situated beside a small lake. Tears of disappointment streaked down my cheeks and as others approached I began walking. I happened to encounter a bronze plaque that stated that the well-known evangelist Billy Graham had also found peace in this place.

As the sun warmed that beautiful, tranquil setting, I considered another psalm about the Rock. "Be to me a rock of strength, a stronghold to save me. For You are my rock and my fortress; for Your name's sake You will lead me and guide me" (Psalm 31:2–3 NASB).

Over fifty times in scripture the word *rock* is used in reference to God. He is steadfast, immovable, and unchangeable.

Lord, You remain that Rock on which my faith stands firm. Amen.

EVENING

Renewal of All Things

Peter answered him, "We have left everything to follow you! What then will there be for us?" Jesus said to them, "Truly I tell you, at the renewal of all things, when the Son of Man sits on his glorious throne, you who have followed me will also sit on twelve thrones, judging the twelve tribes of Israel."

Matthew 19:27–28 NIV

None of us will just occupy space in heaven. Our God is always productive. And this job to which Jesus refers, that of judging the twelve tribes of Israel, will be given to the disciples. Have you ever speculated as to what you might do in heaven? Well, don't worry; it's not going to be anything like what you've done on earth. Your "boss," after all, will be perfect. And the tasks you perform will be custom tailored to you. "Job satisfaction" will finally fit into our vernacular.

Lord, I can't even imagine what You have in store for me in heaven. Please keep me faithful to complete the duties You've called me to on earth. Amen.

DAY 208

MORNING
Hold On to Hope

The prospect of the righteous is joy,
but the hopes of the wicked come to nothing.
PROVERBS 10:28 NIV

Trusting in Jesus gave you new life and hope for eternity. So how do you respond when life becomes dark and dull? Does hope slip away? When no obviously great spiritual works are going on, do not assume God has deserted you. Hold on to Him even more firmly and trust. He will keep His promises. Truly, what other option do you have? Without Him, hope disappears.

Dear heavenly Father, the day I met You was the day I received life anew. My soul now overflows with hope, love, peace, and joy. Thank You for saving me! Amen.

EVENING
Who Is the Rightful Heir?

Abraham had two sons, one by the bondwoman and one by the free woman. But the son by the bondwoman was born according to the flesh, and the son by the free woman through the promise.
GALATIANS 4:22–23 NASB

God had promised Abraham a son, but at eighty-six years old, Abraham had become weary of waiting (Genesis 16:16). To him, it was apparent that Sarah, his wife, was barren. So, at Sarah's urging, Abraham sought out her slave girl Hagar, and she conceived. Abraham's action led to much dissension within his home. And by the time Sarah conceived the son of promise, the household was in a complete upheaval. God promised to make both sides great nations (Genesis 21:9–13).

Paul now uses these two sons to illustrate the status of the unbeliever versus her changed relationship once she commits her life to Christ. Once we were slaves to sin, but with our redemption in Christ we become free.

Lord, through the line of Isaac men and women are truly blessed. For Christ Himself would be that seed from whom redemption would come (Galatians 3:13–18). Amen.

DAY 209

MORNING

Everyday Blessings

But the eyes of the LORD are on those who fear him, on those whose hope is in his unfailing love.

PSALM 33:18 NIV

The Lord of all creation is watching our every moment and wants to fill us with His joy. He often interrupts our lives with His blessings: butterflies dancing in sunbeams, dew-touched spiderwebs, cotton candy clouds, and glorious crimson sunsets. The beauty of His creation reassures us of His unfailing love and fills us with hope. But it is up to us to take the time to notice.

May I always be aware of Your lovely creation, Father God. Your artistry never fails to amaze me! Amen.

EVENING

Moses Is in Glory

And behold, two men were talking with Him; and they were Moses and Elijah, who, appearing in glory, were speaking of His departure which He was about to accomplish at Jerusalem.

LUKE 9:30–31 NASB

In case you've been feeling sorry for Moses, who never got to enter the Promised Land, just look at what God had in store for him. These verses tell us that Moses and Elijah appeared in glory. But what does that really mean?

We are not now what we will become. For whether we die or are taken up by what is referred to as the Rapture, the Lord will someday allow this "earthsuit" of ours to fall away and issue us our "eternity suit."

In spite of your life, are you assured of your salvation?

Oh Lord, I am so grateful that my place with You is already reserved! Amen.

DAY 210

MORNING

"Blessed are those who mourn,
for they will be comforted."

MATTHEW 5:4 NIV

How often do we think of mourning as a good thing? But when it comes to sin, it is. Those who sorrow over their own sinfulness will turn to God for forgiveness. When He willingly responds to their repentance, mourning ends. Comforted by God's pardon, transformed sinners celebrate—and joyous love for Jesus replaces sorrow.

Heavenly Father, thank You for replacing my sorrow with joy! Your unconditional love floods my soul. You are good! Amen.

EVENING

Loving Jesus

Looking unto Jesus the author
and finisher of our faith.

HEBREWS 12:2 KJV

God is writing a story of faith through your life. What will it describe? Will it be a chronicle of challenges overcome, like the Old Testament story of Joseph? Or a near tragedy turned into joy, like that of the prodigal son? Whatever your account says, if you love Jesus, the end is never in question. Those who love Him finish in heaven, despite their trials on earth. The long, weary path ends in His arms. Today, write a chapter in your faithful narrative of God's love.

God, thank You for helping me write my story. May my story touch the lives of others and be a light pointing them to You! Amen.

DAY 211

MORNING

A Call to Holiness

"When you enter the land which the LORD your God gives you, you shall not learn to imitate the detestable things of those nations."

DEUTERONOMY 18:9 NASB

Our two sons became immediately fascinated with the role-playing game Dungeons and Dragons. While our older son got a part-time job, which severely limited his free time, his younger brother went deeper and deeper into this seductive game.

About the same time, our church encouraged adults and high schoolers to sign up for the seminar "Basic Youth Conflicts." By the time the concluding all-day Saturday session rolled around, each one of us had been convicted by the Holy Spirit concerning our own "pet sins." All the way home that last evening our younger son spoke about how the game had usurped the time he used to spend with the Lord.

We watched as he pulled out a metal trash can and burned every one of the game's expensive books. From that moment Jeff never looked back.

Is God receiving all the glory in your life?

Lord, You know better than I what things will draw my time and attention away from You. Give me the courage to obey You. Amen.

EVENING

First Love

But you must stay deeply rooted and firm in your faith. You must not give up the hope you received when you heard the good news.

COLOSSIANS 1:23 CEV

Do you remember the day you turned your life over to Christ? Can you recall the flood of joy and hope that coursed through your veins? Ah, the wonder of first love. Like romantic love that deepens and broadens with passing years, our relationship with Jesus evolves into a river of faith that endures the test of time.

Father, I am so thankful that You are faithful. Though human relationships may fail, You are a constant companion in my life. Thank You! Amen.

DAY 212

MORNING
JOY: Jesus Occupying You

May all who fear you find in me a cause for joy, for I have put my hope in your word.

PSALM 119:74 NLT

Have you ever met someone you immediately knew was filled with joy? The kind of effervescent joy that bubbles up and overflows, covering everyone around her with warmth and love and acceptance. We love to be near people filled with Jesus-joy. And even more, as Christians we want to be like them!

Lord, show me how to radiate Your joy in the presence of others. I want to be a light for You. Amen.

EVENING
Forever Joy

We don't look at the troubles we can see now. . . . For the things we see now will soon be gone, but the things we cannot see will last forever.

2 CORINTHIANS 4:18 NLT

A painter's first brushstrokes look like random blobs—no discernible shape, substance, or clue as to what the completed painting will be. But in time, the skilled artist brings order to perceived chaos. Initial confusion is forgotten in joyful admiration of the finished masterpiece. We often can't see past the blobs of trouble on our life canvases. We must trust that the artist has a masterpiece underway. And there will be great joy in its completion.

God, You are the master artist. I trust You to create a masterpiece with my life canvas. Amen.

DAY 213

MORNING
Blessed by God

And God blessed them.

Genesis 1:22 KJV

In the very first chapter of the first book of the Bible, we read that God was already in the business of blessing. He created the world—and then He blessed it. But what are we talking about when we use that familiar word, *blessing*? Did you ever stop to think what it means to be blessed?

God, teach me to better understand the blessing You daily pour into my life. May I not take this familiar word for granted. Fill me with wonder and joy at all the ways You bring life and healing into the world. Amen.

EVENING
Sixfold Blessings

"I will be with you and bless you."

Genesis 26:3 NLT

Merriam-Webster's Dictionary gives these definitions for *bless*:

1. to make sacred
2. to ask for God's help
3. to speak words of approval
4. to give happiness and health
5. to protect and preserve
6. to endow with a gift

God blesses you in all these ways. You are set aside to be God's dwelling place—and that makes you sacred. Through Christ, you have the right to ask God for help and care. He speaks to you; He gives you happiness and health; He protects you; and He gives you countless gifts!

I want still more of Your blessing, Lord. Live in me. Help me. Make me sensitive to hear Your voice. Fill my life with joy and well-being. Keep me safe. Give me all Your gifts! Amen.

DAY 214

MORNING
Paul's Ministry Comes to a Close

Paul, an apostle of Christ Jesus by the will of God, according to the promise of life in Christ Jesus, to Timothy, my beloved son. . . I constantly remember you in my prayers night and day, longing to see you, even as I recall your tears, so that I may be filled with joy. For I am mindful of the sincere faith within you, which first dwelt in your grandmother Lois and your mother Eunice, and I am sure that it is in you as well.

2 Timothy 1:1–5 NASB

As I read Paul's second letter to Timothy, I can identify with his anguish at letting go. Paul had to make sure that Timothy, who suffered from bouts of insecurity, remained strong in the faith. For Timothy would now "carry the torch of faith" and continue bringing the Gospel to all who would listen.

Paul praises Timothy, reminding him of the heritage of belief passed down to him from his mother, Eunice, and grandmother, Lois. And Paul, the ever-present spiritual mentor, expresses his love by referring to Timothy as "my beloved son."

Use me, Lord, to do Your will. Amen.

EVENING
The Blessing Circle

May all. . .enter his circle of blessing and bless the One who blessed them.

Psalm 72:17 MSG

When we look at the Old Testament words translated as *bless* and *blessing*, we find deeper meanings. Two different Hebrew words are used in this psalm. The first one has to do with kneeling down; it's how we bless God. The second is how God blesses us; it means "to lead." These two blessings form a circle that never ends: God leads us, we surrender to God, He leads us even further. . .on and on.

God, I want to bless You today. May each thing I do, even the smallest and most trivial, be an act of surrender to You. As I give You more and more of my life, I know You will lead me closer to You. Amen.

DAY 215

MORNING
Fruitful Blessings

"I will bless him, and will make him fruitful."

GENESIS 17:20 NASB

In this verse, the Hebrew word that we've translated *bless* has to do with making something bear fruit. God blesses us by making our lives productive; we create homes and gardens, we raise children and help others; we write stories, paint pictures, and make music. That's one kind of fruitfulness He gives us. He also, however, makes our spirits bear a different kind of fruit—joy, humility, peace, understanding, and most of all, love.

Bless me, Lord, with productivity, creativity, and the fruit of Your Spirit. May each thing that I do yield eternal fruit in Your kingdom. Amen.

EVENING
Our Triune God

"Hear, O Israel! The LORD is our God, the LORD is one!"

DEUTERONOMY 6:4 NASB

Shema Yisroel Adonai Elohenu Adonai Echad is Hebrew for "Hear, O Israel! The LORD our God is one LORD." The three distinct personalities that comprise the Trinity are all equal within the Godhead: Father, Son, and Holy Spirit. But the word *one* here should be interpreted as in a marriage context when the "two become one."

Genesis 1:1 (NASB) states, "In the beginning God created the heavens and the earth." The Hebrew word for God here is *Elohim*, a masculine plural noun. When God speaks of Himself the plural pronoun is used: "Then God [Elohim] said, 'Let Us make man in Our image, according to Our likeness' " (Genesis 1:26 NASB). All three persons of the Trinity were present.

Only God could have omnisciently conceived of the Trinity. God has always been, and will forever be.

Lord, I rejoice in my wonderful Savior, the Father who sent Him, and the Holy Spirit who gives me insight to understand scripture. Amen.

DAY 216

MORNING
Happiness!

How blessed is the one whom You choose and bring near to You.

PSALM 65:4 NASB

The Hebrew word used here means simply "happy." When God chooses us, He makes us happy. When He brings us near to Him, our hearts fill up with joy. We'll still have the ups and downs that everyone else has, of course. Sorrows will come, and we'll face days that challenge us. But when we look back at our lives as we enter eternity, we'll see clearly: we've been so blessed. God's given us so much to make us happy!

You have given me so much, Lord! When I look at my life and think of all the people, places, and things that give me joy, all I can do is say, "Thank You!" In Your name I pray, amen.

EVENING
Spoken

"Come, you who are blessed by my Father, inherit the Kingdom prepared for you from the creation of the world."

MATTHEW 25:34 NLT

The Greek word translated *blessed* in the New Testament adds another meaning to our understanding. In this verse, the word Jesus uses means "to speak well of, to say words that give or create something good." Speaking is important in the Bible. In Genesis, God spoke the world into being. Jesus is the Word. And your name is on God's lips. He has spoken your very self into being. You are a child of the kingdom!

I can't take this in, Lord—You loved me and spoke my name before the world was created! Your love astounds me! When I doubt myself, remind me that You have chosen to bless me with Your love. Amen.

DAY 217

MORNING
The Blessing of True Identity

This is my beloved Son,
in whom I am well pleased.
MATTHEW 17:5 KJV

This is the blessing the Father gave to Jesus at the beginning of His ministry. It's a spoken affirmation of a reality that already existed. Through grace we, too, can claim this blessing as our own. When you feel down on yourself, when your self-concept feels beaten down to nothing, repeat this blessing to yourself. It affirms your true identity. Christ has made you part of His family, and now you are God's beloved child. He is pleased with you!

Jesus, thank You for bringing me
into Your family, so that I, too,
can call God "Father." Amen.

EVENING
The Eternal Gospel

"Fear God, and give Him glory, because the hour of His judgment has come; worship Him who made the heaven and the earth and sea and springs of waters."
REVELATION 14:7 NASB

Following the resurrection, Jesus prepared to leave this earth and return to heaven. Before going, He delivered a message to His disciples and charged them with a mission: "Go therefore and make disciples of all the nations, baptizing them in the name of the Father and the Son and the Holy Spirit, teaching them to observe all that I commanded you; and lo, I am with you always, even to the end of the age" (Matthew 28:19–20 NASB).

This great commission is extended to all who choose to believe in Christ.

Lord, while there is still time, please provide imaginative ways in which we can speak forth Your Word of Truth to all those whom we love. We are grateful that You will never leave us or forsake us (Hebrews 13:5). Amen.

MORNING

The cup of blessing which we bless, is it not the communion of the blood of Christ?

1 CORINTHIANS 10:16 KJV

The Greek word used here means "consecration"; in other words, to commit something totally to God. This adds another element to our understanding of blessing: something that is blessed is completely surrendered to God. We commune in our hearts with Christ—we share intimately with Him His absolute self-giving on the cross—and this consecrates us. Our hearts are God's. We have drunk from Christ's cup of sacrifice and blessing.

Jesus, I want to consecrate my life, my self, to You. Help me to give myself away to You and to others. Use me to do Your work, I pray. Amen.

EVENING

God's Abundance

God is able to bless you abundantly.

2 CORINTHIANS 9:8 NIV

The literal meaning of these Greek words adds still another layer to our understanding of God's blessings. When Paul wrote this sentence to the Corinthians, he was talking about God's power—something that is over and above anything else we've ever encountered—to give grace and kindness to us that are also over and above anything we can even imagine. God's blessings are as abundant as His power to shower them upon us. None of our fears and doubts can ever limit either one!

Lord, when my thoughts are negative and full of doubts, remind me that Your power is unlimited—and Your blessings are more abundant than I can even imagine. Amen.

DAY 219

MORNING

The Secret of Material Blessings

Be harmonious. . .kindhearted, and humble in spirit; not returning evil for evil or insult for insult, but giving a blessing instead; for you were called for the very purpose that you might inherit a blessing.

1 PETER 3:8–9 NASB

These verses contain two meanings of the Greek word for *blessing*: first, speaking well of others (this is one way we bless others, by affirming them with our words, rather than gossiping, insulting, boasting, or quarreling), and second (the consequence of the first), tangible good things in our ordinary lives.

Jesus, remind me, please, to use my words for blessing others. May I use my words to build up rather than tear down. Amen.

EVENING

Body and Soul

Beloved, I pray that in all respects you may prosper and be in good health, just as your soul prospers.

3 JOHN 1:2 NASB

The New Testament makes clear that God sends both physical and spiritual blessings into our lives. He wants our lives to be healthy and prosperous—emotionally, physically, financially, spiritually. We tend to separate the spiritual world from the physical one, but the Bible shows us a perspective where each sort of blessing flows into all the others. As we are spiritually blessed, our physical lives will be blessed as well.

Lord, bless me, body and soul. Fill me with Your life-giving love. Make me truly whole, truly healthy, so that I can better serve You. Amen.

DAY 220

MORNING

Already Blessed

God. . .has blessed us in the heavenly realms with every spiritual blessing in Christ.

EPHESIANS 1:3 NIV

That's pretty amazing. Right now, in the world of eternity—the spiritual world—you and I already possess all that God has to give to us. We don't have to wait for these blessings. We don't have to wait until we die and go to heaven. We don't have to earn them first, and we don't have to work hard to become "more spiritual." They're already ours, right now.

Thank You, God, that You have already given me all that I need. Show me how to live daily in eternity's world, claiming the blessings that are mine in Christ. Amen.

EVENING

Spiritually Strong

I long to see you so that I may impart to you some spiritual gift to make you strong.

ROMANS 1:11 NIV

In this verse, Paul is talking about a particular kind of blessing: a spiritual gift. The Greek word is *charisma*, a grace-gift that empowers us to work on behalf of God's kingdom. It's given to us freely; we don't have to do anything to earn it. We can't see this kind of blessing, but we can feel its power. It fills our lives with love, joy, and peace. We are spiritually strong. We have abundant life.

I ask You today, dear Lord, for the spiritual gifts that will empower me to serve You and others with love and joy and strength. Amen.

DAY 221

MORNING
Trusting God in All Circumstances

"The LORD your God has multiplied you, and behold, you are this day like the stars of heaven in number. May the LORD, the God of your fathers, increase you a thousand-fold more than you are and bless you, just as He has promised you!"

DEUTERONOMY 1:10–11 NASB

The Israelites were two million strong when they left Egypt, and now in "the fortieth year, on the first day of the eleventh month" (Deuteronomy 1:3 NASB), Moses proclaimed to them what the Lord had commanded.

The people had been in this same place forty years earlier, but the Israelites disobeyed God by refusing to fight for the land and to trust God for the victory.

Therefore, God announced that this entire generation of rebellious people—with two exceptions, Caleb and Joshua—would not see the Promised Land. Even Moses, who had displayed a lack of faith, would not set foot there. God demands trust from His people and His spiritual leaders.

Do you trust God for everything?

Dear Heavenly Father, let my trust in You never waver. Give me wisdom and courage for this day. Amen.

EVENING
Thriving

I am like an olive tree, thriving in the house of God. I will always trust in God's unfailing love.

PSALM 52:8 NLT

Children need love to thrive. So do all of us older folks. Without love, our hearts would be sad and lonely. Our lives would be narrow and unfulfilling. In fact, love is the most important of all the many spiritual blessings we've received. All God's blessings, both spiritual and physical, are wrapped up in His love. Because He loves us, He will never stop blessing us. His love never fails.

God, when I look back on my life, I see that You have never failed me in the past. Thank You that Your blessings have no end. Amen.

DAY 222

MORNING

The Ultimate Love

This is how God showed his love among us: He sent his one and only Son into the world that we might live through him.

1 JOHN 4:9 NIV

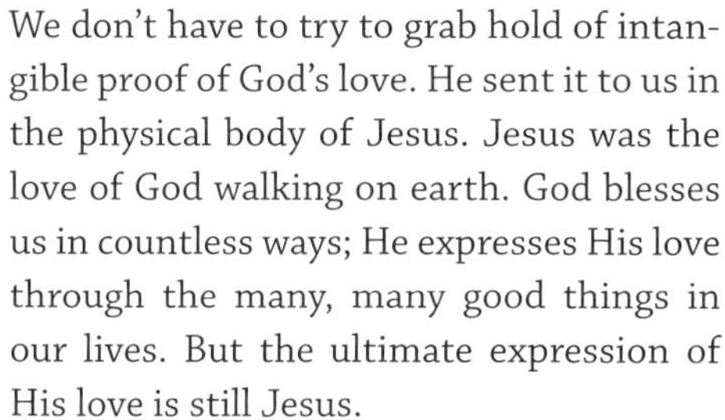

We don't have to try to grab hold of intangible proof of God's love. He sent it to us in the physical body of Jesus. Jesus was the love of God walking on earth. God blesses us in countless ways; He expresses His love through the many, many good things in our lives. But the ultimate expression of His love is still Jesus.

Jesus, thank You for coming to earth to show us God's love in physical form. Help me to become more like You, following Your example of love. Amen.

EVENING

Matthew, the Tax Collector

After that He went out and noticed a tax collector named Levi sitting in the tax booth, and He said to him, "Follow Me." And he left everything behind, and got up and began to follow Him. And Levi gave a big reception for Him in his house; and there was a great crowd of tax collectors and other people who were reclining at the table with them.

LUKE 5:27–29 NASB

Oh no, not the dreaded tax man! Yet Levi responded to Christ's invitation to follow Him. Christ changed his name from Levi to Matthew, which means "gift of God." Whatever flaws Matthew possessed prior to this time no longer mattered.

Because of his record-keeping skills and attention to detail, Matthew made an excellent and meticulous Gospel writer. He'd been regenerated by Christ, and the Lord could use his talents to further the kingdom.

Lord, after all these years, attitudes remain the same about tax collectors. Please help me to see them as You saw Matthew, as people who know You or are in need of a Savior. Amen.

DAY 223

MORNING

God's love has been poured out into our hearts through the Holy Spirit.

ROMANS 5:5 NIV

God's love touches our entire lives. Even better, He pours His love into our very being. We are like a cup that God never stops filling up with His love. Love is a constant stream flowing into us until that love runs over and spills out to others. Because we have been blessed with God's unfailing love, we can pass that blessing on to others.

I ask You, Lord, that You increase my capacity to hold Your love! Make me open to the life-giving stream of Your Spirit—and may it flow through me to everyone around me. Amen.

EVENING

Reliable

We know and rely on the love God has for us. God is love.

1 JOHN 4:16 NIV

When we talk about God's love, it's not just a pretty phrase or some lofty theological concept. The Greek word translated here as *know* implies firsthand experience. We know God's love because it touches us personally. The more we allow ourselves to experience His love, the more we will be able to trust that love. We can put our full weight on it, knowing that God will never jerk it out from under us. How could He, when His very nature is love?

I'm relying on Your love tonight, God, to get me through all the things I have to face in the days ahead. I know I can count on You. Your love will give me everything I need. Amen.

DAY 224

MORNING
Secure

Such love has no fear, because perfect love expels all fear. If we are afraid, it is for fear of punishment.

1 JOHN 4:18 NLT

Sometimes love hurts. Even the people who love us most let us down—and we let them down. When we say or do the wrong thing, they may pull back from us. We fear we might lose their love. We worry they'll leave us, even if it's only through death. But God's love is perfect. It will never let us down. He never pulls away from us, no matter what we do. We are totally secure.

Loving Lord, how can I thank You enough for all the ways Your love has filled my life? I ask that You drive all fear from my heart. Make me ever more confident in You. Amen.

EVENING
For as Long as It Takes!

Love is patient, love is kind. . .bears all things, believes all things, hopes all things, endures all things.

1 CORINTHIANS 13:4, 7 NASB

We usually think of these verses as a description of how we should love others (which, of course, they are). But these familiar words also describe how God loves us. He is patient with us, no matter how many times we fall on our faces, no matter how long we take to learn something. He never stops believing in us. He's willing to put up with us for as long as it takes!

Others have let me down, Lord. They didn't mean to, I know, but nevertheless they hurt me. But You have never stopped being patient with me. You've never stopped believing in me. You're always there with me, going through everything by my side. I am so grateful! Amen.

DAY 225

MORNING

Jesus Is Tempted by Satan

And the devil said to Him, "If You are the Son of God, tell this stone to become bread." And Jesus answered him, "It is written, 'MAN SHALL NOT LIVE ON BREAD ALONE.' "

LUKE 4:3–4 NASB

Have you ever found yourself so tempted to sin that you ached all the way to your soul? Christ understands that pull toward evil.

Satan wasn't just present in the wilderness to "bug" the Lord Jesus Christ. This was a full-on, frontal attack. And the stakes were high. For if Christ succumbed to Satan's snare, He would be ineligible to make that perfect sacrifice on the cross as the Lamb of God without blemish.

Lord, I thank You for Your Son's perfect victory over Satan. Amen.

EVENING

At Home in the Love of Jesus

"Just as the Father has loved Me, I have also loved you; abide in My love."

JOHN 15:9 NASB

Jesus loves you just as much as His heavenly Father loves Him. Think about it. The Son of God, the Word that existed before the beginning of the world, loves you infinitely, unconditionally, with all His heart. What a blessing! The only thing He asks in return is that you make His love your home—that you seek out the place where your heart is close to His.

Teach me, Jesus, to make my home in Your love. Remind me not to seek my security anywhere else but in You. Amen.

DAY 226

MORNING
Relentless Love

I am convinced that nothing can ever separate us from God's love. Neither death nor life, neither angels nor demons, neither our fears for today nor our worries about tomorrow—not even the powers of hell can separate us from God's love.

ROMANS 8:38 NLT

You can turn your eyes away from God. You can insist on shutting your heart against Him. But God's love is unstoppable and relentless. It leaks into the cracks of your heart. It waits patiently for you to turn around and notice it's there. It is always ready to bless you.

Over and over, I turn away from You, God. I forget about You. I seek my own selfish way. And yet Your love never gives up on me. You are always with me, patiently waiting for me to turn back to You. Amen.

EVENING
Simply Love

God is love, and all who live in love live in God, and God lives in them.

1 JOHN 4:16 NLT

We often make our spiritual lives so complicated. We focus on theology. We believe *our* church has got it right, and we worry about those folks in the church down the road who have got it all wrong. But the Bible says it's really quite simple: when we live in love, we are living in God. God is living in us. His blessing flows through us and out into the world.

Remind me, God, to focus more on love than on being right. Help me to put love for others ahead of my opinions. Teach me to live in You. Amen.

DAY 227

MORNING
A Well of Joy

When he arrived and saw this evidence of God's blessing, he was filled with joy.

ACTS 11:23 NLT

One of the spiritual blessings God gives us is joy—and all His other blessings increase that joy. Joy is like a spring of water that keeps spilling into our lives. Just when we think the spring has run dry, when we feel as though we'll never feel joy again, joy wells up. At first, it may just be a tiny trickle—but then it grows into a rushing stream that fills our hearts once more.

Today, Lord, show me the evidence of Your blessing in my life. Fill me with Your joy. Amen.

EVENING
Why Mary and Joseph Married

"Every daughter who comes into possession of an inheritance of any tribe of the sons of Israel shall be wife to one of the family of the tribe of her father, so that the sons of Israel each may possess the inheritance of his fathers."

NUMBERS 36:8 NASB

The Gospels of Matthew and Luke present Christ's genealogy. Although Joseph was not Christ's father, he belonged to the tribe of Judah, just as Mary did. Both came from a godly line.

Mary had led a life of purity, revering God's Word and looking forward to the Savior whom God had promised. When God sent an angel to announce His plan, Mary responded in obedience.

Mary and Joseph married because they loved each other, but more importantly, both of them loved God and desired to be a part of His purpose for man. And within this environment of submission, Israel's inheritance—the Savior—remained secure.

Lord, we know that Joseph loved Mary and both were chosen by You. Yet they also obeyed You in their choice of a life partner. Amen.

DAY 228

MORNING
God's House of Joy

Strength and joy are in his dwelling place.

1 CHRONICLES 16:27 NIV

When we feel as though we're too weak to accomplish anything, we often feel blue and depressed. Our self-concepts suffer. We measure ourselves against others around us and come up lacking. But it doesn't have to be that way. When we stop focusing on our own lack and instead turn our eyes to God, He welcomes us with open arms into His house—a place where joy and strength go hand in hand.

Today, God, I want to dwell in Your house of joy. No matter how busy I get, please remind me that I'm always at home in You. Fill me with Your strength, so that I'm able to meet the day's demands. May Your love and joy flow out of me to others. Amen.

EVENING
Strong Hearts

"Don't be dejected and sad,
for the joy of the LORD is your strength!"

NEHEMIAH 8:10 NLT

The Hebrew word used in this verse is *chedvah*, meaning "rejoicing, gladness." Depression weakens our hearts and separates us from others. But we have a relationship with the Creator of the universe, and He shares His eternal gladness with us. His joy makes us strong, able to face the challenges of life, able to reach out to others. Just as God shares His gladness with us, we are meant to share our joy with everyone we meet.

Creator, Lord of love, thank You that You share with me Your joy. When sadness and despair threaten to overwhelm me, may I find emotional strength in You. Amen.

DAY 229

MORNING
Blessed with Laughter

*You make known to me the path of life;
you will fill me with joy in your presence,
with eternal pleasures at your right hand.*

PSALM 16:11 NIV

Here, the Hebrew word is *samach*, which means joy in the sense of "mirth"—the sort of happiness that makes you laugh out loud. Our faith is not meant to be a gloomy, stern thing, filled with disapproval and a constant "No." Instead, those of us who follow Jesus say "Yes!" to life. We enjoy life! We smile and laugh a lot—because we know the pleasures God shows us will last throughout eternity.

*Bless me with laughter today, Lord.
May my happiness be infectious,
spreading to everyone with
whom I interact today. Amen.*

EVENING
A Refuge from Our Despair

Hear my cry, O God; give heed to my prayer. From the end of the earth I call to You when my heart is faint; lead me to the rock that is higher than I. For You have been a refuge for me, a tower of strength against the enemy. Let me dwell in Your tent forever; let me take refuge in the shelter of Your wings.

PSALM 61:1–4 NASB

King David, writer of this psalm, composed it as a song, acknowledging God as his Rock. Although David's trials may differ from yours, you, too, can use strong coping mechanisms.

First, David acknowledged that God remained all-powerful, despite life circumstances. And second, David looked back at God's past rescues. "O my God, my soul is in despair within me; therefore I remember You from the land of the Jordan, and the peaks of Hermon, from Mount Mizar" (Psalm 42:6 NASB).

Lord, I search for a way through the torrents of despair. How precious is the knowledge that You hear and care. Amen.

DAY 230

MORNING

Pursued by Joy

Gladness and joy will overtake them,
and sorrow and sighing will flee away.

ISAIAH 35:10 NIV

The Old Testament is filled with "joy words" that express different shades of meaning. In this verse, the Hebrew word *suws* contains within it the meanings of gladness, mirth, and rejoicing that we've already mentioned, but it has an added ingredient: "welcome." This is joy that runs after us with open arms. Even when we are deep in depression, wandering down dark and dreary paths, it catches up with us. Its presence—God's presence—chases away all our sadness.

Today, Lord, if sadness and depression creep up on me, please chase them away with Your love and gladness! Amen.

EVENING

Springtime Joy

Shout for joy to the LORD, all the earth,
burst into jubilant song.

PSALM 98:4 NIV

This verse uses yet another Hebrew word: *patsach*, which means "to makes something burst open, to break forth." It makes me think of a spring day, when green buds are opening on every twig, and every bird and frog is singing at the top of its lungs. God blesses us with springtime joy, the sort of joy that can't be contained. It breaks open our hard hearts, letting joy and life spill out of us into the world.

Break open my hard heart, Lord, so that Your joy will burst out of me into the world. Tonight, as I lie in my bed waiting for sleep, teach me to sing Your song of love and happiness. Amen.

DAY 231

MORNING
Abundant Goodness

"Serve the Lord your God with joy and a glad heart, for the abundance of all things."

Deuteronomy 28:47 NASB

We often think of the Old Testament as being a bit gloomier than the New Testament, but look at all the verses that promise joy! Here our gladness is connected with the great bounty of blessings God has given to us. I'm reminded of a short verse by Robert Louis Stevenson: "The world is so full of a number of things, I'm sure we should all be as happy as kings." If we open our eyes, we'll see that God has filled our lives with abundant goodness.

Give me a glad heart, Lord, that delights in all the countless blessings You have given me. Teach me to daily find joy in You. Amen.

EVENING
God in Action

When the righteous see God in action, they'll laugh, they'll sing, they'll laugh and sing for joy.

Psalm 68:3 MSG

This Hebrew word for joy is *alats*, meaning "exults, rejoices in triumph." God is at work in our lives. His Spirit is moving and acting in amazing ways. What a blessing to know that the Creator of the world is working on our behalf, in a personal, intimate, ongoing way! How can we help but laugh and sing when we see Him triumph over the forces of darkness?

Remind me, Holy Spirit, that I don't need to be afraid when I see all the darkness in our world. You are moving in the world, bringing Your peace and reconciliation in ways I can't see. I can go to sleep happy, and look forward to joy and laughter tomorrow. Amen.

DAY 232

MORNING

One Calling in the Desert

The word of God came to John, the son of Zacharias, in the wilderness. And he came into all the district around the Jordan, preaching a baptism of repentance for the forgiveness of sins.

LUKE 3:2–3 NASB

As John came into the district around the Jordan River, the religious leaders used their influence to attempt to dissuade the people from the truth about the Messiah. John called them a "brood of vipers" (Luke 3:7 NASB). And then he added, "Therefore bear fruits in keeping with repentance, and do not begin to say to yourselves, 'We have Abraham for our father,' for I say to you that from these stones God is able to raise up children to Abraham" (Luke 3:8 NASB).

The religious leaders called themselves Abraham's children. Yet being Abraham's children required that they display faith.

John's exhortations were aimed at the "wilderness of men's souls." How many churchgoers do you know who claim the faith yet exist in a wasteland of sin?

Lord, You sent John to proclaim Your beloved Son. Help me to proclaim Your Word and love to anyone, anywhere. Amen.

EVENING

Lift Up Your Voice!

They shall lift up their voice, they shall sing for the majesty of the LORD, they shall cry aloud.

ISAIAH 24:14 KJV

There's a lot of singing going on in the Old Testament! Here the Hebrew word *ranan* means a happiness that's expressed vocally, with shouts of joy, with loud singing. Unfortunately, we haven't all been blessed with beautiful singing voices—but we *have* all been blessed by God in ways that make us sing! Even if we can't carry a tune, He's glad to hear our voices lifted up in praise.

Tonight, loving God, I lift up my heart to You in song and praise. You fill me with wonder and joy. Amen.

DAY 233

MORNING

God Gave Israel the Land

Then the LORD spoke to Moses, saying, "Among these the land shall be divided for an inheritance according to the number of names. . . Each shall be given their inheritance according to those who were numbered of them. But the land shall be divided by lot. They shall receive their inheritance according to the names of the tribes of their fathers."

NUMBERS 26:52–55 NASB

God picked for Himself a people, the Jews. And He blessed them with this land as an inheritance. It's not too late for Israel's enemies to repent. Yet with each new wave of terrorism and attacks against Israel, we know that nothing short of divine intervention will free the Jews from annihilation.

Christ is coming back as the ultimate judge and rescuer of Israel. The time is now to be sure of our commitment to Jesus Christ and that of our loved ones.

Lord, I pray that men and women repent while there is yet time. I look forward to the establishment of Your perfect kingdom. Amen.

EVENING

The Bridegroom

As a young man marries a young woman,
so will your Builder marry you;
as a bridegroom rejoices over his bride,
so will your God rejoice over you.

ISAIAH 62:5 NIV

Imagine you're at a wedding. Now picture the way the groom looks at the bride as she walks down the aisle toward him. Can you see his look of total love and joy? His face tells everyone there how much he loves this woman, how glad he is to join his life with hers. That's how God loves *you*. You fill His heart with joy. He loves you so much that He wants to give Himself totally to you.

Oh God, it's hard for me to imagine that You can possibly love me so much. When I have failed You so often, how can I still make You happy? Teach me to accept Your love, even when I feel unworthy. Help me to trust it more and more. Amen.

DAY 234

MORNING
Anointed with Joy

Your God has anointed you,
pouring out the oil of joy.
HEBREWS 1:9 NLT

We find more promises of joy in the New Testament. The Greek word used here is *agalliao*, which contains within it the sense of both joyful welcome and exceeding gladness. It brings to mind the image of my mother's expression when I returned home for a Christmas gathering. As I came through the door, her face lit with such welcome as she hurried to give me whatever she could to make me happy. That's the sort of loving joy God pours over us!

Pour Your joy over me today, Lord.
Anoint me with Your happiness! Amen.

EVENING
Homecoming

Well done, thou good and faithful
servant. . .enter thou into the joy of thy lord.
MATTHEW 25:21 KJV

The word Jesus uses is *chairo*. It implies cheerfulness, a calm delight that's also closely connected to grace, God's undeserved, freely given blessings. We need to be careful not to get turned around in our understanding: the faithful servant didn't *earn* the Lord's joy with his hard work. Joy was simply the home that lay at the end of the road, the natural end point to his lifetime of service—a place of blessing and grace waiting for him to come home.

Lead me home, Jesus. Show me the road
to the joy You have prepared for me. Amen.

DAY 235

MORNING
Leap for Joy!

"Blessings await you when people hate you and exclude you and mock you and curse you as evil because you follow the Son of Man. When that happens, be happy! Yes, leap for joy!"

LUKE 6:22–23 NLT

This is quite a promise! The word Jesus uses is *skirtaó*, which means literally "leap for joy." It's also the word used when a baby "quickens," when the mother first feels the movement of life. So Jesus is saying this: if you follow Him and feel misunderstood and separated from everyone around you—that's the very moment new joy will leap into life!

Leap into my life today, Jesus! Even when no one else understands me, fill me with Your joy. Amen.

EVENING
Anna, the Prophetess

And there was a prophetess, Anna the daughter of Phanuel, of the tribe of Asher . . . . She never left the temple, serving night and day with fastings and prayers. At that very moment she came up and began giving thanks to God, and continued to speak of Him to all those who were looking for the redemption of Jerusalem.

LUKE 2:36–38 NASB

Anna had faithfully served in the temple her entire life. And despite her advanced age, she remained there even after others had gone home for the evening. She was a prophetess; she foretold the truths of God to the people. No wonder He used her life.

God had promised Anna that she would see the Messiah before she died. She waited eighty-four years, biding her time in service to the Lord. And He kept His word. Let us strive to follow Anna's prayerful example, and we, too, will be blessed by God.

Lord, call my heart to faithfulness and prayer. May I serve as an example to encourage others. Amen.

DAY 236

MORNING

Overflowing Joy

I am exceeding joyful in all our tribulation.

2 CORINTHIANS 7:4 KJV

Paul confirms what Jesus already told His followers: in the midst of trouble, when no one understands us, when problems are everywhere we turn, we are blessed with joy! This joy isn't something small and weak, and it isn't merely a stiff-upper-lip endurance. Instead, the Greek word (*chara*) means joy that's abundant, overflowing—joy so great it can't even be measured. God's blessings are never limited by human problems—and He does nothing by half measures!

No matter what I have to face today,
Jesus, bless me with Your joy! Amen.

EVENING

Inexpressible

You love him even though you have never seen him. . .you trust him; and you rejoice with a glorious, inexpressible joy.

1 PETER 1:8 NLT

From the world's perspective, it might seem as though Jesus is our imaginary friend. After all, we can't see Him, can't hear Him. But we know His presence is real because He has blessed us with a joy that lies beyond words. *Aneklálētos* is the word Peter uses here, a joy that's impossible to convey with words. It can't be grasped with language, can't be pinned down with any of our human concepts. But it's real!

I love You, Jesus. I am learning to trust
You more and more. And one day,
I will see You face-to-face! Amen.

DAY 237

MORNING
The Spiritual Blessing of Peace

"Peace I leave with you; My peace I give to you. . . . Do not let your heart be troubled, nor. . .fearful."

JOHN 14:27 NASB

Jesus shares with us His own peace. Imagine that! We have access to the same peace of mind and heart He experienced during His life on earth. It's the legacy He left us, His going-away gift when He went back to His Father. *"Don't* let *yourself be troubled,"* He tells us, indicating that we have a choice in the matter. All we have to do is accept this spiritual blessing He's shared with us.

Remind me, Jesus, not to dwell on worries and fears today. Instead, may I choose Your peace. Amen.

EVENING
Peace Covenant

I give unto him my covenant of peace.

NUMBERS 25:12 KJV

We humans make a lot of promises. We also break a lot of promises. Even when we start out with the best of intentions, we all too often find that we can't follow through with whatever we promised. God's promises are different from ours, though. When the Bible talks about a covenant, it's referring to a binding promise that can never be broken. God's promise of peace is a solid thing, firm and unchanging. It's a covenant that will never be broken.

Thank You, God, that Your covenant peace is so firm and solid that I can build my entire life on it. Amen.

MORNING

So Israel joined themselves to Baal of Peor, and the LORD was angry against Israel. The LORD said to Moses, "Take all the leaders of the people and execute them in broad daylight before the LORD, so that the fierce anger of the LORD may turn away from Israel."

NUMBERS 25:3–4 NASB

God had watched over Israel in war and in peace. He was delivering them to a land flowing with milk and honey; He had promised them a Messiah. But if the Israelites continued to kill their children by sacrificing them to Baal, the line to Christ would be wiped out before He ever arrived on the scene.

God was forced to purge from Israel those who chose to lead others astray.

If you're a parent, you probably devote much time and energy to keeping your children from getting involved in things that would harm them. In the same way, God, our loving parent, must pull in the reins when we drift too far from His truth.

Lord, shine Your beacon of truth on those who are in leadership, that they may never lead others astray. Amen.

EVENING

Peace in the Desert

The LORD's justice will dwell in the desert, his righteousness live in the fertile field. The fruit of that righteousness will be peace. . .quietness and confidence forever.

ISAIAH 32:16–17 NIV

God's justice is simply the way He does things: fairly, without favoritism, ordering all things according to His own nature, creating peace and quiet confidence in our lives. The Hebrew word used here is *shalom*. It's more than freedom from conflict; it's also health and safety and completeness. It's ours not only in the midst of productive days like "fertile fields" but also in our empty "desert days."

May Your peace and wholeness fill me, Lord, and Your justice find a home in both my productive days and the empty days when I feel useless. Teach me to rely on You rather than myself. Amen.

DAY 239

MORNING
Forget Fear

"Go in peace. Your journey has the LORD's approval."

JUDGES 18:6 NIV

In this verse shalom means freedom from fear. We may not fear for our physical safety, but we often live with a constant, nagging anxiety, a sense that doom and gloom is hanging over us and the people we love. God wants to take that anxiety away from us. The word translated here as *approval* means literally "to go in front of." Knowing God precedes us into the future, we can let go of all our worries. We can go in peace.

What peace there is in knowing, Lord, that You are going in front of me each step of the way! Amen.

EVENING
John the Baptist Is Born

They were both righteous in the sight of God, walking blamelessly in all the commandments and requirements of the Lord. But they had no child, because Elizabeth was barren, and they were both advanced in years.

LUKE 1:6–7 NASB

Zacharias could be found day after day in the temple, obediently "performing his priestly service before God" (Luke 1:8 NASB).

One day, as he offered incense before the altar, an angel of the Lord appeared and said, "Do not be afraid, Zacharias, for your petition has been heard, and your wife Elizabeth will bear you a son, and you will give him the name John" (Luke 1:13 NASB).

Now Zacharias asked, "How will I know this for certain?" (Luke 1:18 NASB). Fulfillment of that promise still looked impossible to him.

So, poor Zacharias was struck "dumb." Elizabeth did become pregnant, just as the angel had said. And during her sixth month, her cousin Mary came to tell her that she, too, was carrying a child. One day their sons would meet by the Jordan River. This was God's perfect plan, the fulfillment of His promises.

Lord, restore my hope in You today. Amen.

DAY 240

And He said to her, "Daughter, your faith has made you well; go in peace and be healed."

MARK 5:34 NASB

In the New Testament, instead of the Hebrew word *shalom*, we have the Greek word *eiréné*. Much like shalom, its meaning is far deeper than simply freedom from conflict. This peace means that all the essential parts of our lives are joined together. It means that we have been healed, body and soul. All the broken pieces of our hearts have been put back together. In Christ, we have been made whole.

Jesus, I thank You that You are healing all my hidden wounds, the ones I don't like others to see. You are making me whole. Amen.

EVENING
Guarded by Peace

Then you will experience God's peace, which exceeds anything we can understand. His peace will guard your hearts and minds as you live in Christ Jesus.

PHILIPPIANS 4:7 NLT

We all crave peace. We long for that quiet sense that all is as it should be. It seems like too much to ask, though. After all, everyone has their share of troubles. But God's peace is deeper, wider, and greater than any peace we can imagine. We can't understand it—but we can experience it. It will guard our thoughts and emotions, even in the middle of heartache and trouble.

Tonight, Jesus, guard my heart and mind. Keep fear and worry out. Circle me with Your peace. Amen.

DAY 241

MORNING

Surrender

The mind governed by the Spirit is life and peace.

Romans 8:6 NIV

All through the Bible, God promises peace to His people. And yet our lives and our hearts are all too often shaken by conflict and fear. How can we access the peace that God promises? How can we experience it as something more than a fleeting emotion? The apostle Paul gives us the answer here: we need to surrender our thoughts to the Holy Spirit. This isn't easy. It takes discipline. In 2 Corinthians 10:5, Paul calls it "taking every thought captive." But it's well worth the effort!

Help me, Holy Spirit, to surrender my every thought to You. Live in me. Fill me with Your peace. Amen.

EVENING

Where Do You Take Refuge?

When I am afraid, I will put my trust in You. In God, whose word I praise, in God I have put my trust; I shall not be afraid. What can mere man do to me?

Psalm 56:3–4 NASB

David wrote this psalm when the Philistines had seized him in Gath. These Philistines had been enemies of the Israelites for a long time. At one point they'd even stolen the ark of the covenant! They'd probably never forgiven David for killing their giant, Goliath. I wonder if David reflected during his present predicament, remembering the time in his youth when he'd faced that giant with only five smooth stones and a sling. He had called upon his God to deliver him, and the Lord had prevailed (1 Samuel 17:37–50).

Where do you go for refuge? I run to the arms of my loving Father, just as David did in his own crisis. And He always comes through.

O Lord, You alone are my Refuge and Strength. Help me to come to You first in a crisis. Amen.

DAY 242

MORNING

Taught by God

I will instruct you and teach you in the way which you should go; I will counsel you with My eye upon you.

Psalm 32:8 NASB

Another spiritual blessing that we're promised is God's guidance. This seldom means that we hear His voice speaking clearly, directly. He doesn't write His directions in big letters across the sky. Instead, He teaches us—and teaching is a process that's often long and slow. We have so much to learn, but God sees our lives clearly, and He has promised to teach us everything we need to know.

Some days, God, I feel like such a slow student. I don't understand what You're teaching me. Thank You that You are such a patient teacher and You won't ever give up on me. Amen.

EVENING

Dawn

"The people living in darkness have seen a great light; on those living in the land of the shadow of death a light has dawned."

Matthew 4:16 NIV

We often feel as though we're stumbling around in the dark. We'd like to follow God, but we're overwhelmed by sorrows and discouragement. We don't know which way to turn. But if we're patient, even the darkest nights give way to the dawn. God's light will rise in our lives once again—and all the shadows will disappear.

Tonight, God, the world is dark—
but I know Your dawn is coming.
I'm waiting for Your light. Amen.

DAY 243

MORNING
Joseph of Arimathea

Joseph of Arimathea came, a prominent member of the Council, who himself was waiting for the kingdom of God; and he gathered up courage and went in before Pilate, and asked for the body of Jesus.

MARK 15:43 NASB

Today's scripture reading, along with parallel passages from the other three Gospels, discloses that Joseph of Arimathea had become "a secret disciple of Christ." Yet now, accompanied by Nicodemus, another member of the ruling council of religious leaders, Joseph of Arimathea displayed an incredible boldness of character. For Joseph requested Christ's body for burial; then he and Nicodemus lovingly prepared their Lord for His burial.

Christ nurtured the faith of both these men, safely reserving them for His divine purpose within the realm of authority in which He had placed them. They were needed for just such a time, because down through the ages to come the faith of other believers would hinge on the fact that Christ really died and really was resurrected.

Lord, the tomb is empty, and the grave clothes left behind signify for all time that You have risen from the dead. And because You live, we can face whatever tomorrow brings! Amen.

EVENING
Spiritual Ears

Whether you turn to the right or to the left, your ears will hear a voice behind you, saying, "This is the way; walk in it."

ISAIAH 30:21 NIV

Can you imagine how wonderful it would be if we could actually hear God's voice in our ears, whispering, "*Go this way. Go that way. Now go* this *way.*" Maybe we depend too much on our five senses, though. We need to practice using our spiritual senses. If we want to hear God's voice, we need to listen with the ears of our spirits.

Father, sharpen my spiritual ears. Make me more sensitive to Your voice. Amen.

DAY 244

MORNING
God Knows Best

This is what the LORD says—your Redeemer, the Holy One of Israel: "I am the LORD your God, who teaches you what is good for you and leads you along the paths you should follow."

ISAIAH 48:17 NLT

Sometimes we get in our heads that God likes to say no. We hesitate to ask for His direction because we're afraid He'll tell us we can't do something we want to do. But that's not the way God works. His guidance always is a yes to life, to health, to joy, to blessing.

Holy One, show me the path that leads to life and health, to joy and blessing. I want to follow You. Amen.

EVENING
Bringing Us to Completion

Being confident of this, that he who began a good work in you will carry it on to completion until the day of Christ Jesus.

PHILIPPIANS 1:6 NIV

No matter how many times we fail, no matter how many times we mess up, we know God hasn't written us off. He's still working on us. He still loves us. Those of us who have been adopted into God's family through believing in His Son, Jesus Christ, can be confident that God won't give up on us. No matter how messed up our lives may seem, He will continue working in us until His plan is fulfilled, and we stand before Him, perfect and complete.

Dear Father, thank You for not giving up on me. Help me to cooperate with Your process of fulfilling Your purpose in me. Amen.

DAY 245

MORNING
God's Word

Your word is a lamp to guide my feet and a light for my path.

PSALM 119:105 NLT

The Hebrew translated as *word* refers to any sort of communication. So how does God communicate with us? The obvious answer is through the Bible; scripture sheds light into our hearts and minds, helping us to see the right way to go. Christ is also called the Word, and He is the embodiment of God's communication with humans. As we study the life of Jesus in the Gospels, as we open our hearts to His Spirit, His light will guide us.

Communicate Your message of love and light to me, God, I pray. Guide my path. Amen.

EVENING
Heart Searching

Search me, O God, and know my heart; try me and know my anxious thoughts; and see if there be any hurtful way in me, and lead me in the everlasting way.

PSALM 139:23–24 NASB

Asking for divine guidance isn't like consulting a Magic 8 Ball. We don't get immediate answers. Instead, we need time alone with God, time when we open our hearts to Him. We have to be honest—with Him and with ourselves—willing to see our unhealthy thoughts and wrong behavior. Only then will He be able to bless us with His guidance.

Lord, show me the unhealthy, hurtful thoughts and actions that I've been harboring. Guide me into Your life and wholeness. Amen.

DAY 246

MORNING

He Won't Let You Down

I tell you that Christ has become a servant of the Jews on behalf of God's truth, so that the promises made to the patriarchs might be confirmed.

ROMANS 15:8 NIV

Everyone has been hurt at one time or another by a broken promise. When that happens, it is best to forgive and go on. People are just people. They mess up. But there is One who will never break His promises to us—our heavenly Father. We can safely place our hope in Him. Choose to place your hope in God's promises. You won't be discouraged by time—God's timing is always perfect. You won't be discouraged by circumstances—God can change everything in a heartbeat. He is faithful.

Lord, I choose this day to place my trust in You, for I know You're the one true constant. Amen.

EVENING

The Blessing of Insomnia!

I will praise the LORD, who counsels me; even at night my heart instructs me.

PSALM 16:7 NIV

Do you ever lie awake, worrying? Do you sometimes dread those long, sleepless hours when everything looks darker than it does during the day? It doesn't have to be that way. Instead, whenever we have a bout of insomnia, we can use the time to open our hearts to God. If we surrender each worry to God, He can use this time to speak to our hearts.

Here, Lord—take all my worries, every one of them! Get them out of the way, so that I can hear Your voice in my heart. Amen.

MORNING

For God, who commanded the light to shine out of darkness, hath shined in our hearts, to give the light of the knowledge of the glory of God in the face of Jesus Christ.

2 CORINTHIANS 4:6 KJV

Humans have always loved light. Since the beginning of the twentieth century, starting with Einstein, physicists have been discovering amazing things about light that make it even more mysterious, even more wonderful. And God created it! If He could create light out of darkness and nothingness, He can shine the blessing of spiritual light into even the darkest hearts.

God, I will never understand how miraculous You are, how powerful. Your ways are a mystery to me—but I know You love me. Fill me, I pray, with the light of Your love. Fill me with Jesus. Amen.

EVENING

Barabbas Is Released

Pilate answered them, saying, "Do you want me to release for you the King of the Jews?" . . . But the chief priests stirred up the crowd to ask him to release Barabbas for them instead.

MARK 15:9, 11 NASB

Why did the chief priests incite the people to choose Barabbas?

The priests were but players in the great drama prophesied hundreds of years earlier in the Old Testament. Jesus Christ would be sentenced to death by Pilate even though Pilate found Him without guilt. Jesus Christ must die for the sins of humankind.

Today we know the truth. And we can share, without fear, without guilt, the kingship of Jesus Christ.

What would I have shouted if I had been part of that crowd? And what affirmation do I give You today, Lord? Amen.

DAY 248

MORNING
Showered with Blessing

"I will bless my people and their homes. . . . And in the proper season I will send the showers they need. There will be showers of blessing."

Ezekiel 34:26 NLT

When we think of blessings, often what comes to mind are things like money, good health, a nice house, a car. God has nothing against those blessings—but He doesn't send them based on the power of positive thinking or the "law of attraction." Instead, when we let go of what we want, when we surrender everything to God, He showers us with exactly what we need.

God, I give You my life and everything it holds. I know You will bless me. I know You are blessing me. You give me exactly what I need, when I need it. Amen.

EVENING
Strength in the Lord

The Lord is my light and my salvation—whom shall I fear? The Lord is the stronghold of my life—of whom shall I be afraid?

Psalm 27:1 NIV

At times, this world can be a tough, unfair, lonely place. Since the fall of man in the garden, things have not been as God originally intended. The Bible assures us that we will face trials in this life, but it also exclaims that we are more than conquerors through Christ who is in us! When you find yourself up against a tribulation that seems insurmountable, *look up*. Christ is there. He goes before you, stands with you, and is backing you up in your time of need. You may lose everyone and everything else in this life, but nothing has the power to separate you from the love of Christ. Nothing.

Jesus, I cling to the hope I have in You. You are my Rock, my Stronghold, my defense. I will not fear, for You are with me always. Amen.

MORNING

A young man was following Him, wearing nothing but a linen sheet over his naked body; and they seized him. But he pulled free of the linen sheet and escaped naked. They led Jesus away to the high priest; and all the chief priests and the elders and the scribes gathered together.

MARK 14:51–53 NASB

Suddenly you awake at one in the morning to the sound of the doorknob being turned, followed by the sound of creaking boards. Your heart leaps into your throat. What do you do?

When John Mark, the writer of this Gospel, learned that Jesus had been captured by the Roman guards and a trial was pending, he grabbed the sheet off his bed and ran to observe the events himself.

We know John Mark escaped the threatening situation. Yet Jesus Christ remained in the eye of the storm, well aware of the situation yet in perfect sync with the Father. When fear paralyzes, help is only a prayer away.

Lord, I believe in all that You are, both God and man. Amen.

EVENING

Blessed by Worship

"Worship the LORD *your God, and his blessing will be on your food and water. I will take away sickness from among you."*

EXODUS 23:25 NIV

The word translated *worship* in this verse actually means "serve" or "work for," in the way that a farmer works the land or an employee works for her employer. It means serving God with our actions—and with our thoughts. When we do, He has promised to bless the food we eat and the water we drink. He will bless our bodies, and He will heal our hearts.

I want to serve You, Lord God. Show me how. Amen.

MORNING
Opened Floodgates

"Test me in this," says the LORD Almighty, "and see if I will not throw open the floodgates of heaven and pour out so much blessing that there will not be room enough to store it."

MALACHI 3:10 NIV

The "law of attraction" says to think about what you want; focus your thoughts on it, and the Universe will give it to you. God tells us something different. He says surrender all your demands. Let go of all your ideas about what you need to be happy. When you do, He will pour more blessings into your life than you can even grasp.

Take my heart, Lord; take my life; take my home and my work; take the people I love; take my thoughts and ideas. I give it all to You, the whole kit-and-caboodle. Let there be nothing left to block the floodgates of Your blessing. Amen.

EVENING
More Circles of Blessing

"The LORD your God. . .is giving you power to make wealth."

DEUTERONOMY 8:18 NASB

The Hebrew words used here are talking about wealth and strength that are tied together. The meaning hints at a well-equipped army that has all the supplies it needs to be a powerful force. This works both ways: God blesses us with strength that enables us to bring good things into our lives—and we're made stronger by the good things with which we've been blessed. It's a blessing circle (the opposite of a vicious circle).

Lord God, create circles of blessing in my life that spread out into the world, bringing Your abundance to more and more of Your creation. Amen.

DAY 251

MORNING

First Things First

Those who seek the LORD lack no good thing.

PSALM 34:10 NIV

The psalmist is reminding us again of what our priorities should be. We don't need to worry about material blessings. We don't need to focus our thoughts on them. Instead, we need to turn all our attention to the Lord. When we do, He will take care of our material needs. He will make sure we don't lack anything. When He is our priority, we can leave everything else up to Him.

Today, Lord, I seek only You. Remind me not to worry about money. . .or what people think of me. . .or anything else. You can take care of all that for me. Amen.

EVENING

Where Credit Is Due

It is not that we think we are qualified to do anything on our own. Our qualification comes from God.

2 CORINTHIANS 3:5 NLT

It's easy to seek God when we feel like failures, but when success comes our way, we like to congratulate ourselves rather than give God the credit. When we achieve great things, we need to remember that it is God's grace through us that brought about our success.

Father, every good thing I do comes from You. Thank You for allowing me to collaborate with You to do Your work. It is an honor to be used by You. Amen.

DAY 252

MORNING

Sibling Rivalry

Then the LORD. . .called Aaron and Miriam. . . . He said, "Hear now My words: If there is a prophet among you, I, the LORD, shall make Myself known to him in a vision. I shall speak with him in a dream. Not so, with My servant Moses, he is faithful in all My household."

NUMBERS 12:5–7 NASB

God speaks face-to-face with Moses, and Aaron and Miriam become jealous. So God comes down in a pillar of cloud. When the cloud is withdrawn from over the tent of meeting, Miriam's skin has become leprous.

God leaves Miriam to mull over her rebellious and questioning spirit for seven days. And then the Lord graciously heals her, at the request of Moses.

How could she even think of asking God to explain Himself? But don't we all do the same thing when the going gets rough? How about, "If there's a God then why is there so much suffering?"

The power to make a choice between good and evil is a gift from God. What we do with the gift is up to us.

Lord, please help me understand that Your actions are always in my best interest. Amen.

EVENING

An Abundant God

The LORD will grant you abundant prosperity.

DEUTERONOMY 28:11 NIV

The Bible tells us again and again that God blesses abundantly, both spiritually and materially. Jesus' miracles embodied this aspect of God's nature. Look at the way He turned water into wine at the wedding in Cana, where the wine was better than anything that had yet been served. Think about when He fed the five thousand—and not only was there enough to go around, but there were leftovers. God will always bless us with more than enough!

Jesus, when I feel as though there's never enough—not enough time, not enough money, not enough energy—remind me that You can turn water into wine; You can multiply meager resources; You can turn not-enough into abundance. Amen.

DAY 253

MORNING
The Blessing Storehouse

The Lord will open the heavens,
the storehouse of his bounty, to send rain
on your land in season and to bless
all the work of your hands.
Deuteronomy 28:12 NIV

Most of us go to work every day, in one form or another. We work in offices, schools, factories, and hospitals; in yards and homes; on farms, boats, and roadways. Some of us like our work. Some of us are doing the work only for the paycheck. Either way, God has promised to reach into the enormous warehouse where He keeps His blessings—and rain them down on our jobs.

Today, Lord, bless the work of my hands.
Use even the simplest tasks I do
to give You glory. Amen.

EVENING
What If?

The Lord will keep you from all harm—
he will watch over your life.
Psalm 121:7 NIV

Feeling safe and secure rests not in the world or in other human beings but with God alone. He is a Christian's help and hope in every frightening situation. He promises to provide peace to everyone who puts their faith and trust in Him. What are you afraid of today? Allow God to encourage you. Trust Him to bring you through it and to give you peace.

Dear Lord, hear my prayers, soothe me with Your words, and give me peace. Amen.

DAY 254

MORNING

God's Pleasure

Let them shout for joy, and be glad. . .
let them say continually, Let the Lord
be magnified, which hath pleasure in
the prosperity of his servant.

Psalm 35:27 KJV

God's not stingy. He doesn't like to see us suffer. It makes Him happy to bless us with prosperity. When we truly believe we have a God who loves us like that, we can stop worrying so much about our bank accounts. Instead of stressing out every time we sit down to pay our bills, we can praise God, knowing it gives Him pleasure to supply what we need.

I praise You, God, for all the ways
You fill my life with Your richness. Amen.

EVENING

Sinners from Birth

Behold, I was brought forth in iniquity,
and in sin my mother conceived me.

Psalm 51:5 NASB

You need to get straight in this passage what God's Word is *not* saying. The union of man and woman, within the bounds of marriage, is absolutely God's design and purpose. These verses are not alluding to the act of love that produces a child. Rather, David is stating that each of us is born with the same sin nature as Adam.

David spoke from the depths of his guilty, broken heart. He had viewed the lovely Bathsheba as she prepared to bathe on her rooftop. Hypnotized by her beauty, he "took her to bed." And when she became pregnant, he plotted a murderous solution that would send her husband, Uriah, to the front lines of battle.

Admitting our own sinful state is the first step toward a more sincere Christian walk. And acknowledging the sin in our children makes us more effective Christian parents.

David didn't acknowledge his sin until You
sent Nathan the prophet to convict his
soul. What will it take for me, Lord? Amen.

DAY 255

MORNING

God's Riches

God shall supply all your need according to his riches in glory by Christ Jesus.

PHILIPPIANS 4:19 KJV

Our material needs can seem overwhelming. We're so aware of what we lack. Whether it's money or physical strength, social skills or artistic talent, we're more likely to feel poor than rich. We tend to feel that we lack more than we have. But think about where all our blessings come from—God's "riches in glory." We can be certain that whatever we truly need, God has more than enough to give us!

Remind me, God, to rely on Your riches—Your storehouse of grace—rather than my own. My bank account can be depleted—but Yours never can! Amen.

EVENING

God Revealed

For ever since the world was created, people have seen the earth and sky. Through everything God made, they can clearly see his invisible qualities—his eternal power and divine nature.

ROMANS 1:20 NLT

The world of nature is another vehicle for God's blessings. The earth and the sky are filled with lovely and amazing things—enormous trees and tiny fern fronds; flaming sunsets and star-strewn skies; birdsong and whale song; summer thunderstorms and the minuscule intricacies of snowflakes. Each beautiful thing reveals God's wonder and power and loveliness.

Oh what loveliness I see in Your world, God! Thank You for making Your creation so beautiful. Amen.

DAY 256

MORNING

Walking in the Light of God's Goodness

The fear of the LORD prolongs life, but the years of the wicked will be shortened. The hope of the righteous is gladness, but the expectation of the wicked perishes. The way of the LORD is a stronghold to the upright.

PROVERBS 10:27–29 NASB

Instead of being a cause of terror in our hearts, the phrase "fear of the Lord" means to reverence and honor Him as God. For He alone is God, righteous and wise enough to intervene and effect positive changes in our lives. Instilling this truth in our children enables them to know the ways of the Lord.

God's very nature is goodness. Therefore, everything that stems from Him reflects His character. This knowledge should cause hope to flood our lives. Unshaken by the winds of change, we can stand firm in the face of any kind of adversity, like a boat anchored to its strong moorings.

Lord, show us how to raise children who reflect the goodness of Your character! Amen.

EVENING

God's Metaphors

"God, who helps you. . .who blesses you with blessings of the skies above, blessings of the deep springs below."

GENESIS 49:25 NIV

The next time you look up at a blue, blue sky, remember that it is an expression of God's blessing. When you feel the sun on your face or moonlight pours through your window, think of God's light shining in your heart. When you see water spilling clear and bright out of the earth, remember that Jesus is a well of living water springing up within you.

Remind me to see You, God, in light and water, in sunshine and moonlight. May everything I see remind me of You. Amen.

DAY 257

MORNING
Shouts of Joy

*He will yet fill your mouth with laughter
and your lips with shouts of joy.*

Job 8:21 NIV

Do you remember the last time you laughed till you cried? For many of us, it's been far too long. Stress tends to steal our joy, leaving us humorless and oh so serious. But lightness and fun haven't disappeared forever. They may be buried beneath the snow of a long, wintery life season, but spring is coming. Laughter will bloom again, and our hearts will soar as our lips shout with joy. Grasp that hope!

Father God, thank You for the hope of joy. I know that because I trust in You, as sure as spring follows winter, joy will again bloom in my heart. Amen.

EVENING
Lessons from Nature

"But ask the animals what they think—let them teach you; let the birds tell you what's going on. Put your ear to the earth—learn the basics. Listen—the fish in the ocean will tell you their stories. Isn't it clear that they all know and agree that God is sovereign, that he holds all things in his hand—Every living soul, yes, every breathing creature?"

Job 12:7–11 MSG

If we pay attention, we can learn a lot from nature. The birds, the fish, the wild animals, the very soil itself, all have stories to tell about God's blessings.

Open my heart, God, so that everything I see in nature teaches me more about You and Your love. Amen.

DAY 258

MORNING

God's Masterpieces

The Lord God made all sorts of trees grow up from the ground—trees that were beautiful and that produced delicious fruit.

Genesis 2:9 NLT

At the beginning of the Bible in the book of Genesis, we learn that God created the natural world. Nature is His masterpiece, an endlessly beautiful expression of divine creativity. Each tree—pines and oaks, palms and willows, maples and tamarinds—all of them are God's love poems. They speak to us of His unending power and love.

Remind me, Lord God, that every tree and leaf, each flower and fruit, are truly Your masterpieces, revealing Your love. Amen.

EVENING

Some Will Be Singing

And they sang the song of Moses, the bond-servant of God, and the song of the Lamb, saying, "Great and marvelous are Your works, O Lord God, the Almighty; righteous and true are Your ways, King of the nations!"

Revelation 15:3 NASB

Those who are victorious over the adversities of the last days on earth will have much to celebrate. This victorious number will include many Jews who come to believe in Christ as their Messiah. And in true Israelite fashion, they will express their jubilation in song, just as King David did. For the covenant God made with His people stands for all time: "He has sent redemption to His people; He has ordained His covenant forever; holy and awesome is His name. The fear of the Lord is the beginning of wisdom; a good understanding have all those who do His commandments; His praise endures forever" (Psalm 111:9–11 NASB).

Lord, You alone are worthy of our worship. I praise You with all my heart and look forward to the day when I will worship You in heaven. Amen.

DAY 259

MORNING
Granter of Dreams

Hope deferred makes the heart sick,
but a dream fulfilled is a tree of life.
PROVERBS 13:12 NLT

As a teenager, I dreamed of one day writing a book. But life intervened, and I became a wife, mother, occupational therapist, and piano teacher. My writing dream was shelved. Twenty-five years later, after my youngest chick flew the coop, God's still, small voice whispered, *"It's time."* Within five years, the granter of dreams delivered over seventy articles and nine book contracts. What's your dream? Be brave and take the first step.

Heavenly Father, please give me courage so that I will have the confidence to take the first step in following the dreams You planted deep within my heart. Amen.

EVENING
Nature's Bounty

O LORD, how manifold are thy works!
in wisdom hast thou made them all:
the earth is full of thy riches.
PSALM 104:24 KJV

The earth brims over with God's abundance: countless fish in the sea, thousands of species of flowers and butterflies and feathered creatures; trillions of tiny creatures too small for us to see; sunset after sunset and sunrise after sunrise; ocean and desert, forest and rivers. Everywhere we turn, we see beauty that tells us of the bountiful blessings of our Lord.

Lord, each time I see something beautiful—a sunset, a silvery cloud, a delicate flower, a bird on the wing, moonlight on water—turn my heart to You. Knit me closer to Your Spirit. Amen.

DAY 260

MORNING
Never Take a Drink?

Again the LORD spoke to Moses, saying, "Speak to the sons of Israel, and say to them, 'When a man or woman makes a special vow, the vow of a Nazirite, to dedicate himself to the LORD, he shall abstain from wine and strong drink.' "

NUMBERS 6:1–3 NASB

When I became a Christian at age twenty-nine, drinking was the first thing to go out of my life. Along with all the warnings against strong drink that I read in the Bible, there was family history. My father had been an alcoholic.

After making a decision to follow Christ, I recognized the risk of potentially harming the young children my husband and I were raising. Like a Nazirite submitting to his vow, I refused to provide a breeding ground in which this substance might interfere with the plans God desired for my life and future. And the Lord has remained faithful to provide all the inspiration I need.

Whatever is preventing me from seeing only You, Lord, provide the strength I require to set it aside. Amen.

EVENING
Love That Never Fails

The earth is full of his unfailing love.

PSALM 33:5 NIV

Nature's beauty can take our breath away. Even in the midst of a city, nature's green life bursts out, and science has revealed to us still more of the mystery and wonder within the natural world. We humans often forget our vital connection to the rest of the earth, but we live in a beautiful world where each thing is dependent on everything else, a living, interconnected network that reveals God's love—a love that flows through the very structure of all life.

God, thank You for all the ways in which Your love flows through creation. Use me, I ask, to protect the life that shares this planet with me. Amen.

DAY 261

MORNING

Wordless Praise

The beast of the field shall honour me. . .
because I give waters in the wilderness,
and rivers in the desert.

ISAIAH 43:20 KJV

Deer and woodchucks, chipmunks and rabbits, snakes and spiders, dragonflies and prairie dogs: each creature in its own way praises and honors God. Wordlessly, even without human intelligence and reasoning, they show us that God provides for His creation even in the most barren lands. His blessings reach into the wild, secret places. He forgets none of His creation and blesses it all.

Lord, I make my life so complicated
sometimes. Teach me to praise and honor
You with the simplicity of Your creatures.
I know that You will supply my
needs, just as You do theirs. Amen.

EVENING

Heaven and Earth Are the Lord's

Behold, the heaven and the heaven of
heavens is the LORD's thy God, the earth
also, with all that therein is.

DEUTERONOMY 10:14 KJV

Sometimes we forget that the earth is the Lord's. He has entrusted it to our care, but it is still His. When we exploit it, when we pollute the sky, when we pour poison into its waters, we are damaging something that belongs to God, not us. We are failing to honor and respect the great blessings He has given us through the natural world.

Make me a force for good, God.
Give me wisdom and strength
to honor Your creation. Amen.

DAY 262

The chief priests and the scribes and the elders came to Him, and began saying to Him, "By what authority are You doing these things, or who gave You this authority to do these things?" And Jesus said to them, "I will ask you one question, and you answer Me, and then I will tell you by what authority I do these things. Was the baptism of John from heaven, or from men? Answer Me."

MARK 11:27–30 NASB

The Pharisees, the Jewish religious leaders, made sure the Mosaic laws were adhered to. They read the laws day and night, probably looking for ones that had been broken. The scribes were given the task of recording every "jot and tittle" of the Word of God. Both groups not only knew the law but also understood what the Messiah would do when He came.

Jesus Christ cannot be fooled. He knew the hearts of the Pharisees and scribes, and He knows your heart, too.

Jesus, You spoke plainly about who You are. Help me hear. Amen.

EVENING

Seeing the Lord in Nature

The LORD wraps himself in light as with a garment; he stretches out the heavens like a tent. . . . He makes the clouds his chariot and rides on the wings of the wind. He makes winds his messengers.

PSALM 104:2–4 NIV

When you look up at the Milky Way sparkling across a night sky, you are seeing God's tent. Look at the sun streaming over the hills: you are seeing the Lord's garment. See the clouds that tower up in the sky before a storm: those are God's chariots. Listen to the wind blowing through the trees: you are hearing God's voice.

Teach me to see and hear You, Lord God, in the endless beauty of nature. Cleanse my vision; sharpen my eyes; and open my heart to Your messengers, Lord of all creation. Amen.

DAY 263

MORNING
The Missing Pieces

Trust the LORD with all your heart, and don't depend on your own understanding.

PROVERBS 3:5 NCV

Life is confusing. No matter how hard we try, we can't always make sense of it. We don't like it when that happens, and so we keep trying to determine what's going on, as though we were trying puzzle pieces to fill in a picture we long to see. Sometimes, though, we have to accept that in this life we will never be able to see the entire image. We have to trust God's grace for the missing pieces.

Dear Lord, my own understanding is awfully limited, and yet I still sometimes try to depend on it. Help me to trust You with 100 percent of my heart. Amen.

EVENING
Go with Joy

For ye shall go out with joy, and be led forth with peace: the mountains and the hills shall break forth before you into singing, and all the trees of the field shall clap their hands.

ISAIAH 55:12 KJV

The Bible tells us that humans and nature are connected. Another verse (Romans 8:22) speaks of the way in which the natural world groans and suffers because of sin. Here, the psalmist tells us that when we are set free to live in the Lord's joy and peace, the hills will hum a song of joy, and the trees will applaud. The earth is blessed when we are blessed.

May the blessings You pour into my life, Lord, ripple out from me, blessing as well the earth and all it holds. Amen.

MORNING

"Look at the birds of the air, that they do not sow, nor reap nor gather into barns, and yet your heavenly Father feeds them. Are you not worth much more than they? . . . Observe how the lilies of the field grow; they do not toil nor do they spin, yet I say to you that not even Solomon in all his glory clothed himself like one of these."

MATTHEW 6:26, 28–29 NASB

If you're worried about your finances, spend some time watching a robin—or looking at a flower. Both of them have something to tell you.

Remind me, Father, that You will always care for me, filling my life with beauty and abundance. Amen.

EVENING

God Orders a Census

"Take a census of all the congregation of the sons of Israel, by their families, by their fathers' households, according to the number of names, every male, head by head from twenty years old and upward, whoever is able to go out to war in Israel, you and Aaron shall number them by their armies. With you, moreover, there shall be a man of each tribe, each one head of his father's household."

NUMBERS 1:2–4 NASB

The Israelites, who were constantly at odds with the Gentile nations surrounding them, needed to know the strength of their army. So God showed Moses a systematic way to determine this number.

Notice that men were conscripted to serve Israel's army from the time they were twenty years old until they were no longer able to serve. In doing so, they would be preserving their nation clear into the time in history when the Messiah would finally be born.

Lord, with You everything has a plan. In a world that is filled with nebulous thinking, I can rely on Your consistency. Amen.

DAY 265

MORNING

Tree of Life

Jesus said, "How can I describe the Kingdom of God? What story should I use to illustrate it? It is like. . .the smallest of all seeds, but it becomes the largest. . .it grows long branches, and birds can make nests in its shade."

MARK 4:30–32 NLT

When Jesus looked for something to help His followers understand complicated ideas, He often turned to the natural world. These symbols are still there around us; every tree we look at can remind us we belong to a kingdom that grows in miraculous ways.

May Your kingdom continue to grow in my life, God, spreading out wide branches covered with green leaves. Amen.

EVENING

Worship

"Worthy are You, our Lord and our God, to receive glory and honor and power; for You created all things, and because of Your will they existed, and were created."

REVELATION 4:11 NASB

Enjoying the blessings of nature is also a form of worship. The awe and delight we feel when we see a towering mountain, a storm-tossed ocean, or a field of wildflowers can turn our hearts to God. When that happens, we're caught in another blessing circle: the more we worship God through nature's blessings, the more we are blessed!

God, You bless me with nature's beauty. May I bless You with my praise! Amen.

DAY 266

MORNING
My Refuge

God is our refuge and strength,
always ready to help in times of trouble.
PSALM 46:1 NLT

What is your quiet place? The place you go to get away from the fray, to chill out, think, regroup, and gain perspective? Mine is a hammock nestled beneath a canopy of oaks in my backyard. . .nobody around but birds, squirrels, an occasional wasp, God, and me. There I can pour out my heart to my Lord, hear His comforting voice, and feel His strength refresh me. We all need a quiet place. God, our Refuge, will meet us there.

Father, thank You for my special place. . .
the place I love to go and spend time
in Your presence. Amen.

EVENING
Jesus Prophesies His Death

Those who followed were fearful. And again He took the twelve aside and began to tell them what was going to happen to Him, saying, "Behold, we are going up to Jerusalem, and the Son of Man will be delivered to the chief priests and the scribes; and they will condemn Him to death and will hand Him over to the Gentiles. They will mock Him and spit on Him, and scourge Him and kill Him, and three days later He will rise again."
MARK 10:32–34 NASB

Christ's disciples couldn't cope with the thought of His leaving and therefore became fearful. Jesus encouraged them with the hope of His resurrection.

And when He had risen from the dead, "He opened their minds to understand the Scriptures, and He said to them, 'Thus it is written, that the Christ would suffer and rise again from the dead the third day, and that repentance for forgiveness of sins would be proclaimed in His name to all the nations, beginning from Jerusalem. You are witnesses of these things' " (Luke 24:45–48 NASB).

Lord, when grief overwhelms us,
let us remember Your death provides
our hope of eternal life. Amen.

DAY 267

MORNING
Community of Believers

"For where two or three gather in my name, there am I with them."

MATTHEW 18:20 NIV

We all need time alone with God, but we also need each other. Jesus and His followers taught that the Church—a community built on relationships—is God's presence on earth. Together, we are the body of Christ. Together, we can bring hope and love to those who are poor in spirit and body. And Jesus has promised to be with us. Even if our "church" is only two friends praying together, supporting each other in the Lord's work, we bless one another.

Thank You, Jesus, for Your living body here on earth. May I contribute to its health and strength. Amen.

EVENING
The Words of the Wise

The words of the wise bring healing.

PROVERBS 12:18 NLT

None of us knows everything. No matter how mature we are in Christ, we all have times when our own knowledge runs out. We find ourselves confused, overwhelmed, weak. Times like those, we need friends and teachers, counselors and pastors who can share their wisdom with us. We need to be humble enough to ask for help—and then we need to be willing to open our minds and hearts to the healing we need.

Thank You for the many wise people You have brought into my life, Lord. May I not be too proud to seek their counsel. Amen.

MORNING

"The LORD our God has allowed a few of us to survive as a remnant."

EZRA 9:8 NLT

Remnants. Useless by most standards, but God is in the business of using tiny slivers of what's left to do mighty things. Nehemiah rebuilt the fallen walls of Jerusalem with a remnant of Israel; Noah's three sons repopulated the earth after the flood; four slave boys—Daniel, Shadrach, Meshach, and Abednego—kept faith alive for an entire nation. When it feels as if bits and pieces are all that has survived of your hope, remember how much God can accomplish with remnants!

Father God, thank You for proving that there is hope. . .even in the remnants! Amen.

EVENING

In Memory of the Righteous

The memory of the righteous is blessed, but the name of the wicked will rot.

PROVERBS 10:7 NASB

Not long ago I attended the funeral of the mother of one of my husband's coworkers.

Warmth, love, and appreciation greeted my husband and me from the moment we set foot in the chapel, which overflowed with guests. This large family had assembled to provide a magnificent send-off for their precious "Nanay." Amid the battles of World War II, she was widowed at twenty-seven and left with three small children. Yet those difficult days of grief and hardship became her stepping-stones to faith in Christ. Later she remarried and was blessed with five more children.

This woman had lost so much. And yet, blessed with true wisdom, she turned to the Lord for solace and found in Him the foundation on which to build her life. To leave a rich legacy of love one must be dearly acquainted with the author of love, our heavenly Father.

Lord, I am blessed by the memory of righteous women. Help me to live in such a worthy manner, that I might be remembered for following after You all my days. Amen.

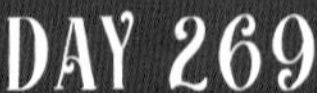

DAY 269

MORNING

The Blessing of True Love

Love never gives up. Love cares more for others than for self. Love doesn't want what it doesn't have. Love doesn't strut, doesn't have a swelled head, doesn't force itself on others, isn't always "me first," doesn't fly off the handle, doesn't keep score of the sins of others, doesn't revel when others grovel, takes pleasure in the flowering of truth, puts up with anything. . .always looks for the best, never looks back, but keeps going to the end.

1 CORINTHIANS 13:4–7 MSG

How blessed we are when others love us like that!

Thank You, Jesus, for bringing so much love into my life through my friends and family. Help me to return their love, so that they are as blessed by me as I am by them. Amen.

EVENING

The Kiss of Peace

Love and faithfulness meet together; righteousness and peace kiss each other.

PSALM 85:10 NIV

The New Testament has a lot to say about the way God blesses us through our relationships with others—but so does the Old Testament. The psalmist tells us that love and faith go hand in hand. Living in peace with others is the road to righteousness. Here's another of those blessing circles! God blesses us when we live out our faith by loving others—and when we treat others with love, making an effort to resolve disagreements, our faith is strengthened.

Lord, remind me that I cannot be faithful to You if I don't truly love others; I cannot be righteous if I'm not at peace with those around me. Amen.

DAY 270

MORNING
Increasing Visibility

"Where then is my hope?"

Job 17:15 NIV

On hectic days when fatigue takes its toll, when we feel like cornless husks, hope disappears. When hurting people hurt people, and we're in the line of fire, hope vanishes. When ideas fizzle, efforts fail; when we throw the spaghetti against the wall and nothing sticks, hope seems lost. But we must remember it's only temporary. The mountaintop isn't gone just because it's obscured by fog. Visibility will improve tomorrow and hope will rise.

God of hope, I am thankful to know You. . .and to trust that because of You, hope will rise. Amen.

EVENING
Jesus Is Transfigured

Jesus took with Him Peter and James and John. . . . And He was transfigured before them; and His garments became radiant and exceedingly white, as no launderer on earth can whiten them. Elijah appeared to them along with Moses; and they were talking with Jesus.

Mark 9:2–4 NASB

We can't even imagine what glory these disciples beheld. Their human eyes were allowed to view Jesus virtually transformed into a supernatural form.

The Greek word for this phenomenon of transfiguration is *metamorphoó*, from which we derive our word *metamorphosis*. Christ performs the miracle of metamorphosis in us when we come to believe in Him as Lord and Savior. He transforms us, quickening our spirits so that we are destined to spend eternity with God in heaven. It's a change on the inside that is displayed on the outside—for the unbelieving world to see.

Lord, transform me today, by Your almighty power, into a bold witness of Your Gospel message. Amen.

DAY 271

MORNING
The Blessing of Friendship

A friend loves at all times,
and a brother is born for adversity.
PROVERBS 17:17 NASB

When things are going our way, we may be tempted to think we are so strong that we don't need anyone's help. We may consider ourselves so spiritually mature that we can go it alone, "just me and the Lord." But sooner or later, all of us face times when everything seems to fall apart. We can't cope with life, and even our faith falters. When a friend quietly offers us her hand, that's the moment when we truly understand the blessing of friendship!

Thank You, Lord, for the friends with
whom You've blessed my life. I know
I couldn't make it without them. Amen.

EVENING
Painful Blessings

As iron sharpens iron,
so a friend sharpens a friend.
PROVERBS 27:17 NLT

Our friends can bring out the best in us. Sometimes that's a pleasant experience. We bask in the knowledge that someone truly understands and appreciates us. But a real friend doesn't only stroke our egos. He also speaks the truth to us, even when it's difficult for us to hear. He hones us, the way a knife is made sharper and more useful by being rubbed against another knife. And sometimes that can be painful!

Remind me, God, not to get defensive
and angry when a friend offers me honest
criticism. May I be open to hear
what You need to tell me. Amen.

DAY 272

MORNING

Commandments or Suggestions?

"I am the LORD who sanctifies you. . . .
You are therefore to keep all My statutes
and all My ordinances and do them,
so that the land to which I am bringing
you to live will not spew you out."

LEVITICUS 20:8, 22 NASB

When God gave His laws to Moses, He expected them to be observed.

But how could sinful men ever comply consistently with these laws? Therefore, throughout Old Testament history, humanity was to look forward in time and trust God for the coming Messiah; His death would finally cleanse them from their sin. Abraham believed this and passed the "promise" on to his descendants. Isaac then brought this seed of expectation to Jacob. And on and on the Word of the Lord progressed.

However, so did man's sin. Our hope lies in the fact that Jesus Christ has paid the penalty for all our sin. And if we confess our sins to Him, then He is faithful and just to forgive us (1 John 1:9).

Lord, having a relationship with You is
the only way we can keep Your commands.
Help us to relinquish our wills to You. Amen.

EVENING

Heartfelt Blessings

The pleasantness of a friend springs
from their heartfelt advice.

PROVERBS 27:9 NIV

Down through the years, God uses our friends to bless us again and again. We feel joy in their company, laughing and having fun together. In times of sorrow and discouragement, we are comforted by their love and faith in us. Their prayers strengthen us. And most of all, we benefit from their wisdom. God has taught each of us unique insights, and we are blessed when our friends share with us their hearts' wisdom.

Thank You, God, for the wisdom You
have given my friends. May I never be so
full of myself that I refuse to
learn from them. Amen.

DAY 273

MORNING

Lord of the Dance

Remember your promise to me;
it is my only hope.

PSALM 119:49 NLT

The Bible contains many promises from God: He will protect us (Proverbs 1:33), comfort us (2 Corinthians 1:5), help in our times of trouble (Psalm 46:1), and encourage us (Isaiah 40:29). The word *encourage* comes from the root phrase "to inspire courage." Like an earthly father encouraging his daughter from backstage as her steps falter during her dance recital, our Papa God wants to inspire courage in us, if we only look to Him.

Promise keeper, You are the one true source of courage. Thank You for Your promises and for giving me courage when I need it most. Amen.

EVENING

Entertaining Angels

Do not neglect to show hospitality to strangers, for by this some have entertained angels without knowing it.

HEBREWS 13:2 NASB

In the New Testament, the Greek word translated *hospitality* literally means "love of strangers"—and the word for *angel* means "messenger." The author of Hebrews is telling us that it's not only our friends who bless us. Sometimes God sends strangers into our lives with a message we need to hear. Are our hearts open when we meet someone who seems different from us? Are we willing to hear God speaking through that person?

Help me, God, to hear Your voice speaking to me, even through people I would never have thought would carry Your message to me. Remind me to open my heart and my home to those who are different from me. Amen.

MORNING

Jesus left that place and went to the vicinity of Tyre. He entered a house and did not want anyone to know it; yet he could not keep his presence secret. In fact, as soon as she heard about him, a woman whose little daughter was possessed by an impure spirit came and fell at his feet.

MARK 7:24–25 NIV

Shocking headlines assault us almost daily, relating the horrors children have inflicted upon other children. Even during the time of Christ, diabolic forces knew no age barriers.

A Gentile woman of Syrophoenician heritage sought out Jesus. A desperate woman, she recognized that her little daughter was demon possessed.

She not only displayed faith in His ability to heal, but she believed that she had the right to ask Him for assistance. Jesus came to bring the good news to the Jews first. But this woman, a Gentile, said she needed Jesus' touch, too. And He responded to her faith. Ask Jesus to touch your life this day.

Lord, You are Messiah to all, Jews and Gentiles, and I know You will never turn me away. In this I rejoice! Amen.

EVENING

Keys to the Kingdom

"It gives your Father great happiness to give you the Kingdom."

LUKE 12:32 NLT

Sometimes when we pray, we act as though God is a stingy, distant authority figure. We plead with Him to give us the things we need. We beg Him to bless us. But we don't need to pray like that. Instead, we can pray with confidence. We don't have to beg. It makes God happy to bless us. God's kingdom is rich and full, immense and lovely—and He wants to give us the whole entire thing!

Thank You, Father, that You are already in the process of giving me everything I need! Amen.

DAY 275

MORNING
Smiling in the Darkness

The hopes of the godless evaporate.

JOB 8:13 NLT

Hope isn't just an emotion; it's a perspective, a discipline, a way of life. It's a journey of choice. We must learn to override those messages of discouragement, despair, and fear that assault us in times of trouble and press toward the light. Hope is smiling in the darkness. It's confidence that faith in God's sovereignty amounts to something. . . something life changing, lifesaving, and eternal.

Father God, help me smile through the darkness today. Thank You for hope. Amen.

EVENING
Heart's Desire

Take delight in the LORD, and he will give you the desires of your heart.

PSALM 37:4 NIV

Sometimes it feels as though we have an empty place inside us that can never be filled, no matter how many things we get. That empty place is real, but material possessions can never fill it up. The Bible says that God put eternity into our hearts. Deep inside our innermost beings we yearn for all that eternity holds, all its abundance and beauty. Only God can give us the deepest, real desires of our hearts.

When I feel empty inside, God, remind me not to turn to anything but You to fill me. Food, drink, other people, distractions, possessions—none of them can make me whole. Only You can. Amen.

DAY 276

MORNING
God's Plans

"For I know the plans I have for you," declares the Lord, "plans to prosper you and not to harm you, plans to give you hope and a future."

Jeremiah 29:11 NIV

The future scares us sometimes. We can't predict what sorrows and loss lie ahead. On the other hand, we *can* predict some of the losses that will come—like aging and the eventual deaths of those we love—and that's almost worse! But we don't need to live in fear. Instead, we can read and reread this verse! No matter what this world tells us, God always keeps His promises.

I trust Your plans for my life, Lord. No matter what happens, I know You will bless me and heal me—and You will use me in Your kingdom. Amen.

EVENING
Small but Mighty

He has. . .exalted the humble.

Luke 1:52 NLT

God delights in making small things great. He's in the business of taking scrap-heap people and turning them into treasures: Noah (the laughingstock of his city), Moses (stuttering shepherd turned national leader), David (smallest among the big and powerful), Sarah (old and childless), Mary (poor teenager), and Rahab (harlot turned faith-filled ancestor of Jesus). So you and I can rejoice with hope! Let us glory in our smallness!

I feel so very small today, God. Please remind me that because I am Yours, I am worthy. And that's all that matters! Amen.

DAY 277

MORNING
The Wise of Heart

The wise of heart will receive commands, but a babbling fool will be ruined. He who walks in integrity walks securely, but he who perverts his ways will be found out.

PROVERBS 10:8–9 NASB

For years James Dobson, president of Focus on the Family, has warned parents about the pitfalls ahead for their strong-willed children. Personally, we raised our three kids with one hand on the radio and the other on the Bible. Dr. Dobson's radio ministry has given us hope and kept us sane.

My repeated prayer for all our children was this: "Lord, protect them and surround them with Your angels. And if they're disobedient, let them be found out."

Our kids were convinced that I had spies stationed all over the city. No matter what they did, I knew about it within hours. And I can assure you, it was a direct result of this prayer.

Is there a young person in your life who needs your prayers today?

Lord, help us to stress honesty, obedience, and the truth of Your Word to our kids and to shower them with unconditional love so that they can grow to maturity in a secure emotional place. Amen.

EVENING
Praise Song

Let all that I am praise the LORD*; may I never forget the good things he does for me. He forgives all my sins and heals all my diseases. He redeems me from death and crowns me with love and tender mercies. He fills my life with good things.*

PSALM 103:2–5 NLT

Since all these eternal blessing are ours, our entire being should sing with praise!

May I never forget, Lord, all You have done for me! Fill my heart and life with a greater awareness of Your blessings, so that every part of me pours out Your praise into the world. Amen.

DAY 278

MORNING

Stay Connected

"Your Father knows exactly what you need even before you ask him!"

MATTHEW 6:8 NLT

We need to pray. The Bible tells us to "pray without ceasing" (1 Thessalonians 5:17 KJV). But we don't pray because God needs to be told what we need. We pray because we need to be in vital connection with God; we need to be always aware that we are living in eternity. But God already knows what we need, better than we do ourselves. We don't need to give directions as to how He should bless us!

Thank You, Father, that You always know exactly what I need. In fact, You know far better than I do! Amen.

EVENING

Richness of Life

The blessing of the LORD makes a person rich.

PROVERBS 10:22 NLT

The Hebrew word used here for *makes rich* is *ashar*, which means "creates abundance." When we talk about blessing, that's what we really mean—the abundant riches, thriving health, overflowing bounty that God pours into our lives in countless shapes and forms, myriad varieties, all the depth and width that's contained in eternity. This richness of life is what God's blessings create for us and in us. This is the life we enter into through Jesus.

Jesus, Your life is an abundant stream of life. Thank You that You give it to me daily. Amen.

DAY 279

MORNING

U-Hauls Don't Follow Hearses

"Lord, make me to know my end,
and what is the extent of my days;
let me know how transient I am."
Psalm 39:4 NASB

As Christians we know that no human possesses the ability to access knowledge of future events. Omniscience belongs to God alone.

God wants us to trust Him for our future. To know our life span would affect us every day of our life. So, God has guarded this secret as a great favor to us.

In a church we used to attend, the pastor was famous for his story about the man who wanted to have a "U-Haul following the hearse" to his funeral. None of us will take the fruits of our labor with us to our eternal destination. Instead, we should concern ourselves with where that final stop will be.

To worry about the future is to be uncertain of your eternity.

Lord, it's so easy to get caught up in the glitter of gold. Give me a daily glimpse of heaven, my real home. Amen.

EVENING

God's Nature

Surely you have
granted him unending blessings.
Psalm 21:6 NIV

Unending. The Bible uses that word over and over, telling us again and again that eternity and blessing are part of God's very nature. His being has no end, no limits. And since God is love (1 John 4:8), His love is constantly flowing around us and into us—an unending stream of blessings.

God, sometimes I am so afraid of all the endings this life holds—the end of careers, the end of friendships, the end of phases of life, the end of life itself. Remind me that in You there are no real endings. Your love is eternal. Amen.

DAY 280

MORNING
God's Faithful Love

I cry out, "My splendor is gone! Everything I had hoped for from the Lord *is lost!" The thought of my suffering. . .is bitter beyond words. I will never forget this awful time, as I grieve over my loss. Yet I still dare to hope when I remember this: The faithful love of the* Lord *never ends! His mercies never cease.*

Lamentations 3:18–22 NLT

God's blessing isn't like an eternal raincoat that protects us from sorrow. Awful times will come. We will grieve over losses. And yet, even then, we can be confident that God's love is faithful. We live in eternity—and God is still blessing us.

Oh God, when all I see is loss and disappointment in my life, remind me that Your faithfulness has not changed. Your love and mercy are still at work. Amen.

EVENING
Keep Breathing, Sister!

As long as we are alive, we still have hope, just as a live dog is better off than a dead lion.

Ecclesiastes 9:4 CEV

Isn't this a tremendous scripture? At first glance, the ending elicits a chuckle. But consider the truth it contains: regardless of how powerful, regal, or intimidating a lion is, when he's dead, he's dead. But the living—you and I—still have hope. Limitless possibilities! Hope for today and for the future. Although we may be as lowly dogs, fresh, juicy bones abound. As long as we're breathing, it's not too late!

God of possibilities, remind me that it's never too late as long as I'm breathing. Because of You, I have hope! Amen.

DAY 281

MORNING

God's Blessing

If you listen obediently to the Voice of GOD. . .GOD, your God, will place you on high. . . . All these blessings will come down on you and spread out beyond you because you have responded to the Voice of GOD, your God: GOD's blessing inside the city, GOD's blessing in the country; GOD's blessing on your children, the crops of your land, the young of your livestock, the calves of your herds, the lambs of your flocks. GOD's blessing on your basket and bread bowl; GOD's blessing in your coming in, GOD's blessing in your going out.

DEUTERONOMY 28:1–6 MSG

All those blessings are yours. God has promised!

May I respond to Your voice, God,
so that Your blessings will come down
on me—and spread out from me
into the lives of others. Amen.

EVENING

You Can Bring Heaven to Earth

"May your Kingdom come soon. May your will be done on earth, as it is in heaven."

MATTHEW 6:10 NLT

God wants you to be a part of His work on earth. He longs for you to exercise your faith in His will. This is because God has included us in His plans through our prayers. Our prayers enable us to access God in heaven. What a privilege!

If you want something from heaven to come to earth, pray. Entreat God to make it happen.

God, use me to build Your kingdom on earth.
I know that praying alone is not enough.
Make me an active part of what
You want to do in the world. Amen.

DAY 282

MORNING

Jets and Submarines

No power in the sky above or in the earth below. . .will ever be able to separate us from the love of God that is revealed in Christ Jesus our Lord.

ROMANS 8:39 NLT

Have you ever been diving amid the spectacular array of vivid color and teeming life in the silent world under the sea? Painted fish of rainbow hues are backlit by diffused sunbeams. Multitextured coral dot the gleaming white sand. You honestly feel as if you're in another world. But every world is God's world. He soars above the clouds with us and spans the depths of the seas. Nothing can separate us from His love.

Your love amazes me, Father. Just when I find myself questioning how You could possibly love me so much, I am reminded of the precious promises of Your Word. Amen.

EVENING

The Lord's Diet Plan

"Speak to the sons of Israel, saying, 'These are the creatures which you may eat from all the animals that are on the earth. Whatever divides a hoof, thus making split hoofs, and chews the cud, among the animals, that you may eat.' "

LEVITICUS 11:2–3 NASB

Moses was chosen by God to deliver dietary restrictions to the Israelites. The one meat you probably already know about is pork. God didn't even want the Israelites to touch it. He told Moses that although it has "a divided hoof, [it] does not chew the cud; it is unclean for you" (Leviticus 11:7 NIV).

Unlike the cow, the pig doesn't take time to ruminate. So what in the world does this have to do with anything?

In those days prior to refrigeration and pasteurization, if the Israelites hadn't obeyed God's dietary laws, most if not all of them would have died from bacterial infections, food poisoning, and so on. God was preserving a nation from which the Messiah would be born.

Lord, Your call to obedience may not always make sense, but help me remember that You have a reason. Amen.

DAY 283

MORNING

Blessed by the Stranger

"For I was hungry and you gave me something to eat, I was thirsty and you gave me something to drink, I was a stranger and you invited me in. . . I was sick and you looked after me, I was in prison and you came to visit me. . . . Truly I tell you, whatever you did. . .you did for me."

MATTHEW 25:35–36, 40 NIV

Strangers aren't only angels in disguise! They're also Jesus Himself. When we give to others in need, we are giving to our Lord.

Jesus, may I never turn You away.
May I always see Your face in others
and respond in love. Amen.

EVENING

Blessed by Those in Need

"When you give a banquet, invite the poor, the crippled, the lame, the blind, and you will be blessed."

LUKE 14:13–14 NIV

When we give to those in need, we may think we are the ones who are doing God's work. And we are, of course; God is using us to bless others. But at the same time, we may find that we're the ones who are blessed the most. Not only will God bless us, but we'll also find that the poor, the sick, the stranger, and the prisoner all have blessings to give us.

Make me a blessing to others, God.
And open me to the blessing You want
to give me through them. Amen.

When everything was hopeless, Abraham believed anyway, deciding to live. . . on what God said he would do.

Romans 4:18 msg

"You can't do that. It's impossible." Have you ever been told this? Or just thought it because of fear or a previous experience with failure? This world is full of those who discourage rather than encourage. If we believe them, we'll never do anything. But if we, like Abraham, believe that God has called us for a particular purpose, we'll go for it despite our track records. Past failure doesn't dictate future failure. If God wills it, He fulfills it.

Help me to have the faith of Abraham, Father God. . .to believe anyway! Amen.

EVENING
Don't Forget to Say Thank You

I always thank my God for you.

1 Corinthians 1:4 nlt

When you thank God for the many blessings He has given you, don't forget the people He has put in your life. Thank Him for your friends and your family, your coworkers and your employers. Thank Him for the people you know casually and for each stranger you pass on the street. Thank Him even for the difficult people you encounter! Each and every one of them can be a vehicle for God's blessing to flow into your life.

God, thank You for all the wonderful and lovable people You have put in my life. And thank You, too, for all the irritating and difficult people! Open my mind and heart to receive Your blessing through them all. Amen.

DAY 285

MORNING
To Touch Jesus' Cloak

A woman who had had a hemorrhage for twelve years, and had endured much at the hands of many physicians. . .after hearing about Jesus, she came up in the crowd behind Him and touched His cloak. For she thought, "If I just touch His garments, I will get well."

MARK 5:25–28 NASB

The wonder is that this woman could survive for twelve long years. In one last-ditch effort, she reaches out to touch the garment of Jesus as He passes by. Somehow she knows that His very holiness can heal her physically.

"Immediately Jesus, perceiving in Himself that the power proceeding from Him had gone forth, turned around in the crowd and said, 'Who touched My garments?' " (Mark 5:30 NASB).

"But the woman fearing and trembling, aware of what had happened to her, came and fell down before Him, and told Him the whole truth" (Mark 5:33 NASB). She's been miraculously healed and now she demonstrates her faith by worshipping at Jesus' feet. Does your faith shine through even in small gestures?

Lord, You heal me when I come to You by renewing my spirit and deepening my faith. I worship Your majesty and power. Amen.

EVENING
Blessed in the Presence of My Enemy

You prepare a feast for me in the presence of my enemies. . . . My cup overflows with blessings.

PSALM 23:5 NLT

We often think of blessings as things we experience in the happy times. When we get a raise, when we are healed from some illness, or when our children and our elderly parents are all happy and healthy, we consider that we've been blessed. But the psalmist reminds us that God blesses even when enemies surround us. God's blessings are just as bountiful on dark days as they are on sunny days.

Let me enjoy Your feast of blessing, God, even in the darkness. Amen.

DAY 286

MORNING

Can You Hear Me Now?

But as for me, I watch in hope for
the LORD, I wait for God my Savior;
my God will hear me.

MICAH 7:7 NIV

If there's anything more frustrating than waiting for someone who never shows, it's trying to talk to people who aren't listening. It's as if they have plugged their ears and nothing penetrates. Mothers are well acquainted with this exercise in futility, as are wives, daughters, and sisters. But the Bible tells us that God hears us when we talk to Him. He shows up when we wait for Him. He will not disappoint us.

When I talk, Lord, I know You will listen.
You will never let me down. Amen.

EVENING

Blessed When We Are Broken

The LORD is close to the brokenhearted;
he rescues those whose spirits are crushed.

PSALM 34:18 NLT

The meanings found in this verse's Hebrew words are rich with blessings: When we've been broken, crushed by life, hurt so badly that we feel we can't survive, the self-existent eternal One is as intimate with us as a close friend, as close by as if He were sitting at our side. When our inner beings are ground down to nothing, He sets us free, He helps us, and He makes us safe. He opens wide all the doors in our lives.

Thank You, eternal Lord, that You are always near to me. You are always loving me, always rescuing me. You'll never abandon me. Amen.

DAY 287

MORNING
Speed-of-Light Blessings

God is our refuge and strength,
an ever-present help in trouble.
PSALM 46:1 NIV

The Hebrew word that's been translated *ever-present* is an interesting one. It carries within it several meanings: something that's diligent and never gives up; something unbelievably fast; something that shouts louder than any other sound. That's the way God's blessings reach us when we're in trouble—unstoppable, breaking the sound barrier, faster than the speed of light. No matter how big the problem, His help will be there when we need it.

I praise You, Lord, for the superpower energy of Your blessings. Nothing can come between You and me. Nothing can interfere with Your presence in my life. Amen.

EVENING
A Woman of Folly

The woman of folly is boisterous, she is naive
and knows nothing. She sits at the doorway
of her house, on a seat by the high places
of the city, calling to those who pass by,
who are making their paths straight:
"Whoever is naive, let him turn in here,"
and to him who lacks understanding
she says, "Stolen water is sweet;
and bread eaten in secret is pleasant."
PROVERBS 9:13–17 NASB

This woman is not only content to wreak havoc on her own life, but she entices those who wanted to go the right way to join her on this road to nowhere. The passage describes her as "naive," because surely if she'd known better she'd have chosen more wisely.

Have you ever felt like this woman? Did you start out with endless options and then begin purchasing tickets to oblivion? With Christ it's not too late to cash in that pass to nowhere. With Christ your life will have direction.

Lord, please provide me with a true picture of myself. Guide me to the place You envision for me. Amen.

DAY 288

MORNING
Unlikely Heroes

*Rahab the harlot. . .Joshua spared. . .
for she hid the messengers whom
Joshua sent to spy out Jericho.*

JOSHUA 6:25 NASB

Rahab was the unlikeliest of heroes: a prostitute who sold her body in the darkest shadows. Yet she was the very person God chose to fulfill His prophecy. How astoundingly freeing! Especially for those of us ashamed of our pasts. God loved Rahab for who she was—not what she did. Rahab is proof that God can and will use anyone for His higher purposes. Anyone. Even you and me.

*When I feel absolutely useless, God,
remind me of Rahab's story. If you could
use Rahab for Your purposes,
You can certainly use me! Amen.*

EVENING
The Blessing of Weakness

I will boast all the more gladly about my weaknesses, so that Christ's power may rest on me. . . . I delight in weaknesses, in insults, in hardships, in persecutions, in difficulties. For when I am weak, then I am strong.

2 CORINTHIANS 12:9–10 NIV

People don't very often say, "God has blessed me so richly by making me so weak." No, we usually think of strength as a blessing—and weakness is more like a curse! But that's not what Paul says here. In the midst of weakness, hardship, and difficulties, he says, we are blessed with God's power.

*Jesus, You know all the ways in which I'm
weak. I don't like to admit my weaknesses,
even to myself—but if You want to use
them as conduits for Your power,
I'll give them all to You. Amen.*

DAY 289

MORNING
Offerings to the Lord

"Speak to the sons of Israel and say to them, 'When any man of you brings an offering to the LORD, you shall bring your offering of animals from the herd or the flock.'"

LEVITICUS 1:2 NASB

God communicated His Word and His desire for proper worship through His chosen leaders. These spokesmen then communicated His message to His chosen people. Before the coming of the Holy Spirit at Pentecost, this chain of command was vital so that God's flock was not misled.

God required proper and orderly worship. Only an unblemished male animal could be used as the burnt offering. Down through the ages men and women were to make a connection between this sacrifice and the one Christ would willingly make on Calvary's cross.

There have not been any animal sacrifices since the temple in Jerusalem was destroyed in AD 70. Since Christ made His atoning sacrifice on the cross, our sins are forgiven based on His shed blood.

Lord, how grateful I am for Jesus, Your unblemished Lamb. Might I willingly become a living sacrifice through service to You as I take the Gospel to this needy world. Amen.

EVENING
Rejoicing in Times of Trial

We can rejoice, too, when we run into problems and trials, for we know that they help us develop endurance. And endurance develops strength of character, and character strengthens our confident hope of salvation. And this hope will not lead to disappointment. For we know how dearly God loves us.

ROMANS 5:3–5 NLT

In this verse, Paul has more to say about the blessings we can find during times of trouble. He spells out what some of them are: endurance, strength of character, hope—and most of all, the confidence that God loves us.

God, in all the trials I've experienced lately, I choose to rejoice. I believe You are using these difficult things to make me strong. Amen.

DAY 290

MORNING
The Blessing of Confidence

Though a mighty army surrounds me, my heart will not be afraid. Even if I am attacked, I will remain confident.

PSALM 27:3 NLT

Confidence is truly one of the blessings we can gain from the hard times we face. It doesn't come to us immediately, but with each challenge we face, we grow more certain of God's power to overcome even the greatest problems. We remember that He did it before—and we can begin to trust that He will do it again. God is bigger than any enemy we face!

I am learning, Lord, that I have nothing to fear. You have taken care of everything! Amen.

EVENING
Cherished Desire

God our Father loves us. He is kind and has given us eternal comfort and a wonderful hope.

2 THESSALONIANS 2:16 CEV

Webster's definition of hope is "to cherish a desire with expectation." In other words, yearning for something wonderful you expect to occur. Our hope in Christ is not just yearning for something wonderful, as in "I hope for a sunny beach day." It's a deep trust with roots that extend from the beginning of time to the infinite future. Our hope is not just the anticipation of heaven, but the expectation of a fulfilling life walking beside our Creator and best friend.

Dear heavenly Father, I want to journey through life in hopeful expectation—always anticipating You'll work in wonderful ways! Amen.

DAY 291

MORNING
God's Castle of Blessing

The LORD *also will be a refuge for the oppressed, a refuge in times of trouble.*

PSALM 9:9 KJV

The Hebrew word translated *refuge* is *sagab*—a stronghold on a high mountain or cliff. Why is the refuge situated like this? Because a stronghold on a mountain or cliff has a good view of any enemies that might approach—and it can be defended more easily if it's attacked. Picture one of those enormous storybook castles in the mountains of Germany, all the towers and the strong wall around the entire thing. That's the sort of refuge God offers us in times of trouble!

Thank You, Lord of all, that You are my Refuge, a Stronghold that can never be breached. No matter what troubles come my way, You will keep me safe. Amen.

EVENING
Blessings during Times of Drought

*"Blessed is the man who trusts. . .*GOD*, the woman who sticks with* GOD*. They're like trees replanted in Eden, putting down roots near the rivers—never a worry through the hottest of summers, never dropping a leaf, serene and calm through droughts, bearing fresh fruit every season."*

JEREMIAH 17:7–8 MSG

God never promises us that troubles won't come into our lives. What He does promise is that no matter how dry and empty our external lives are, He will supply our hearts with the blessing of life. We don't need to worry!

When my life seems empty, when all the things that usually give me pleasure seem to have dried up, remind me, Lord, that my roots are deep in You. You will give me the water of life, even in seasons of drought. Amen.

MORNING

God blesses those who patiently endure testing and temptation. Afterward they will receive the crown of life that God has promised to those who love him.

JAMES 1:12 NLT

It's not easy to feel blessed during hard times. Our emotions tell us that everything is *awful*. But we need patience. The Hebrew word used here has to do with perseverance. That means just putting one foot in front of the other for as long as it takes. That's all God asks of us, while He supplies the blessings, both now and in eternity.

Thank You, God, for lifting the burden of responsibility from my shoulders. It's not my job to fix things; that's Yours. All I have to do is keep persevering, following You a step at a time. Amen.

EVENING

Seeking an Oasis

He changes a wilderness into a pool of water and a dry land into springs of water.

PSALM 107:35 NASB

The wilderness of Israel is truly a barren wasteland—nothing but rocks and parched sand stretching as far as the distant horizon. The life-and-death contrast between stark desert and pools of oasis water is startling. Our lives can feel parched, too. Colorless. Devoid of life. But God has the power to transform desert lives into gurgling, spring-of-water lives. Ask Him to bubble up springs of hope within you today.

When I am feeling parched, Jesus, I trust You'll create a peaceful oasis in my soul. Envelop my spirit in Your hope, Lord. Amen.

DAY 293

MORNING

True Love Means Sacrifice

They spat on Him, and took the reed and began to beat Him on the head. After they had mocked Him, they took the scarlet robe off Him and put His own garments back on Him, and led Him away to crucify Him.

MATTHEW 27:30–31 NASB

Years ago the popular movie *Love Story* coined the unforgettable phrase "Love means never having to say you're sorry." What a fallacy, and more is the pity for those who bought into this lie!

For love demands that we always say we're sorry. How else can relationships be restored? Those two words, "I'm sorry," have the power to keep families and churches together.

To admit fallibility is to make a sacrifice. To have done nothing wrong and to offer the ultimate sacrifice is an act only possible for God's Son. Jesus' offering of His body at Calvary gave eternal life to all who believe in Him.

Is there someone from whom you are estranged who is waiting to hear those two little words? Say you're sorry.

Lord, You sacrificed all You had to provide my eternal salvation. Help me today to express true sorrow for my sins. Amen.

EVENING

Being Honest with God

O LORD, why do you stand so far away? Why do you hide when I am in trouble?

PSALM 10:1 NLT

All of us have experienced the feeling the psalmist describes here. No matter how many verses we read about blessings in the midst of trouble, we don't *feel* blessed. Jesus felt the same way when He hung on the cross—and like the psalmist, He wasn't afraid to express His feelings to His Father. Sometimes bitterness, discouragement, and anger are all we have to offer God. We can be honest with God. He accepts and blesses even our negative emotions.

God, when all I have to give You is anger and despair, remind me that You will accept even that when I offer it up to You. Amen.

DAY 294

MORNING
Feel the Love

Long before he laid down earth's foundations, he had us in mind, had settled on us as the focus of his love, to be made whole and holy by his love.

EPHESIANS 1:4 MSG

Need a boost of hope today? Read this passage aloud, inserting your name for each "us." Wow! Doesn't that bring home the message of God's incredible, extravagant, customized love for you? I am the focus of His love, and I bask in the hope of healing, wholeness, and holiness His individualized attention brings. You too, dear sister, are His focus. Allow yourself to feel the love today.

Long before You laid down earth's foundations, You had me in mind, had settled on me as the focus of Your love, to be made whole and holy by Your love. Thank You, Jesus! Amen.

EVENING
Offerings for the Tent of Meeting

Then the whole Israelite community withdrew from Moses' presence, and everyone who was willing and whose heart moved them came and brought an offering to the LORD for the work on the tent of meeting, for all its service, and for the sacred garments.

EXODUS 35:20–21 NIV

When was the last time your whole community agreed on anything? Imagine everyone's talents, skills, and resources united for a common purpose!

The hearts of God's people were stirred to erect the tent of meeting, following the Lord's command. Leaving all selfish desires behind, they pooled their brooches, earrings, signet rings, bracelets, and other offerings of gold for the Lord. From these articles gemstones were extracted to make the ephod and the breastplate.

As those in Moses' day brought all they possessed, we can surrender our own time and talents.

How is God using you in His Church?

Lord, You've created within me something to be used to further Your kingdom. Please enable me to open my hands willingly in service. Amen.

DAY 295

MORNING
Permission to Mourn

When I heard this, I sat down and cried.
Then for several days, I mourned;
I went without eating to show
my sorrow, and I prayed.

NEHEMIAH 1:4 CEV

Bad news. When it arrives, what's your reaction? Do you scream? Fall apart? Run away? Nehemiah's response to bad news is a model for us. First, he vented his sorrow. It's okay to cry and mourn. Christians suffer pain like everyone else—only we know the source of inner healing. Disguising our struggle doesn't make us look more spiritual. . .just less real. Like Nehemiah, our next step is to turn to the only true source of help and comfort.

Thank You for being big enough, God,
to carry my sorrow. I am thankful
that with You, I can always be real. . .
sharing my every thought and emotion.
And You love me still! Amen.

EVENING
Songs of Deliverance

You are my hiding place; You preserve me
from trouble; You surround me
with songs of deliverance.

PSALM 32:7 NASB

When our hearts are full of doubt and despair, how can we experience God's blessings? Sometimes, we just have to endure our emotions with that one-foot-in-front-of-the-other patience we mentioned earlier. But we do have options, even then. Prayer, scripture, the support of others, and even music can become "hiding places" where we can escape, even temporarily, and experience God's presence.

Show me the places—the activities, the
people, the occasions—where I can hide
from life's challenges and be strengthened
by Your presence, loving Lord. Amen.

DAY 296

MORNING
The Blessing of Scripture

Those who hope in the LORD will renew their strength. They will soar on wings like eagles; they will run and not grow weary, they will walk and not be faint.

ISAIAH 40:31 NIV

Scripture verses like this are good to read over and over during hard times. Write them on note cards and tape them to your car's dashboard or your computer monitor, wherever your eyes go regularly throughout the day. The more you read them, the more they will come to life. . .the more you will believe you are blessed.

Write Your promises on my heart, Lord. Engrave them in my thoughts. May they become entwined with every circumstance of my life, so that they become living realities in my soul. Amen.

EVENING
Pebbles

"I will give you a new heart and put a new spirit within you; and I will remove the heart of stone from your flesh and give you a heart of flesh."

EZEKIEL 36:26 NASB

So many things can harden our hearts: overwhelming loss; shattered dreams; even scar tissue from broken hearts, disillusionment, and disappointment. To avoid pain, we simply turn off feelings. Our hearts become petrified rock—heavy, cold, and rigid. But God can crack our hearts of stone from the inside out and replace that miserable pile of pebbles with soft, feeling hearts of flesh. The amazing result is a brand-new, hope-filled spirit.

God, please take my hard heart and make it soft again. Renew my spirit with Your hope. Transform me from the inside out! Amen.

DAY 297

MORNING

Before He Set the Heavens in Place

"The LORD *possessed me at the beginning of His way, before His works of old. From everlasting I was established, from the beginning, from the earliest times of the earth. When there were no depths I was brought forth, when there were no springs abounding with water. . . . When He marked out the foundations of the earth; then I was beside Him, as a master workman."*

PROVERBS 8:22–24, 29–30 NASB

What existed before anything else? God. And now woman and man come along, filling in a narrow blip of time, and state that all of creation "just simply evolved." Get a clue! God designed, planned, and implemented all that we do see and everything we can't comprehend.

Somehow we have turned around history. Humans are not in charge. God is. And He's still commanding the dawn to happen and the earth to keep spinning and the stars to remain in the sky. Aren't you glad?

Lord, keep me from taking Your magnificence for granted. Let my heart overflow with gratitude for all You are. Amen.

EVENING

Gentle Jesus

Jesus said, "Come to me, all of you who are weary and carry heavy burdens, and I will give you rest. . . . Let me teach you, because I am humble and gentle at heart, and you will find rest for your souls."

MATTHEW 11:28–29 NLT

Jesus longs to lift our burdens from our shoulders. Like a mother worrying over her child, He yearns to do whatever He can to ease our troubled hearts. He knows how hard it is for us—and He'll take the time to teach us all we need to know to trust Him.

Jesus, when I'm weary and overwhelmed, remind me to turn to You. Teach me, Lord. Give me rest. Amen.

DAY 298

MORNING

Peter's Denial

Then Jesus said to them, "You will all fall away because of Me this night, for it is written, 'I WILL STRIKE DOWN THE SHEPHERD, AND THE SHEEP OF THE FLOCK SHALL BE SCATTERED.' But after I have been raised, I will go ahead of you to Galilee." But Peter said to Him, "Even though all may fall away because of You, I will never fall away."

MATTHEW 26:31–33 NASB

Peter was convinced that his faith in Christ was so strong nothing could cause it to crumble. Yet only a few hours later, he cowered when a young servant girl accused him of being one of Jesus' followers. And then he openly denied his Lord.

There have been times when you have disappointed Jesus. Have you asked for forgiveness? Have you realized that upon asking the burden of sin will be lifted forever?

Lord, I have, at one time or another, acted as if I could live any way I wanted. Yet it cost Christ everything to purchase my redemption. Let me willingly come and pray to You. Amen.

EVENING

Following God in the Darkness

"Be strong and courageous! Do not be afraid and do not panic. . . . For the LORD your God will personally go ahead of you. He will neither fail you nor abandon you."

DEUTERONOMY 31:6 NLT

Feeling sad and discouraged is one thing. Panicking is another. Panicked people have stopped thinking. They've relinquished all control, and they've let fear take the driver's seat. We can't always control negative emotions—but we can refuse to let fear drive all sense from our heads. Instead, we can cling to the thought that God's presence is going ahead of us into the darkness.

Lord God, I ask that You give me Your strength and courage. May I hold tight to the assurance that You are with me. Help me not to panic. Amen.

DAY 299

MORNING

Do a Little Dance

Then Miriam. . .took a tambourine and led all the women as they played their tambourines and danced.

EXODUS 15:20 NLT

Can you imagine the enormous celebration that broke out among the children of Israel when God miraculously saved them from Pharaoh's army? Even dignified prophetess Miriam grabbed her tambourine and cut loose with her girlfriends. Despite adverse circumstances, she heard God's music and did His dance. Isn't that our goal today? To hear God's music above the world's cacophony and do His dance as we recognize everyday miracles in our lives?

Make me aware of Your everyday miracles, Father. Help me to listen closely for Your music so I can join in the dance. Amen.

EVENING

Mourning Turned into Dancing

You have turned for me my mourning into dancing.

PSALM 30:11 NASB

Years ago I was drawn to watch Corrie ten Boom one day on television. She spoke about a meeting, long after World War II, with the SS soldier who had stood guard in the showers at her concentration camp. When I heard her speak about extending her hand in a gesture of forgiveness, her words pierced through my soul like a dagger. How could she offer the hand of friendship to him? Lacking her own strength, Corrie prayed to God for Him to give His forgiveness to this man. And when Corrie's hand touched the former soldier's, she likened it to love's lightning going through her arm, to the man, and then back again.

At the time, there were many people whom I felt incapable of pardoning. God's name topped the list. Corrie's words lingered in my mind and heart, making me miserable. But I finally surrendered my life to Christ. And God's power of forgiveness has turned my own mourning into dancing.

Lord, Your "merry saint" Corrie knew joy was a condition of a heart filled with forgiveness. Help me see this, too! Amen.

DAY 300

MORNING

Renewed Hope

I cried out, "I am slipping!" but your unfailing love, O LORD, supported me. When doubts filled my mind, your comfort gave me renewed hope and cheer.

PSALM 94:18–19 NLT

This verse always makes me think of the Gospel story where Peter is walking on the water—and suddenly starts to sink beneath the waves because he's taken his eyes off Jesus and begun to doubt. "Lord, save me!" Peter shouts. And Jesus doesn't scold him for his doubt. Instead, the scripture says, "Immediately Jesus reached out his hand and caught him" (Matthew 14:30–31 NIV).

Catch me, Jesus, whenever I start to slip. Comfort me when I begin to doubt You. Support me when I'm weak. Renew me when I'm hopeless. Save me! Amen.

EVENING

Remember the Sabbath

"Remember the sabbath day, to keep it holy. Six days you shall labor and do all your work, but the seventh day is a sabbath of the LORD your God; in it you shall not do any work."

EXODUS 20:8–10 NASB

During the 1950s in Missouri where I grew up, blue laws virtually shut down the city on Sundays. Merchants finally managed to get these laws overturned, and the stores opened on Sunday. Sales were timed to begin early on the Sabbath, enticing people to make a choice between church and shopping. On a Sunday morning, compare the number of cars at the mall with those at church. This worldly strategy has certainly been effective.

In the very beginning of our marriage, my husband and I made a decision to honor God on Sunday. God has blessed our family over and over for this faithful commitment, providing not only the weekly spiritual guidance we desperately need, but also giving our bodies and souls the rest they require.

Lord, please help me to remember that Your commandments are always for my good. Amen.

DAY 301

MORNING

An Invitation to Dine

"The kingdom of heaven may be compared to a king who gave a wedding feast for his son."

MATTHEW 22:2 NASB

When God sent His Son to earth, He invited all men and women to a wedding feast. Those who accept the invitation become part of the Church. And the Church is the bride of Christ.

The Son is the Bridegroom for whom the wedding feast is prepared. God Himself has laid the groundwork in the hearts that will respond to His Son, Jesus Christ.

There will be an appointed hour in the future when the guests will come to the banquet. And Christ will call them forth to be His Church when all is made ready, after His resurrection and ascension and the coming of the Holy Spirit at Pentecost.

Also, those in attendance receive "wedding clothes." Jesus Christ now clothes them in His righteousness. Those not wearing these garments are cast out because they refused Christ's invitation, and in so doing, have rejected His salvation.

Lord, You've invited me to dine with You. Let me graciously accept my "wedding clothes." Amen.

EVENING

Mother Love

"As a mother comforts her child, so will I comfort you."

ISAIAH 66:13 NIV

Whether we are mothers ourselves, have had a loving mother, or have had a woman in our lives who has loved us like a mother, most of us know that a mother's love is the sort that doesn't ask questions before it rushes to help. If her children are in danger, a mother will do whatever she has to in order to save them. In good times and bad, her whole identity is focused on blessing her children. Remember—that's the way God loves you!

God, thank You for Your mother-love that tirelessly reaches out to save and comfort me. Amen.

MORNING

We are hard pressed on every side, but not crushed; perplexed, but not in despair; persecuted, but not abandoned; struck down, but not destroyed. We always carry around in our body the death of Jesus, so that the life of Jesus may also be revealed in our body.

2 CORINTHIANS 4:8–10 NIV

Paul's decision to follow Jesus didn't bring him the easy life. Instead, he faced prison, shipwreck, and misunderstanding. He could have given up; he could have thrown up his hands and said, "What's the use?" Instead, he identified with Jesus, knowing that in Him, new life always follows death.

Whenever I face life's difficulties, Jesus, remind me to identify with You and Your death, so that You can transform my circumstances with Your resurrection power. Amen.

EVENING

Up Is the Only Out

Let them lie face down in the dust, for there may be hope at last.

LAMENTATIONS 3:29 NLT

The Old Testament custom for grieving people was to lie prostrate and cover themselves with ashes. Perhaps the thought was that when you're wallowing in the dust, at least you can't descend any further. There's an element of hope in knowing that there's only one way to go: up. If a recent loss has you sprawled in the dust, know that God doesn't waste pain in our lives. He will use it for some redeeming purpose.

Help me to recognize the purpose in my pain, Father. I know You have a plan for my life—and that Your plans are good. I trust You, Father. Amen.

DAY 303

MORNING

The Passover Lamb

"Slay the Passover lamb. You shall take a bunch of hyssop and dip it in the blood which is in the basin, and apply some of the blood that is in the basin to the lintel and the two doorposts; and none of you shall go outside the door of his house until morning. For the LORD will pass through to smite the Egyptians; and when He sees the blood on the lintel and on the two doorposts, the LORD will pass over the door and will not allow the destroyer to come in to your houses to smite you."

EXODUS 12:21–23 NASB

This scripture passage paints a comprehensive picture of the Passover. Each year this symbolic Passover meal is re-created. We can celebrate the Passover with joy and thanksgiving, knowing for certain that the long-awaited Messiah has come, and will come again!

Lord Jesus Christ, I thank You for being my promised Messiah and Passover Lamb. I thank You for Your sacrifice so that my sins could be forgiven. Amen.

EVENING

The God of All Grace

Therefore humble yourselves under the mighty hand of God, that He may exalt you at the proper time, casting all your anxiety on Him, because He cares for you. . . . After you have suffered for a little while, the God of all grace. . .will Himself perfect, confirm, strengthen and establish you.

1 PETER 5:6–7, 10 NASB

Here's a summary of how we can experience God's blessings in the midst of trouble: with humility (not insisting on our own way), with patience (putting one foot in front of another), and by giving all our anxiety to God.

Teach me humility, God. Give me patience. And in return, I'll give You all my worries! It doesn't seem like a fair exchange— but I want to become the person You created me to be. Amen.

DAY 304

MORNING

Making God Our Priority

"But we will devote ourselves to prayer and to the ministry of the word."

ACTS 6:4 NASB

As busy women, we've found out the hard way that we can't do everything. Heaven knows we've tried, but the truth has found us out: superwoman is a myth. So we must make priorities and focus on the most important. Prayer and God's Word should be our faith priorities. If we only do as much as we can do, then God will take over and do what only He can do. He's got our backs, girls!

I know I can't do it all, God. I find comfort in knowing that if I put my faith in You wholeheartedly, You will always help me prioritize my to-do list and get the R & R I need. Amen.

EVENING

Ever Wider

A longing fulfilled is a tree of life.

PROVERBS 13:12 NIV

Take stock of your life. What were you most hoping to achieve a year ago? (Or five years ago?) How many of those goals have been achieved? Sometimes, once we've reached a goal, we move on too quickly to the next one, never allowing ourselves to find the grace God wants to reveal within that achievement. With each goal reached, His grace spreads out into your life, like a tree whose branches grow ever wider.

God, help me to find the balance between moving forward and looking back. Give me moments to pause and reflect on how far I have come with Your grace. Amen.

DAY 305

MORNING

Blessings for Your House

"Put your entire trust in the Master Jesus. Then you'll live as you were meant to live—and everyone in your house included!"

ACTS 16:31 MSG

God's blessings are not just for us. When we trust Jesus, our lives find a healthy balance. Blessings flow out around us, into our families, our homes, and our workplaces. As we surrender to God all the people and things that concern us most, we will see Him pour out His love and grace.

Jesus, help me to put my entire trust in You. I want to live as You meant for me to live—and I want the people who live with me to share Your blessings. Amen.

EVENING

Sprouts

"For there is hope for a tree, when it is cut down, that it will sprout again."

JOB 14:7 NASB

Have you ever battled a stubborn tree? You know, one you can saw off at the ground but the tenacious thing keeps sprouting new growth from the roots? You have to admire the resiliency of that life force, struggling in its refusal to give up. That's hope in a nutshell, sisters. We must believe, even as stumps, that we will eventually become majestic, towering evergreens if we just keep sending out those sprouts.

Father God, help me continue to hope that I will grow into the woman You created me to be—just like the majestic, towering evergreen. Amen.

DAY 306

MORNING

Pharaoh Admits His Sin

Then Pharaoh sent for Moses and Aaron, and said to them, "I have sinned this time; the LORD is the righteous one, and I and my people are the wicked ones."

EXODUS 9:27 NASB

One would think that with an admission like this, especially from an unbelieving ruler, the man had finally seen the light. Pharaoh sounds ready to commit his heart and soul to the almighty God. Wrong!

Pharaoh's heart had not yielded to God's authority. Three more plagues would come upon the people because their leader refused to honor the true God.

Pharaoh would pay a terrible price for his sins. In the end, his stubbornness would cause the loss of his own precious son. This would be the final curse in Egypt, the death of every firstborn son.

Lord, it's so easy to see Pharaoh's obstinate streak. Give me strength to admit when I'm wrong. Give me strength to come to You in repentance. Amen.

EVENING

The Voice of Experience

I was young and now I am old, yet I have never seen the righteous forsaken or their children begging bread. They are always generous and lend freely; their children will be a blessing.

PSALM 37:25–26 NIV

These are worrisome days. We worry about our jobs and the economy. We worry about what the world will be like by the time our children are entering the work world. We worry about our retirement. But the psalmist is the voice of experience who tells us we don't need to worry. We can trust that we and our children will be blessed with enough to bless others.

When worries start to overwhelm me, Lord, remind me that You have never forsaken Your people—and You never will. Amen.

DAY 307

MORNING
It's Up to You!

I place before you Life and Death, Blessing and Curse. Choose life so that you and your children will live.

DEUTERONOMY 30:19 MSG

We may feel as though we're at the mercy of fate. Some of us are lucky, some of us are unlucky, and there's nothing we can do about it. But God says that's not how things work. Instead, we each have a choice to make. When we choose life, we will find blessings everywhere we turn. But if we choose death, we will see only curses in the same circumstances. Which do we want for our children?

I choose life, God, not death. I choose Your blessings, not curses. And I want to share Your abundant life with the next generation. Amen.

EVENING
Trusting God with Our Children

"For I will fight those who fight you, and I will save your children."

ISAIAH 49:25 NLT

Until I had children, I didn't worry much. News of wars and accidents, illnesses and disasters didn't make me turn cold with fear. I got on planes without being anxious they might crash, and I wandered fearlessly through city streets. Once I had children, though, the world was full of dangers. For the first time, I learned what it really meant to trust God. I had to accept that I couldn't keep my children safe—but He could, all the way into eternity.

Only You, Lord, have the power to keep my children safe. I am helpless to protect them from all life's dangers—and so I trust them to You! Fight on their behalf, I pray. Save them from the enemy of their souls. Amen.

DAY 308

MORNING
Makeover

Since I was worse than anyone else, God had mercy on me and let me be an example of the endless patience of Christ Jesus.

1 Timothy 1:16 CEV

Saul was a Jesus hater. He went out of his way to hunt down believers to torture, imprison, and kill. Yet Christ tracked him down and confronted him in a blinding light on a dusty road. Saul's past no longer mattered. Previous sins were forgiven and forgotten. He was given a fresh start. A life makeover. We, too, are offered a life makeover. Christ offers to create a beautiful new image of Himself in us, unblemished and wrinkle-free.

Thank You for new beginnings and fresh starts, God. You have erased my sins, and now I walk free in Your unending grace! Amen.

EVENING
Fit for Service

Then Moses said to the Lord, "Please, Lord, I have never been eloquent, neither recently nor in time past, nor since You have spoken to Your servant; for I am slow of speech and slow of tongue."

Exodus 4:10 NASB

Moses heard God's voice clearly calling him to this position. Why was he balking at the task?

Remember that Moses was nothing but a murderer with the best of intentions when God first met him at that burning bush. Perhaps he took a momentary look back at his life before the Lord got hold of him.

The passage continues: "Then the anger of the Lord burned against Moses, and He said, 'Is there not your brother Aaron the Levite? . . . He shall speak for you to the people' " (Exodus 4:14, 16 NASB). Now if this was God's plan all along, why was He angry with Moses? Because the Lord wanted Moses to understand that He could and would meet all of his needs.

Lord, I am inadequate to understand Your perfection. Please help me see that Your help is like owning a store that has everything I need in utterly limitless supply. Amen.

DAY 309

MORNING
Divine Education

"All your children will be taught by the LORD, and great will be their peace."

ISAIAH 54:13 NIV

Whether or not we have our own children, most of us have children we love. As much as we love them—and we really do!—we all, if we're honest, know that in one way or another we've let these children down. So it's good to know that God will fill in the gaps we've left in our children's education. As we surrender to God both our love for them and the mistakes we've made, God will bless them with His peace.

Forgive me, Lord, for all the times I've failed the children in my life. Make up for my failures, I pray. Use other people and circumstances to help them grow in ways I haven't been able to do. Bless these children with peace of heart all the days of their lives. Amen.

EVENING
Coming Home Again

"Your children will come back to you from the distant land of the enemy."

JEREMIAH 31:16 NLT

Teenagers can be a challenge. Adolescents are struggling hard to find their identities. In the process, they often refuse to be anything like the adults who love them. That's healthy, a part of growing up—but their rejection of our deepest beliefs can be both painful and terrifying. Once again, God asks us to surrender these children into His hands, in new ways than ever before. He will go with them where we can't go, and He will bring them back again. His blessings never cease.

God, I put the teenagers in my life into Your hands. Go with them, wherever they go, and keep them safe, body and soul. Amen.

DAY 310

MORNING
Snippets of Hope

I also pray that you will understand the incredible greatness of God's power for us who believe him.

EPHESIANS 1:19 NLT

Daydreams are snippets of hope for our souls. Yearnings for something better, something more exciting, something that lifts our spirits. Some dreams are mere fancy, but others are meant to last a lifetime because God embedded them in our hearts. It's when we lose sight of those dreams that hope dies. But God offers us access to His almighty power—the very same greatness that brought His Son back from the dead. What greater hope is there?

Thank You for the dreams you wove into my heart, Father God. Please help me keep those dreams for the future alive. Amen.

EVENING
Forsaken by God?

My God, my God, why have You forsaken me? Far from my deliverance are the words of my groaning.

PSALM 22:1 NASB

Have you ever cried out to God with such despair? I have. While my clenched fists beat against my bedroom wall, twelve years' worth of tears—a maelstrom of anger, hurt, and frustration—flowed freely.

He showed me the cross. The year was 1973. I left my knapsack of grief on the bloodstained ground beneath His wooden cross. And I never looked back. He has met my every need in surprising, miraculous, and incredible ways.

Jesus, separated from the Father because of our sin, reached the ear of God with His own desperation. He experienced for us this ultimate terror. . .so that we would never be forsaken or walk alone on the road that leads to Calvary.

Where are you? On the road, walking toward Him? Sitting down, too bewildered to even formulate questions? Or are you kneeling, as I did, right at His bleeding feet?

Lord, no matter what hazards are down the road, You've got a signpost ready to hang on whatever misleading marker is already in the ground. The Son is shining ahead! Amen.

DAY 311

MORNING

Jesus Loves the Little Children

Then he took the children in his arms
and placed his hands on their
heads and blessed them.

MARK 10:16 NLT

The Gospels show us that Jesus loved children. He expressed His love to the children around Him much the same as we do to our children: with hugs and pats and kind words. He affirmed them and let them know they were important. He blessed them. Jesus is no longer walking our earth, calling children to Him for physical hugs. But He hasn't stopped blessing children. He never will.

Jesus, so many children in our world face physical and emotional suffering. Thank You that You are with these children. Find ways, I pray, to bless them and heal them. May they know Your love is real. Amen.

EVENING

Easy as ABC

God has done all this, so that we will look
for him and reach out and find him.
He isn't far from any of us.

ACTS 17:27 CEV

God is near. But we must reach out for Him. There's a line that we choose to cross, a specific action we take. We can't ooze into the kingdom of God; it's an intentional decision. It's simple, really—as simple as ABC. A is Admitting we're sinful and in need of a Savior. B is Believing that Jesus died for our sins and rose from the grave. C is Committing our lives to Him. Life everlasting is then ours.

God, You are always within reach. For that, I am so very thankful. I look forward to eternal life in Your presence. Amen.

DAY 312

MORNING

Who Is Christ to You?

"But what about you?" he asked. "Who do you say I am?" Simon Peter answered, "You are the Messiah, the Son of the living God."

MATTHEW 16:15–16 NIV

Jesus knew that once He was gone His followers would be scattered and most would die for their faith in Him. Therefore, it was crucial that they understand exactly who Christ was.

Six days after this conversation with Peter, a miraculous event occurred. Jesus took Peter, James, and John up a high mountain. And there He was transfigured before them. "His face shone like the sun, and his clothes became as white as the light" (Matthew 17:2 NIV). Moses and Elijah appeared with Jesus and spoke with Him.

A bright cloud overshadowed them and a voice from heaven said, "This is my Son, whom I love; with him I am well pleased; Listen to him!" (Matthew 17:5 NIV). Just the awesome sound of God's voice caused the disciples to fall on their faces in fear.

Jesus Christ: Son of God, Son of Man, Redeemer, displayed His glory to these disciples. Do you know Him as Savior?

Lord, let me declare as Peter did, "You are the Christ, the Son of God." Amen.

EVENING

Long-Term Blessings

"So there is hope for your descendants," declares the LORD. "Your children will return to their own land."

JEREMIAH 31:17 NIV

We are often shortsighted, but God always takes the long perspective. He not only looks into the future; He also is building it right now. At this very moment, He is blessing you in ways that will one day bless your children and their children and *their* children. His blessings flow down through the generations. We may look at the present moment and feel discouraged—but God does long-term work.

I am so grateful, so humbled and amazed, Lord, that right now, in the midst of the daily troubles and frustrations of my life, You are working to build hope, not only in my life but also in the lives of generations to come. Amen.

DAY 313

MORNING
Aim High

My aim is to raise hopes by pointing the way to life without end.

TITUS 1:2 MSG

No woman is an island. We're more like peninsulas. Although we sometimes feel isolated, we're connected to one another by the roots of womanhood. We're all in this together, girls. As we look around, we can't help but see sisters who need a hand, a warm smile, a caring touch. And especially hope. People need hope, and if we know the Lord—the source of eternal hope—it's up to us to point the way through love.

I have so many women in my life who are constant reminders of the one eternal source of hope—You, Father God. Thank You for placing these beautiful women in my life. Amen.

EVENING
A Thousand Generations

"Know therefore that the LORD your God, He is God, the faithful God, who keeps His covenant and His lovingkindness to a thousandth generation."

DEUTERONOMY 7:9 NASB

Most of us worry about our children. We may worry, too, about our grandchildren and even our great-grandchildren. God says He will be faithful not only to them but also to a thousand generations into the future. That's hard to comprehend—but remember, you are here today because God was also with the thousand generations that came before you. He's not going to fail your children or grandchildren. . .or great-great-great-grandchildren!

Faithful God, thank You that You have created a chain of blessing that reaches back through past generations—and stretches far ahead into the future. Amen.

DAY 314

MORNING
God's Promise to Our Children

"I will pour out my Spirit on your descendants, and my blessing on your children."

Isaiah 44:3 NLT

We'd like to give so many things to the children we love: health. . .safety. . .happiness . . .security. Most of all, we wish we could send our love with them wherever they go throughout their entire lives. We long to wrap them up forever in our arms the way we could when they were small. We can't, of course. That's one of the hard lessons of parenthood. But God's Spirit will do what we can't.

Holy Spirit, I trust the children I love into Your care. Bless them even when I am no longer around to help them. Keep them close to You. Amen.

EVENING
Home Sweet Home

My people shall dwell in a peaceable habitation, and in sure dwellings, and in quiet resting places.

Isaiah 32:18 KJV

God has also promised to bless our homes. He's not talking about a vague, "spiritual" blessing that's hard to truly grasp. He's promising us something concrete that exists in the real world: a home where we can feel safe, where we can rest and be quiet. So the next time you look around your house and see worn carpets, clutter, or smudgy windows, remember that your home is blessed by God—and He lives there with you!

Thank You, God, for sharing my home with me—for making it a place of peace and safety. Help me to rest tonight in Your presence. Amen.

DAY 315

MORNING
Fill 'Er Up

"What strength do I have,
that I should still hope?"
JOB 6:11 NIV

Run, rush, hurry, dash: a typical American woman's day. It's easy to identify with David's lament in Psalm 22:14 (NASB): "I am poured out like water. . .my heart is like wax; it is melted within me." Translation: I'm pooped; I'm numb; I'm drained dry. When we are at the end of our strength, God doesn't want us to lose hope of the refilling He can provide if we only lift our empty cups to Him.

Fill me up, Lord! I need Your heavenly
presence. . .Your strength. . .Your comfort.
Thank You for the hope you provide
in the daily-ness of life! Amen.

EVENING
A Life Turned Around

The man said, "Who made you ruler and judge over us? Are you thinking of killing me as you killed the Egyptian?" Then Moses was afraid and thought, "What I did must have become known."
EXODUS 2:14 NIV

Moses had killed an Egyptian. Was it right? No. God Himself administers true justice, in His own time, to those who deserve punishment.

Later, God revealed His plan to Moses, a plan to bring the Israelites out of Egypt. So when Moses asks God, "Who am I that I should go to Pharaoh and bring the Israelites out of Egypt?" it comes from the heart of one who has murdered and knows his guilt before God. But instead of rebuke Moses hears, "I will be with you. . . . I AM WHO I AM" (Exodus 3:11–12, 14 NIV). This is the same "I Am" who calls you to serve Him today.

Lord, Moses felt unworthy to serve You
because of his great sin. Forgive me of
my sins and focus my life on You. Amen.

DAY 316

MORNING

Paid in Full

Do your best. Work from the heart for your real Master, for God, confident that you'll get paid in full when you come into your inheritance.

COLOSSIANS 3:24 MSG

Paul understood how frustrating it can be to work hard and get paid little, to feel as though no one is appreciating your full effort and skill. In this verse, he reminds us again: no matter what our job or profession, we work for Christ. Even on those days when we hate our jobs—and we all have at least a few of those days!—He will bless our efforts.

Bless my work, God. Remind me that I do it for You. Use even the most ordinary and boring tasks to build Your kingdom. Amen.

EVENING

The Work of Righteousness

And the work of righteousness will be peace, and the service of righteousness, quietness and confidence forever.

ISAIAH 32:17 NASB

What if every day when we started our work, we remembered that we're serving God and His kingdom? If instead of obsessing about success or failure, our paycheck or a promotion or any other earthly goal, we focused all our hearts and minds on building the kingdom of God? If we did that, this verse promises, we'll be blessed with peace—a quiet and eternal confidence that we are doing the work God needs us to be doing.

Tonight, Lord, I give You tomorrow's work. Help me to surrender to You all my worry and striving, all my pride in my own achievement, and my despair at my failures. Let me sleep tonight with a sense of quiet peace, confident that You will use my work as You see fit. Amen.

DAY 317

MORNING

Laugh a Rainbow

"When I see the rainbow in the clouds, I will remember the eternal covenant between God and every living creature on earth."

GENESIS 9:16 NLT

Ever feel like a cloud is hanging over your head? Sometimes the cloud darkens to the color of bruises, and we're deluged with cold rain that seems to have no end. When you're in the midst of one of life's thunderstorms, tape this saying to your mirror: "Cry a river, laugh a rainbow." The rainbow, the symbol of hope that God gave Noah after the flood, reminds us even today that every storm will eventually pass.

The rainbows You place in the sky after a storm are lovely reminders of the hope we have in You, God. Because of You, I know that the storms of life are only temporary. . .and You will bring beauty from the storms. Amen.

EVENING

Embrace Life!

Take your everyday, ordinary life—your sleeping, eating, going-to-work, and walking-around life—and place it before God as an offering. Embracing what God does for you is the best thing you can do.

ROMANS 12:1 MSG

Our attitudes shape our emotions. They also shape what we see in the world around us. If we look at the world with angry, suspicious eyes, we see slights and insults everywhere we turn. But if we look at each aspect of our lives as an offering to God, we will find blessings instead of curses. When we open our hearts and embrace life, we are blessed.

Take from me, God, my tendency to get irritated, to become hurt or defensive. Fill me instead with a willing acceptance of each thing in my life. I surrender it all to You. Amen.

MORNING

Then Joseph said to his brothers, "Please come closer to me." And they came closer. And he said, "I am your brother Joseph, whom you sold into Egypt. Now do not be grieved or angry with yourselves, because you sold me here, for God sent me before you to preserve life."

GENESIS 45:4–5 NASB

How many of us could forgive as Joseph did? His jealous siblings kidnapped him, threw him into a pit, and then allowed him to be sold into slavery. Yet Joseph trusted that from God's perspective—not his own—his trials had a purpose.

Is there a hurt so deep inside that you have never shared it with another human being? Perhaps someone in your own family has rejected or betrayed you. Remember the pain suffered by Joseph; remember the anguish of Jesus Christ, who was betrayed by one as close as a brother, Judas Iscariot. God knows your pain and He is strong enough to remove any burden.

Lord, sometimes I want to enjoy my agony a while longer. Show me the brilliance of Your forgiveness that I might trust You in the trial and not miss the outcome You've planned. Amen.

EVENING

The Greatest Blessing

Praise the Lord; praise God our savior! For each day he carries us in his arms.

PSALM 68:19 NLT

When we count our blessings, we usually list the good things in our lives. We may remember to include spiritual blessings like peace and joy and a sense of the Lord's leading. But do we remember the greatest blessing of all? God—the Creator of the universe—is present with us every minute of every day! What greater blessing could there possibly be than that?

Thank You, Savior God, for carrying me in Your strong arms. Teach me to rely on You. I praise Your constant, loving presence in my life. Amen.

DAY 319

MORNING

Comfort in the Truth of God's Word

Do not snatch your word of truth from me,
for your regulations are my only hope.

PSALM 119:43 NLT

Bibles wear and tear. Papers get discarded. Hard drives crash. But memorizing scripture assures us that God's Word will never be lost. His truth will always be at our disposal, any moment of the day or night when we need a word of encouragement, of guidance, of hope. Like a phone call from heaven, our Father communicates to us via scripture implanted in our hearts. But it is up to us to build the signal tower.

Your Word is a never-ending source of hope in my life. When troubles come, I find comfort, peace, strength, love. . . Whatever my soul thirsts for, I know I will find it in the Bible. Amen.

EVENING

Inner Treasure

We now have this light shining in our hearts,
but we ourselves are like fragile clay jars
containing this great treasure.

2 CORINTHIANS 4:7 NLT

God is not only present in the world around us; He is also present in our hearts, in our inner beings. Imagine that! The same God who made the stars, who keeps our sun burning and our earth turning around the sun, who waters and nourishes all the life on our planet—that God lives inside you. You carry treasure within your very being.

Shine from me, God. Fill my clay jar with Your treasure. May others see You in me and be blessed. Amen.

DAY 320

MORNING
All I Want

"You are my place of refuge.
You are all I really want in life."

PSALM 142:5 NLT

Earlier, we spoke of the refuge God offers us in trouble, the blessings that come to life even in the midst of sorrow and hardship. In this verse, the psalmist reminds us that in good times *and* bad, God Himself is our safe place. When we believe He is the only thing we truly need, we no longer have to worry about death and loss and failure. We can rest in the knowledge that we are blessed with His presence—no matter what.

Teach me, gracious God, not to cling to people and things. Remind me that so long as I have You, I have everything. Amen.

EVENING
The Shelter of God's Love

In the shelter of your presence. . .you keep them safe. . .from accusing tongues.

PSALM 31:20 NIV

We all worry about what other people think of us. We want people to like us. We want them to approve of us. We want to impress them. When we succeed in doing all that, we feel good about ourselves—but when we don't, we often feel less worthy, full of despair and self-doubt. We don't have to live like that. Instead, we can live in the shelter of God's presence, knowing that His love is always with us.

Shelter me, Lord, from the negative opinions of others. Help me to rely only on You for my worth. Amen.

DAY 321

MORNING
Rescued from My Enemies

He reached down from on high and took hold of me; he drew me out of deep waters. He rescued me from my powerful enemy, from my foes, who were too strong for me. They confronted me in the day of my disaster, but the LORD was my support.

PSALM 18:16–18 NIV

David wrote this psalm at a time when he was being pursued by Saul. Imagine David's terror as he and his band of loyal followers huddled within the concealing walls of caves for shelter while Saul sought to slaughter him. During this time of desperation, David learned to lean on God's power, convinced in his heart that He alone could rescue him from harm.

Have you ever known such desperation? Did you realize that He could act in your behalf, despite the obvious circumstances?

The very nature and character of God demands that He rescue those whom He loves. When confronted with a crisis, like David, you can put your life in His hands.

Lord, when all is lost, I thank You that You reach out to me with Your mighty hand of rescue. Your welcoming hand is a lifeline in any storm. Amen.

EVENING
How Should I Talk to God?

"This, then, is how you should pray: 'Our Father in heaven, hallowed be your name, your kingdom come, your will be done, on earth as it is in heaven. Give us today our daily bread. And forgive us our debts, as we also have forgiven our debtors. And lead us not into temptation, but deliver us from the evil one.' "

MATTHEW 6:9–13 NIV

Jesus gave us an example of how to pray in His famous petition that was recorded in Matthew 6:9–13. We don't need to suffer with an anxious heart or feel ensnared by this world with no one to hear our cry for help. We can talk to God, right now, and He will listen. The act of prayer is as simple as launching a boat into the Sea of Galilee, but it's as miraculous as walking on water.

God, how wonderful it is that You hear me when I call out to You, and that You answer with exactly what I need. Amen.

DAY 322

MORNING

Why Jesus Spoke in Parables

And the disciples came and said to Him, "Why do You speak to them in parables?"

MATTHEW 13:10 NASB

Jesus' main purpose in coming to earth was to communicate God's love by His perfect words and actions. Certainly He could clearly articulate a point when He desired. So why did He shroud many of His teachings behind a veil of curious stories?

Jesus Himself explains: "Therefore I speak to them in parables; because while seeing they do not see, and while hearing they do not hear, nor do they understand" (Matthew 13:13 NASB). Who was Jesus talking about? Only moments before, He'd been conversing with the scribes and Pharisees. And although they had great knowledge of God's Word, they refused to see its very fulfillment before their eyes. Everything Jesus did and said confirmed that He was their long-awaited Messiah. Yet they closed their eyes and stopped up their ears.

Yet to those who He knew would respond, He provided plain words. How open have you been to God's Word?

Lord, Your truth surrounds me. Please lift my eyelids to see it and stir my heart to respond to Your Word. Amen.

EVENING

God Is Doing Something New

"See, I am doing a new thing! Now it springs up; do you not perceive it? I am making a way in the wilderness and streams in the wasteland."

ISAIAH 43:19 NIV

Imagine that desert, dry and barren—with no hope of even a cactus flower to bloom—suddenly coming to life with bubbling pools of pure water. That is what God promises us. He is doing something new in our lives. He is making a path through what feels impassable, and He will command a stream to flow through the wilderness of our pasts, places where we had only known the wasteland of sin and a landscape of despair. Have faith and bring your empty buckets to the stream.

Father, thank You for Your provision, hope, and joy. Without You, life is dry and hostile. Come into my life and quench my thirst. You are the only One who can fulfill me. Amen.

DAY 323

MORNING

Normal Life

"My Presence will go with you,
and I will give you rest."

EXODUS 33:14 NIV

Sometimes life seems so *hard*. We face one challenge after another: sickness, problems with our parents or our children, financial worries, car trouble, broken relationships. We say to ourselves, *When will life get back to normal?*—but it never does. Finally, we have to accept that these endless challenges *are* normal life, so we'll need to look somewhere else for relief. When we turn to God, we find His presence already there, offering us rest even in the midst of all life's challenges.

God, remind me that You are the only true source of peace and rest in my life. Help me to rely on You to keep me steady through all of life's ups and downs. Amen.

EVENING

God's Contagious Joy

You will fill me with joy in your presence,
with eternal pleasures at your right hand.

PSALM 16:11 NIV

Life isn't *all* hard! God longs to share with us His own joy. Think about how easy it is to catch a good mood from your spouse or a close friend. It's the same with God. His presence is never sad or gloomy. It's not disapproving and stern. His joy is greater than any human's. When we spend time in His presence, we catch His joy. We find pleasures that will last throughout all eternity.

Keep me near to You, Lord, so that I can share Your joy. May I "catch" happiness and peace from being close to You. Amen.

DAY 324

MORNING

Which Way Do I Go?

I will instruct you and teach you in the way you should go; I will counsel you with my loving eye on you.

PSALM 32:8 NIV

God says, *"I will instruct you and teach you in the way you should go; I will counsel you with my loving eye on you."* That is truly what we need in a noisy world that may offer little reliable or usable advice. God not only promises to guide us, to teach us the way we should go, but He plans on doing it with a loving eye on us. For the most loving counsel, listen to the voice of God. He's talking to you, and He has something important to say that will change your life.

Wonderful Counselor, help me to be receptive to Your voice and to always trust in Your guidance. Amen.

EVENING

Screaming God's Name

The LORD is near to all who call upon Him.

PSALM 145:18 NASB

The Hebrew word that's translated *call* in this verse doesn't mean that we're calling God the way we call a dog. It's not the same thing as calling a friend on the phone. Instead, the word is a lot stronger. It means to scream God's name out loud so that everyone around us can hear. It's an affirmation of our faith in God's very identity. God's presence is already there with us—but a call like that changes our own hearts so that we finally *know* He's there.

God, I know You're not deaf. I'm shouting Your name at the top of my lungs, though, because I want to change my own attitude. I want to make room for You in my heart. Amen.

DAY 325

MORNING

Joseph Honors God

Now Joseph was well-built and handsome, and after a while his master's wife took notice of Joseph and said, "Come to bed with me!" But he refused.

GENESIS 39:6–8 NIV

Joseph could neither dishonor Potiphar, an Egyptian officer of Pharaoh's, nor disobey his God. But day after day Potiphar's wife kept after Joseph, hoping to wear down his resistance. But when Joseph's outer garment fell away as he fled, she proceeded to act like a scorned woman and had Joseph thrown into jail.

But God had a plan. Through an incredible chain of events Joseph was found innocent and released from prison after he correctly interpreted the king's disturbing dream. Eventually Joseph's position was restored, and he created a stockpile of grain that saw both Egypt and Joseph's restored family through a great famine—the one he had predicted in that dream.

Joseph's moral stand preserved the very ancestral line leading up to Jesus Christ.

Lord, I can't look ahead to see how a critical moment of obedience fits into Your overall plan. Please give me Your strength when my human desires threaten to overpower me. Amen.

EVENING

The Angel of God's Presence

The angel of His presence saved them.

ISAIAH 63:9 NASB

God is always with us. He understands how limited our perceptions are, though, so sometimes He sends "angels" into our lives whom we can touch with our hands, hear and see with our physical ears and eyes. The Hebrew word used here is *malak*: a messenger, an ambassador, an envoy. Our lives are full of people who can make real to us the presence of God. They carry His messages. We just need to listen.

God, thank You for sending so many of Your messengers into my life. My friends, my family—even my pets!—carry Your love to me. Through them, I hear Your voice. Amen.

DAY 326

MORNING

Divine Imaginings and Sublime Aspirations

He has made everything beautiful in its time. He has also set eternity in the human heart.

ECCLESIASTES 3:11 NIV

Let's join hands. Let's celebrate. God has made everything beautiful in its time. He has also set eternity in the human heart. Never sit in the gutter when the steps of paradise are at your feet! So, widen your scope. See beauty in all things great and small. Soar free. Imagine beyond the ordinary. Love large. Forgive lavishly. Hope always. Expect a miracle.

Father, give me a contagious enthusiasm for life. You have given me everything I need. Amen.

EVENING

Stop Being Afraid!

"Be strong and courageous! Do not be afraid or discouraged. For the LORD your God is with you wherever you go."

JOSHUA 1:9 NLT

The Bible is constantly telling us not to be afraid. There are at least 145 verses that communicate that meaning in one form or another, as though God is trying very hard to get the message across: *"I AM with you. Why are you so worried? Please trust Me!"* He is patient with our fear—but He longs to take it from us.

You know how easily I become scared and worried. So much in life makes me anxious. I can't talk myself out of being like this, no matter how hard I try—so instead, I'm just giving all my fear to You. Take it, Lord God; replace it with Your strength and courage. Amen.

DAY 327

MORNING

Remain in Jesus

"If you remain in me and I in you,
you will bear much fruit;
apart from me you can do nothing."
JOHN 15:5 NIV

Many of us believe independence is a good thing. We feel we should be able to "go it alone," that we should be strong enough to "stand on our own two feet." Jesus wants us to look at things differently. He wants us to open our tight grip on our lives and instead take His hand. He knows that only then will we be able to live truly productive lives, lives that are blessed with spiritual and physical blessings.

I give up, God. On my own,
I just keep failing. I can't do it.
But You can! Amen.

EVENING

Living the "What-If" Blues

And we know that in all things God
works for the good of those who love him,
who have been called according
to his purpose.
ROMANS 8:28 NIV

All of life's "not knowing" can prompt a lot of "what-ifs." Pray for wisdom and guidance, knowing that God will give them to you freely and lovingly. But if you still take a wrong turn, embrace His promise that He will work all things for good for those who love Him. Hard to imagine, but the Lord really does mean "all things." Praying and embracing His promises will go a long way in keeping you on the right road, as well as easing those "what-if" blues.

God, I'm so grateful You can turn evil
into good and sorrow into joy. Amen.

MORNING

Do not fret.

PSALM 37:1 NIV

Instead of fretting, delight in the Lord, and He will give you all your heart's desires. Especially if one of those desires is to be free from fretting. And even if you've prayed, breathed, and tried to relax, and the worries still come—like houseflies that just refuse to find their way back out the screen—then don't fret about fretting. Trust. Commit. Be still. Wait. Refrain. Turn. Give generously. Lend freely. Do good. Hope. Consider. Observe. Seek peace. Just don't fret.

Dear God, You know our hearts and the worries that prey on our minds. Please help us to stay busy doing good and to grow in trust and patience. Please help us to let go of control we never had to start with. Amen.

EVENING

Loving-Kindness

Yet the LORD will command his lovingkindness in the day time, and in the night his song shall be with me, and my prayer unto the God of my life.

PSALM 42:8 KJV

Think of it—God is with you each moment of the day! He's in the car or on the bus with you as you go to work or run errands. He sits at the table with you while you eat. He never leaves you; His love and kindness are always right there beside you. And at night, when you go to bed, He's singing you His lullaby.

May I fall asleep tonight, loving Lord, with the sound of Your lullaby in my heart. Fill my thoughts with prayer as I drift into sleep. Amen.

DAY 329

MORNING
Our Advocate and Defender

"Therefore everyone who confesses Me before men, I will also confess him before My Father who is in heaven."

MATTHEW 10:32 NASB

Busy with friends her own age, my older sister didn't usually accompany my younger sister and me on our morning trek to school.

However, when we returned home one day relating that two big kids had threatened to beat us up the next day, she rallied to the cause. As she instructed, we traversed our normal route while she lagged watchfully a short distance behind.

Suddenly, the two boys jumped out of the bushes ahead. And just like a superwoman, our sister pounced on them, easily overpowering both and giving them bloody noses in the process. It felt so incredible to have an invincible defender!

If we know Jesus Christ and have responded to His invitation to receive Him as Savior, Jesus remains forever our Advocate. Know that you are so precious to Jesus that He gave His life for you. Doesn't it feel incredible to have Jesus as your defender?

Lord, how reassuring it is to know You mightily defend not only my body but also my soul against attack. Amen.

EVENING
The Answer Is No One

The LORD is my light and my salvation—whom shall I fear?

PSALM 27:1 NIV

When you accept Christ as your Savior, you get certain things in return. You get an understanding of good and evil—and you get the knowledge that you are on the side of good. You get a clearer vision of the darkness in your life—and you get a friend who is always with you, no matter how dark things seem to be. And you get peace—through knowing your place before God. That you stand in His grace, blameless and pure, and you have a place in heaven created just for you. A place no one can take away.

Dear Jesus, help me to feel You at my side. Amen.

MORNING

The people who walk in darkness will see a great light; those who live in a dark land, the light will shine on them.

ISAIAH 9:2 NASB

The Israelites had no idea that such a great depth of darkness had overtaken them until they were in the midst of it. God previously had provided them with great light, for He communicated directly with their leaders. But the Israelites chose to act as though the switch of truth had never been turned on. They were caught up in the dark snare of idolatry.

Are you refusing to act on God's insight, insisting on pursuits that distract you from worshipping Him? How we spend our time is but a habit, and habits can be changed by making a new pattern for our actions. Walk in the light, as your Father intended.

Lord, change the desire of my heart to seek and know You better. Take my life and use me for Your purposes. Amen.

EVENING

Pilgrims

Blessed are those whose strength is in you,
whose hearts are set on pilgrimage. . . .
They go from strength to strength,
till each appears before God in Zion.

PSALM 84:5, 7 NIV

Pilgrims are people who go on long journeys, with God as their only destination. In a sense, our entire lives can be pilgrimages. Even though God is *always* with us, we perceive our life as a journey toward Him, with stopping places along the way. Again and again, God meets us anew—all the way to heaven.

Journey with me, God, as I travel through my life. Teach me new things along the way. Meet me in new ways at each phase of the journey. My heart is set on You, for You are both my companion along the way and my destination. Amen.

DAY 331

MORNING
God's Promise

"I'll stay with you, I'll protect you wherever you go. . . . I'll stick with you until I've done everything I promised you."
GENESIS 28:15 MSG

We really can't hear it enough—God will stay with us! He's not going to get tired of us and walk away. He's not going to give up on us because we keep making stupid mistakes. He doesn't get bored or angry, and He's never inattentive or preoccupied with something else. There's no danger too big or too small for Him to handle. He'll stick with us for eternity!

Creator God, thank You for sticking with me over the course of my life. I am so grateful for Your promises at work in my soul. Amen.

EVENING
Planting

"I planted the seed, Apollos watered it, but God has been making it grow."
1 CORINTHIANS 3:6 NIV

Have you ever hesitated to engage in a spiritual discussion with a person because you didn't know how he would take it or you felt like you didn't have the time required to build a relationship with him? Of course, in an ideal world we'd have time to sit and chat with everyone for days, and the coffee would be free. But the fact that our world isn't ideal should not prevent us from planting a seed. You just never know what might happen to it. And that makes for some exciting gardening.

Dear God, thank You for allowing me to work for Your kingdom. Help me to plant more seeds. Amen.

DAY 332

MORNING
Our Song

By day the LORD directs his love, at night his song is with me—a prayer to the God of my life.

PSALM 42:8 NIV

All through the Bible, we find people worshipping God through song. They sing to God about winning battles and the birth of babies. They sing songs of lament and songs of praise, songs sinking with sorrow and songs bouncing with joy. There is, of course, a whole book devoted just to this exercise: Psalms. . . . By day God guides us, and at night He still leaves the doors of communication open. What do you think His song is saying to you? What do you want to sing to Him?

Dear God, help me listen for Your song, and help me find the words to sing praise to You every day. Amen.

EVENING
Homes and Hugs

"The eternal God is a dwelling place, and underneath are the everlasting arms."

DEUTERONOMY 33:27 NASB

All of us need a home, a place where we feel we belong, a place of safety where we can let down our guards and rest. But no set of four walls will ever be as true a home as God's presence! All of us also need hugs from the people who love us. We need the comfort of being enveloped by love. But no human hug is as strong as God's.

God, You are my heart's home— and Your eternal arms embrace my entire being with love. Amen.

DAY 333

MORNING
Glad Hearts

You have. . .made him glad with the joy of your presence.

Psalm 21:6 NIV

The psalmist wasn't afraid to yell at God; the Psalms are full of anger, rage even. They express the long-ago poet's despair, frustration, and resentment. But the psalmist also experienced the joy of living in God's presence. In between all those angry psalms, verse after verse assures us that our God is a joyful God, a God of gladness—and in His presence we, too, will be glad.

Just being with You, Lord, makes me happy. Keep me close to You all through the busy hours that lie ahead. Amen.

EVENING
Our Great Contender

Do not be far from me, Lord. Awake, and rise to my defense! Contend for me, my God and Lord. Vindicate me in your righteousness, Lord my God.

Psalm 35:22–24 NIV

Our Lord God is the greatest warrior of all time. He is our guide, our leader, our defender, our Shield. He is all-powerful, all-knowing, all-mighty, and all-good. Why would we ever hesitate to call on Him? Why would we ever think that our own strength could somehow be diminished by being supported by the Creator of the universe? The next time you find yourself facing a battle, don't wait. Don't try to do it on your own. Don't stand up by yourself. Ask God to contend for you.

Almighty God, please defend me from my enemies and help me fight my battles. Amen.

DAY 334

MORNING
Who Are the Faithful?

Help, LORD, for the godly man ceases to be, for the faithful disappear from among the sons of men.

PSALM 12:1 NASB

Who are the faithful? They are the ones who continue to follow God, no matter what obstacles are thrown in their path. One of the faithful, a dear friend who has debilitating multiple sclerosis, is one of the most joyful Christians I know.

Another friend has led a Bible study for years, despite the fact that her husband is frequently out of work and their finances are at times nearly nonexistent.

By now you have probably decided that it doesn't pay to become one of my friends. But I must reassure you that neither of these women consider shrinking back from following Christ. Instead, they agree with the apostle Paul that these present circumstances and trials are but "light and momentary" compared with the peace we will have in Christ for all eternity (2 Corinthians 4:17 NIV).

Lord, I have watched people carry burdens that, humanly speaking, should be unbearable. Yet with these trials You give them incredible joy. I praise You for all You are! Amen.

EVENING
Body and Soul

But if the Spirit of Him who raised Jesus from the dead dwells in you, He who raised Christ Jesus from the dead will also give life to your mortal bodies through His Spirit who dwells in you.

ROMANS 8:11 NASB

We already mentioned that the living God lives inside us. This isn't only a spiritual promise. This verse from Paul's pen tells us that the Spirit of God—the same powerful Spirit who brought Jesus back to life—lives in our physical bodies. Our arms and legs, brains and lungs, hearts and intestines are all the dwelling place of God!

Fill my physical body with Your energy and life, God. May Your Spirit use my body to do Your work on earth. Amen.

DAY 335

MORNING

Above All

Above all, love each other deeply,
because love covers over a multitude of sins.

1 PETER 4:8 NIV

How deep does your love go? Does it go as far as the distance that grows between two people? Does it cover little insults? Is it deep enough to silence words that should not be said? How deep does your love go? Does it go deep enough to trust? Can it cover over deceit? Does it go deep enough to swallow up betrayal? How deep does Jesus' love go?

Dear Jesus, help me to love
as You love. Amen.

EVENING

Making God Visible

No one has seen God at any time;
if we love one another, God abides in us,
and His love is perfected in us.

1 JOHN 4:12 NASB

In this verse, John is describing the "angel of God's presence" that we spoke of earlier. Not only do others carry God's message of love to us in visible, tangible ways, but we, too, are called to be God's "angels," His ambassadors who carry His love into the world in all sorts of concrete ways. When we do, He is present with others—and He is present with us!

Lord God, make me a messenger of Your
love. Help me to carry Your Spirit of joy
and reconciliation into the world.
Remind me that I am Your ambassador
to everyone I meet, and You are
counting on me to represent
You faithfully. Amen.

MORNING

"I will ask the Father, and He will give you another Helper, that He may be with you forever."

JOHN 14:16 NASB

The disciples had the amazing privilege of Jesus' physical presence. They walked with Him and talked with Him. They knew His voice and the shape of His hands. They saw His smile and looked into His eyes. But then they faced an awful emptiness when He was no longer physically with them. Jesus understood how they were going to feel. He promised them—and us—that though He can no longer be seen or touched, His Spirit would never leave them.

Thank You, Jesus, for sending Your Spirit to help us when we feel alone. I rely on Your presence in the hours ahead. Amen.

EVENING

God's Love Songs

"The LORD your God is living among you. He is a mighty savior. He will take delight in you with gladness. With his love, he will calm all your fears. He will rejoice over you with joyful songs."

ZEPHANIAH 3:17 NLT

On the darkest, dreariest days—those days when just getting out of bed seems to take all your strength—remember: God is there with you, living in the midst of your life. You make Him happy, so happy that He's singing you love songs. Let His love calm and comfort your heart.

Tonight, Lord, I long to hear Your love songs. Sharpen the ears of my spirit, so that I can hear Your voice. Comfort me with Your love. Calm my troubled heart. Amen.

DAY 337

MORNING
Morning Orders

"Have you ever given orders to the morning, or shown the dawn its place, that it might take the earth by the edges and shake the wicked out of it?"

JOB 38:12–13 NIV

God poses many rhetorical questions, all to show the might and wonder and mystery of the Almighty. In these words are some amazing ideas that really cause us to stop and consider who God is. And that is what we should do, especially when we face our worst trials. Stop and consider who God is. That no matter what happens, He will not leave us. And that He alone has the answers for us.

Thank You, God, for providing glimpses of You in Your Word. Amen.

EVENING
A Furious Storm

When He got into the boat, His disciples followed Him. And behold, there arose a great storm on the sea, so that the boat was being covered with the waves; but Jesus Himself was asleep. And they came to Him and woke Him, saying, "Save us, Lord; we are perishing!"

MATTHEW 8:23–25 NASB

The disciples were in the midst of a storm. Yet Jesus was with them in the boat. They woke Him, in the throes of panic, sure that the waves would swallow them up. Jesus took the disciples to the height of the storm's raging fury, yet all the time He was with them. Later on in this chapter, Jesus rose up and rebuked the winds and sea and everything became perfectly calm. Yes, the storms of life will attempt to ravage me, but Christ is there amid the frenzy, ready to deliver by just the power of His Word. He will carry me safely to the other side of the shore.

Lord, keep my eyes focused not on the storms of life, but on Your incredible power to deliver me from them. Amen.

DAY 338

MORNING

King Forever and Ever

The LORD is King forever and ever;
nations have perished from His land.

PSALM 10:16 NASB

Satan, whose dominion is the world, has devoted all his efforts to eradicating Christianity. Yet, while the evil one's influence can seem as ugly as any ink stain, Satan's mark on this earth will not be permanent. The reason? God's Son, Jesus Christ, lives forever within those who call upon His name. And despite the efforts of the evil one, Jesus will remain King and will one day soon come back to claim this earth for His own, forever and ever.

Are you assured of your place in Christ's kingdom?

Lord, as this world becomes increasingly evil, reflecting the one who holds its "title deed," remind me that You're coming back to claim all that is rightfully Yours. Amen.

EVENING

Glue

He is before all things,
and in him all things hold together.

COLOSSIANS 1:17 NIV

Have you ever felt like your life was falling apart? We need to know that there is Someone who is holding us together, even when we feel like falling apart. Jesus has been with us since the beginning. He is "the beginning and the firstborn from among the dead" (v. 18 NIV). He can handle our struggles. And He can put us back together again, even if we let everything fall. There is always hope in Him.

Dear Jesus, thank You for being a friend I can always count on. Help me remember to trust You with all the details of my life. Amen.

DAY 339

MORNING
Learn It by Heart!

"The LORD himself goes before you and will be with you; he will never leave you nor forsake you. Do not be afraid; do not be discouraged."

DEUTERONOMY 31:8 NIV

Here's that same message again: "Do not be afraid!" Learn this verse by heart. Repeat it whenever you feel discouraged or anxious. Say it so many times that it wears a groove in your mind and in your heart. . .until you begin to truly believe that God will never leave you.

When my heart is fearful and discouraged, Lord, remind me that You are there. You will never leave me, and You are at work in my life. Amen.

EVENING
Both Far and Near

"Am I a God who is only close at hand?" says the LORD. "No, I am far away at the same time. . . . Am I not everywhere in all the heavens and earth?"

JEREMIAH 23:23–24 NLT

Some people say God is too holy to be present in the ordinary world, while others insist He is in nature, in human faces, in our own minds and bodies. In this verse, God says, *"You're both right! I'm right here with you*—and *I'm far too great to be contained by your small world. But it doesn't matter. Far or near, I am everywhere!"*

God, thank You that You are a great God, beyond my ability to comprehend—and thank You that You are also a loving God, who makes a home in my own heart. Amen.

DAY 340

MORNING

He Wrote Them Both

God has made the one as well as the other.

Ecclesiastes 7:14 NIV

We need to learn to see God's grace not just in what He does for us, but in what He doesn't do. And we need to realize that the bit of the world we see is just one small piece of a very large story. So when we are standing in the middle of the book and the chapter is a sad and dreary one, we need to remember at least these two things: first, there are many pages to come; and second, it is by God's grace we are living this story, good or bad as it may be.

Dear author of my life, help me to remember to trust You to write my story. Amen.

EVENING

A Message from the Holy One

A Message from. . .God, who lives in Eternity, whose name is Holy: "I live in the high and holy places, but also with the low-spirited, the spirit-crushed."

Isaiah 57:15 MSG

The theological term for a God who lives high above our physical world is *transcendence*, while *immanence* is the word for a God who is present everywhere we turn. In this verse, God tells us again, "*Yes, I'm high and holy—but not so high that I'll ever leave you, even when you're feeling sad and crushed by life.*"

Thank You, God of eternity, that You are both transcendent and immanent—both high and holy, and gentle and near. Amen.

DAY 341

MORNING
False Prophets

"Beware of the false prophets, who come to you in sheep's clothing, but inwardly are ravenous wolves. You will know them by their fruits. Grapes are not gathered from thorn bushes nor figs from thistles, are they?"

MATTHEW 7:15–16 NASB

God gave us a way to recognize the true teachers from the "wolves." "You will know them by their fruits," scripture says. Those who abide in Christ preach the message that is consistent with the one Christ Himself taught—that salvation comes to us by the grace of God, and is obtained through the belief that Christ's blood, shed on Calvary's cross, has cleansed us from our sin.

Don't be afraid to ask questions. True teachers will always be pleased to give straightforward answers.

Lord, there are so many voices. Please help us to hear Yours so that we won't be led astray by the wolves in sheep's clothing who make a mockery out of Your great sacrifice for us. Amen.

EVENING
Father God

You are the helper of the fatherless.

PSALM 10:14 NIV

Some of us were blessed with great fathers. These were men who enriched our lives as role models, trainers, encouragers, supporters, huggers, comforters, and friends. But if your father was never there for you or is now gone, run to your Father God and spend some time with Him. Let Him heal the places in you that are hurting and give you the confidence that comes from the only person in the world who has loved you since before the day you were born—and will continue to love you forever.

---

*Dear Father,
hear and bless Your children. Amen.*

DAY 342

MORNING
Glimpses of God

"You will seek Me and find Me when you search for Me with all your heart."
JEREMIAH 29:13 NASB

If God's always there, why can't we feel Him? If He's real, why doesn't He give us more proof of His presence? People have asked these questions for thousands of years. They're a part of human experience. But here's the answer: the life of faith wasn't meant to be easy. You have to give everything you have inside you—and only *then* will you begin to catch glimpses of God's presence, glimpses that will make you seek Him even harder.

God, show me all that I'm still holding on to, all that comes between You and me. Point out to me the places where I'm still clinging to my own sense of control. I want to get everything out of the way that keeps me from finding You. Amen.

EVENING
He's Not Far Away!

"That they would seek God, if perhaps they might grope for Him and find Him, though He is not far from each one of us."
ACTS 17:27 NASB

This verse comes from one of Paul's sermons, preached to people who were not familiar with the God of Israel. He was trying to put the God he loved into terms they would understand. Paul is acknowledging that seeking God feels like groping around in the dark—and he's promising that even though all we see is darkness, God is standing right there next to us.

Thank You, God, that even when You seem far away, You are still as close as ever. Thank You that even when all I see is darkness, You are right there with me. Amen.

DAY 343

MORNING
To Get the Prize

Everyone who competes in the games goes into strict training.
1 CORINTHIANS 9:25 NIV

We are in the race of life. Time is short, but the days are long. We have a lot to do, and we never know when our life will come to an end. All of us are running to the same finish line. It's important that we run our races in a way that shows we are serious about getting the prize—eternal life with Christ. We need to show that we are running toward something worth sacrificing for. And we need to be prepared for whatever falls in our paths—including other runners.

Dear God, please help me "run in such a way as to get the prize" (1 Corinthians 9:24 NIV). Amen.

EVENING
Building a House for God

In him you too are being built together to become a dwelling in which God lives by his Spirit.
EPHESIANS 2:22 NIV

This verse from one of Paul's letters hints at how we can become more aware of God's presence with us. The important word is *together*. Living in the presence of God is not something we do alone. In our relationships with others, in the love we express and receive, we are constantly building a place where God will live among us.

Teach me, Lord, to get along with others—both the people I like and the people I don't, both the people who agree with me and the people who don't. Remind me that as I build loving relationships with others, I am also building a place where Your Spirit will dwell. Amen.

MORNING

He heals the brokenhearted
and binds up their wounds.

PSALM 147:3 NIV

A heart that does not feel cannot be broken. But it also cannot love. And a heart that loves deeply can be wounded deeply. But God is the great Healer. And He knows how to heal deeply. God searches our hearts and finds the holes. Then He carefully, over time, joins the pieces together—with new love, care, and understanding. A broken heart will never be the same as an innocent one. It is forever scarred. But with the scarring comes wisdom, and that wisdom can blossom into compassion for others who have been hurt as well.

Dear Healer, mend the holes in my heart so I can offer my whole heart to You. Amen.

EVENING

Turn Your Ear to Wisdom

For the LORD gives wisdom; from His
mouth come knowledge and understanding.
He stores up sound wisdom for the upright;
He is a shield to those who walk in integrity,
guarding the paths of justice, and He
preserves the way of His godly ones.

PROVERBS 2:6–8 NASB

Every family has at least one relative who cannot get his act together.

Are you smiling yet? Is someone in particular coming clearly into focus? Now, hold that thought. God's Word says wisdom is truly a gift since it comes from the mouth of God, from the very words He speaks. And all God's words have been written down for us through the inspiration of the Holy Spirit. Therefore, those who refuse to accept God's guidance, who refuse to ask for His wisdom—those hapless relatives, perhaps—will never see the light of reality.

Know that if you hold fast to the precepts contained in the Bible, you will walk in integrity. Your feet will be planted on the straight and narrow road.

Lord, I can't change my relatives, but I can change myself. Please give me Your guidance and wisdom. Amen.

DAY 345

MORNING
Until the End of the World

I am with you always,
even unto the end of the world.
MATTHEW 28:20 KJV

These were Jesus' last words to His friends before He left them to return to His Father. The promise He made then to His followers is ours as well. Again and again, we need to remind ourselves and each other that we live in a world where Jesus is real. He lived among us—and He still does. He always will.

Jesus, I am so glad that, like the disciples,
I too can call You my friend—
and that I can claim for myself
the promises You gave to them. Amen.

EVENING
Everywhere!

Where can I go from your Spirit? Where can I flee from your presence? If I go up to the heavens, you are there; if I make my bed in the depths, you are there. If I rise on the wings of the dawn, if I settle on the far side of the sea, even there your hand will guide me, your right hand will hold me fast.
PSALM 139:7–10 NIV

Is there any blessing greater than that expressed by these verses?

Spirit of God, thank You that You
are everywhere. Thank You for
making sure that nothing will ever
separate me from God. Amen.

DAY 346

MORNING
Shine

"Those who are wise will shine like the brightness of the heavens, and those who lead many to righteousness, like the stars for ever and ever."

Daniel 12:3 NIV

The next time you are feeling a little frumpy or gray, a little old and tarnished, thank God for the wisdom you have. Think about the best decisions you made in the past year. Then pick yourself up, put on something shiny (an aluminum foil tiara? a bouquet of silverware?) and take your own photo. Print it out and write beneath it, "I Shine." Then put it somewhere to serve as a reminder that being wise can be beautiful, too.

Dear Lord, thank You for allowing me to shine with wisdom. Amen.

EVENING
Give More

It is more blessed to give than to receive.

Acts 20:35 KJV

God not only wants to bless us, but He also wants us to bless others. In fact, He wants us to think more about giving blessings than we do about receiving blessings. But then something funny happens. When we stop asking for blessings and focus on giving, we'll get more blessings than we would have otherwise. It's one of those paradoxes of God's kingdom—something that doesn't seem to make sense, but is true.

Somehow, Lord, the more I give away, with no thought of return, the more You always bless me. Funny how that works! Amen.

DAY 347

MORNING

A Never-Ending Cycle

God who gives seed to the farmer that becomes bread for your meals. . .gives you something you can then give away, which grows into full-formed lives, robust in God, wealthy in every way, so that you can be generous in every way.

2 CORINTHIANS 9:10–11 MSG

Here's that blessing circle again. The more we give, the more we're blessed. The more we're blessed, the more we have to give. It's like the water cycle, where water evaporates from the earth into the clouds, and the clouds rain water back to earth, a never-ending cycle of life and growth.

Make my life strong and healthy, God, filled with the fruit of Your Spirit, so that You can use it as a resource to abundantly bless others. Amen.

EVENING

True Treasure

Do good. . .be rich in good works. . . be generous and ready to share, storing up. . . the treasure of a good foundation for the future. . .that which is life indeed.

1 TIMOTHY 6:18–19 NASB

This verse explains what real wealth means, as well as the real purpose of wealth. Doing good to others is what makes us truly rich—and it's all meant to be shared! Giving builds the foundation we need not only for our future lives but for life itself. No other treasure lasts.

May I build a foundation of generosity, Lord, so that You can use my life as a treasure house of blessing for others. Amen.

DAY 348

MORNING
Harm for Good

"You intended to harm me, but God intended it for good."
GENESIS 50:20 NIV

Joseph suffered more in his lifetime than any of us probably ever will. But God remembered him, blessed him, and made him a man of great authority in the land so that he was in the position to make wise decisions and save many people from starvation.

Instead of feeling entitled to apologies, Joseph wanted redemption in place of revenge. In response to his brothers wanting security, he replied, "Don't be afraid. Am I in the place of God? You intended to harm me, but God intended it for good to accomplish what is now being done, the saving of many lives" (Genesis 50:19–20 NIV).

Maybe you're in the middle of suffering right now, so deep in it you can't possibly see any good. Take encouragement from Joseph's words. You are not God—you cannot see what He sees. Maybe yet there will be some good that comes out of the harm.

Dear God, help me to trust in Your plans. Amen.

EVENING
Finish Line

I have fought the good fight, I have finished the race, I have kept the faith.
2 TIMOTHY 4:7 NIV

Paul felt his life was coming to an end. As he wrote to his friend Timothy, he spoke of this. He was not boasting; he was just giving his status report, as it were. Good fight fought? Check. Race finished? Check (well, almost). Faith kept? Check. What does your checklist include? What accomplishments make your list? What goals do you want to be known for achieving? What do you want to do, who do you want to become, before your race is finished? Write them down today. Put a check box by each one. Then go and work out your life, faith, and ministry for all you're worth. Godspeed.

Dear Lord, bless the work of my hands and feet. Make me Your servant so that at the end of my life, I can look forward to hearing You say, "Well done." Amen.

DAY 349

MORNING
Vocalizing a Prayer

"And when you are praying, do not use meaningless repetition as the Gentiles do, for they suppose that they will be heard for their many words."

MATTHEW 6:7 NASB

If you can remember the acrostic ACTS, you'll have an excellent formula for prayer: Adoration, Confession, Thanksgiving, and Supplication.

As we come before the Lord, we first need to honor Him as Creator, Master, Savior, and Lord. Reflect on who He is and praise Him. And because we're human, we need to confess and repent of our daily sins. Following this, we should be in a mode of thanksgiving. Finally, our prayer requests should be upheld.

Your prayers certainly don't have to be elaborate or polished. God does not judge your way with words. He knows your heart. He wants to hear from you.

Lord, Your Word says that my prayers rise up to heaven like incense from the earth. Remind me daily to send a sweet savor Your way! Amen.

EVENING
Blessing versus Cursing

"Bless those who curse you. Pray for those who hurt you."

LUKE 6:28 NLT

As His followers, we should take Jesus' words to us very seriously, but we often don't. We feel justified when we complain about people who hurt us. We fume and brood over insults and slights. And it never occurs to us that this is sin, something that damages our relationship with God. We don't realize that we're cursing rather than blessing. Jesus wants even our thoughts to be filled with blessings, not curses.

Fill my mouth and heart, Lord, with blessings for others. May I be quick to affirm others and slow to criticize. May I seek to build up rather than tear down. Amen.

DAY 350

MORNING
Blessing Our Enemies

If you see your enemy hungry,
go buy that person lunch, or if he's
thirsty, get him a drink.
ROMANS 12:20–21 MSG

Not only are we to pray for the people who have hurt us, but we are also to bless them in visible, tangible ways. God asks us to look for opportunities to show them little kindnesses. He wants us to pay attention to what they need, to look for chances to help them in any way we can. This business of blessing our enemies is serious stuff!

When I forget, Lord of love, that You want me to be Your hands and feet on earth, remind me that my prayers should lead to actions. Let me not use prayer as an excuse to not get involved. Amen.

EVENING
Channels of Blessing

"I will save you, and you will be a blessing.
Do not be afraid, but let your
hands be strong."
ZECHARIAH 8:13 NIV

Sometimes we may doubt our own abilities to be a blessing to others. We may feel we don't have anything to offer—or we think that whatever we could offer wouldn't be good enough. God asks us to take our eyes off our faults and inadequacy and simply get busy, our eyes on Him. When we open our hearts and lives, His strength and love can flow through us, out into the world, blessing everyone it touches.

Remind me, Lord, that it is Your Spirit at work in me that has the power to bless others. I'll get out of Your way so You can do Your work through me! Amen.

DAY 351

MORNING

Women Who Loved Well

Charm is deceptive, and beauty is fleeting.

PROVERBS 31:30 NIV

In the end, it will matter to Jesus, of course, that we knew Him as our friend and Savior, but it will also matter that while we walked this earthly life, we loved well. That we saw a need and met it. That we smiled when we wanted to frown. That we were handier with a cup of cool water than a witty comeback. That we chased after a lost soul faster than we chased after a good time. That we loved other people as ourselves. Those things will matter a great deal, and with the power of the Holy Spirit, all those things are within our grasp. They are also ours to give away. Fully, freely—and daily.

Heavenly Father, help me to focus on cultivating those qualities and virtues that are lasting and will make an eternal impact for Your kingdom. Amen.

EVENING

Called

Be harmonious. . .kindhearted, and humble in spirit; not returning evil for evil or insult for insult, but giving a blessing instead; for you were called for the very purpose that you might inherit a blessing.

1 PETER 3:8–9 NASB

We may tell ourselves, "Of course, I know that, I do that." But do we? This is a way of living that's radically different from our customary attitudes and actions. It doesn't leave room for complaining and gossiping. As individuals, we may be called to do many things, but this is the overarching vocation we all share—to bless others with our words, thoughts, and actions.

Remind me, Lord, when I forget that my greatest purpose in this life is to be a blessing to others. Make me kind and humble; help me to live in harmony with everyone; curb my tongue, so that criticisms and negativity don't spill out of me. Use me, I pray. Amen.

DAY 352

MORNING

Bonus and Blessing

"Give away your life; you'll find life given back, but not merely given back—given back with bonus and blessing."

LUKE 6:38 MSG

Here again Jesus is talking about the blessing cycle, that nonsensical kingdom paradox. Give away your very life—because that's the only way you'll have a real life. Give away absolutely everything you have, every thought and thing, every emotion and action—and you'll still never be able to give as much as God gives back to you.

Thank You, Jesus, that as I abandon everything I call mine, putting it all in Your hands, You give me limitless, bountiful life in return. Amen.

EVENING

Behind the Scenes

"When you do something for someone else, don't call attention to yourself. You've seen them in action, I'm sure—'playactors' I call them. . .acting compassionate as long as someone is watching, playing to the crowds. They get applause, true, but that's all they get. When you help someone out, don't think about how it looks. Just do it—quietly and unobtrusively. That is the way your God, who conceived you in love, working behind the scenes, helps you out."

MATTHEW 6:2–4 MSG

Here's how Jesus wants us to bless others—humbly, lovingly, with no focus on ourselves.

Make me real, Jesus. Keep me from being a hypocrite. May Your love fill every crevice of my being, so that all I am is You. Amen.

DAY 353

MORNING
The Trees That Catch the Storm

Brothers and sisters, I could not address you as people who live by the Spirit but as people who are still worldly—mere infants in Christ. I gave you milk, not solid food, for you were not yet ready for it. Indeed, you are still not ready.

1 CORINTHIANS 3:1–2 NIV

Think of the healthiest trees that shoot up from the forest floor. . . They stretch toward the sun and spread their branches wide. But when the storms of life blow through, many times it's those towering oaks that will catch the brunt of the wind. The last thing the enemy of your soul wants is for you to grow in Christ and His wisdom. So, expect storms, and be watchful and ready. But remember, too, that we can stand strong like the oak trees. We can know peace in the midst of the gale. For Christ is the strength in our branches and the light that gives us life!

Jesus, help me to grow strong in the rich, nourishing soil of Your love and grace. Make me a warrior for Your cause. Amen.

EVENING
Sowing Peace

Peacemakers who sow in peace reap a harvest of righteousness.

JAMES 3:18 NIV

One of the ways we bless others is by working to create peace in the world around us. Some of us may be called to take large actions, to write letters and books, make speeches or run for office—but we're all called to build peace in our individual lives in small, tangible ways every single day. In each relationship, each interaction with another (no matter how casual), God asks us to bless the world with His peace and love.

Make me Your peacemaker, Lord. May I carry Your Spirit of reconciliation into the world. Amen.

DAY 354

MORNING
What to Do with Free Will

"If you do what is right, will you not be accepted? But if you do not do what is right, sin is crouching at your door; it desires to have you, but you must rule over it."

GENESIS 4:7 NIV

Every single thing we do every minute of the day involves a choice, and everything has a ripple effect. Everything has consequences. What we eat for breakfast. What books we read, what programs we watch on TV. Where we go, what we spend our time and money on. Sin is always crouching at our door, but with the help of the Holy Spirit, we can ask it to leave. What will your choices be today?

Holy Spirit, guide me in my decisions. Help me to be wise, clearheaded, and motivated by a selfless love for You and others. Amen.

EVENING
All the Lonely People

Be devoted to one another in love. Honor one another above yourselves.

ROMANS 12:10 NIV

As Christians, let's keep an eye out for those lonely souls, the people who need a smile and a helping hand. Those who need a cup of cool water and a listening ear—who need a friend. Let us open our hearts and homes to them. As the book of Romans reminds us, "Be devoted to one another in love. Honor one another above yourselves." This is God's cure for all the lonely people. Amazingly enough, when we reach out to lessen someone else's lonesomeness, perhaps we will ease our own.

Father, give me the desire to live my life for You and for everyone around me. Deepen and enrich my relationships with family and friends. Amen.

DAY 355

MORNING
Fishers of Men

And [Jesus] said to them, "Follow me, and I will make you fishers of men."
MATTHEW 4:19 ESV

When He spoke the words recorded above, Peter and Andrew must have been intrigued. But Jesus didn't invent the phrase "fishers of men." Philosophers and teachers of that day used this term to describe those who captured men's minds.

Why did Christ want these fishermen? Peter and Andrew were men of action who knew how to get a job done without quitting or complaining. Their tenacity would be an asset to Christ's ministry of soul winning.

Jesus came not only to save but also to teach men and women how to have true servants' hearts. The substance of ministry is service.

Lord, show me clearly where I can be of service within my local body of believers. Perhaps there's a small hand in the Sunday school just waiting to be held. Amen.

EVENING
Abundant Life

I am come that they might have life, and that they might have it more abundantly.
JOHN 10:10 KJV

We've talked about many kinds of blessings. In the end, all those blessings, both spiritual and material, can be contained in the blessing Jesus is talking about here—abundant life. Eternal life doesn't merely go on forever. It's a life that has no limits, not in time, not in strength, not in love. It's a life that's deep and rich, full of countless blessings.

Thank You, Jesus, for coming to earth—and thank You for coming into my very being, bringing me Your abundant, eternal life. Amen.

DAY 356

MORNING

Turning Bondage into Balance

It is for freedom that Christ has set us free. Stand firm, then, and do not let yourselves be burdened again by a yoke of slavery.

GALATIANS 5:1 NIV

The Lord wants us to have a sound mind, which means finding balance in life. How can we be warm, giving, creative, fun, and a light to the world if we are frozen solid in an unmovable block of perfectionism? Let Jesus melt the block of bondage that says, "Never good enough," and let us be able to shout the words, "It is good, and it is finished. Praise God!"

Lord, help me not to be a slave to perfectionism, but in all things, let me find balance and joy. Amen.

EVENING

Life Forevermore

The LORD bestows his blessing, even life forevermore.

PSALM 133:3 NIV

Most of us have a vague idea about eternity, an unknown realm beyond death, far off in the future. But the psalmist is speaking in the present tense. Eternal life starts now. The Hebrew word for this life—*chayah*—has a breadth of meaning: to come to life in a new way, to be restored to life after being dead, to be healed, to be kept alive, to be nourished, to recover from illness. And it's all happening *right now*. We don't have to wait until we die!

Lord, thank You for allowing me to experience eternity here on earth. "On earth as it is in heaven" takes on new meaning when I reflect on the truth that eternal life starts now. Amen.

DAY 357

MORNING
Healed

Store my commands in your heart.
If you do this, you will live many years,
and your life will be satisfying.
PROVERBS 3:1–2 NLT

Think about scripture. Dwell on it. Commit it to memory. Fill your mind with it. It will do you good. It will give you life! The Hebrew word that's been translated as *life* and *live* implies being restored to life after a serious illness. It's the sort of life that is so full, so healthy, that it really can't be measured in years. Hear God's words and you, too, will experience this life.

Restore me to Your life, Lord. Make me what You want me to be. Fill my life with Your purpose. Amen.

EVENING
Seeking Wisdom

To receive instruction in wise behavior. . .
to the youth knowledge and discretion,
a wise man will hear and increase in learning,
and a man of understanding will acquire wise
counsel, to understand a proverb and a figure,
the words of the wise and their riddles.
PROVERBS 1:3–6 NASB

When asked by God what he wished for, Solomon answered, "Wisdom." If you'd been asked this question in your early twenties, what would your response have been?

Seventeen-year-old Natalie found the advances of an older man extremely difficult to resist. Disregarding everything she'd learned in Sunday school, Natalie turned instead to a non-Christian girlfriend for advice. "Go for it!" the friend encouraged with gusto.

A decade later that friend has been married and divorced. Natalie herself found out too late that her "boyfriend" already had a wife and baby.

Satan still finds his way into vulnerable areas of our lives. But God is with you, even in times of temptation. He'll give us the power and wisdom to withstand such moral crises.

Lord, surround me with friends who know You and Your Word. Surround me in a crisis so I can hear Your voice of wisdom. Amen.

DAY 358

MORNING

The Time Is Now

But God demonstrates his own love for us in this: While we were still sinners, Christ died for us.

ROMANS 5:8 NIV

In the book of Mark, Jesus said, "The time has come. . . . The kingdom of God has come near. Repent and believe the good news!" (1:15 NIV). Have you embraced this good news? The kingdom of God has come near to you. Why are you waiting? The time is now. Ask the Lord for forgiveness and be free. Believe in Him as Lord and be made right with God. Accept His grace and live with the Lord for all time. Oh, yes, what a joy—to know love the way it was meant to be!

Thank You, Lord Jesus, that even while I was deep in my sin, You gave up your life so that I might truly live. What a sacrifice. What a Savior! Thank You for Your unfathomable mercy, Your immeasurable love. Amen.

EVENING

Blessings Forever

You will make known to me the path of life; in Your presence is fullness of joy; in Your right hand there are pleasures forever.

PSALM 16:11 NASB

This verse mentions blessings we've already discussed—God's guidance, His joy, His presence—but it adds another element to them all: *forever*. Here's how *Strong's Concordance* explains what the psalmist meant when he used that word: "The bright goal in the distance that's travelled toward; splendor, confidence, victory that is perpetual, constant and ongoing." In other words, all of this exists at the end of our journeys on earth. It's also constantly there, right now.

Oh Lord, Your presence goes with me wherever I go, making me happy, guiding me, giving me confidence in Your victory. Thank You that You are here with me now—and You will still be here tomorrow and forever. Amen.

DAY 359

MORNING

The Water of Life

The water that I shall give him shall be in him a well of water springing up into everlasting life.

JOHN 4:14 KJV

In the New Testament, the Greek word used for *life* is *zoé*. HELPS Word-Studies gives this definition for how Jesus is using the word: "Physical and spiritual life, all life throughout the universe, which always and only comes from and is sustained by God's self-existent life. The Lord intimately shares His gift of life with people, creating each in His image which gives all the capacity to know His eternal life."

Jesus, I praise You for pouring Your living water into me. Sustain me always, body and soul, with Your Spirit. Amen.

EVENING

Right People, Right Place, Right Time

And so find favor and high esteem in the sight of God and man.

PROVERBS 3:4 NKJV

God wants you to experience every favor and rich blessing He's prepared. By faith, expect blessing to meet you at every turn. Imagine what your future holds when you become determined to step out to greet it according to God's design. Remain alert and attentive to what God wants to add to your life. Expect the goodness He has planned for you—doors of opportunities are opening for you today!

Lord, thank You for setting favor and blessing in my path; help me to expect it wherever I go and in whatever I do. Amen.

DAY 360

MORNING

The Joyful Path of Life

You have shown me the way of life,
and you will fill me with the joy
of your presence.

ACTS 2:28 NLT

The blessing of eternal life can't be separated from the blessing of God's presence. It can't be separated from His joy, either, and the blessing of His guidance is wrapped up in it, too. Eternal life is our destination, but it's also a path, a path filled with joy, a path we're walking right now, led each step of the way by God's presence with us.

God, You give so much to me. You fill my life with meaning and richness. Best of all, You fill my life with You! Amen.

EVENING

Trusting While Trembling

And straightway the father of the child
cried out, and said with tears, Lord,
I believe; help thou mine unbelief.

MARK 9:24 KJV

When the Lord looks at us, what does He see? Do we trust Him enough to be vulnerable? Are we willing to obey even when we are afraid? Do we believe Him? Do not be afraid to follow Him, and do not let your trembling hold you back. Be willing to take a step of faith. If you are scared, God understands and is compassionate and merciful. Fear does not negate His love for you. Your faith will grow as you trust Him. Let's trust even while trembling.

Dear Lord, help my unbelief. Enable me to trust You even though I may be trembling. Amen.

DAY 361

MORNING
Life beyond Time

"I am the resurrection and the life.
Anyone who believes in me
will live, even after dying."
JOHN 11:25 NLT

When we look at the Greek words in this verse, we find that Jesus is talking about a life that is both inside and outside time. HELPS Word-Studies says that it is what gives time its "everlasting meaning" even while it's also "time-independent." It "does not focus on the future *per se*, but rather on the *quality*." Eternal life is "right *now*, experiencing this *quality of God's life* now as a *present possession*." That's a pretty amazing blessing!

Jesus, thank You that You are mine and I am Yours both inside and outside of time. I don't even understand what that means, not really—but I know that my life in You will never end. Amen.

EVENING
Equipped to Do God's Will

May the God of peace, who through the blood of the eternal covenant brought back from the dead our Lord Jesus, that great Shepherd of the sheep, equip you with everything good for doing his will, and may he work in us what is pleasing to him, through Jesus Christ, to whom be glory for ever and ever. Amen.
HEBREWS 13:20–21 NIV

Hebrews says God will work in us what is pleasing to Him. When He is at work in you, you may be stretched mentally, emotionally, physically, and spiritually to new places. The good news is that He provides you with everything you need. Like a good football coach wants his team to succeed, God wants His children to receive the blessing of living in His perfect will. You are equipped for the ride!

Father, I ask that You equip me to do Your will in my life. Amen.

DAY 362

MORNING

Get Real

The Lord says: "These people come near to me with their mouth and honor me with their lips, but their hearts are far from me. Their worship of me is based on merely human rules they have been taught."

ISAIAH 29:13 NIV

The world is full of hypocrites. To be honest, sometimes the church is, too—hypocrites who profess to know and honor God, but when it comes right down to it, they are only going through the motions of religion. Their hearts are far from Him. Take the time to find out who God is, what He has done for you, and why He is worthy of your devotion. Following God is not about a bunch of man-made rules. He loves you; He sent His Son to die for you; and He longs to have a deep, personal relationship with you. Get real with God and get real with yourself!

Dear God, reveal Yourself to me. Show me who You are and show me how to live so that I honor You not only with my lips, but with my heart as well. Amen.

EVENING

Changed Priorities

"Don't be so concerned about perishable things like food. Spend your energy seeking the eternal life that the Son of Man can give you."

JOHN 6:27 NLT

If we could just remember that we live both inside and outside time, in the same eternal realm with Jesus, we'd stop worrying so much about whether we'll have enough in this world. Our perspective would shift; our priorities would change. We'd live in the stream of never-ending blessing that is God's life, our eyes fixed on Jesus.

Give me eternity eyes, Jesus. Help me to share Your perspective on reality, Most of all, help me to see You! Amen.

DAY 363

MORNING

Leaving It All

"And everyone who has left houses or brothers or sisters or father or mother or children or farms for My name's sake, will receive many times as much, and will inherit eternal life."

MATTHEW 19:29 NASB

God calls us to live in loving relationship with others—and yet when Jesus talks like this, He sounds as though He's saying the exact opposite, as though He wants us to abandon our children and our parents, our homes and our work. What He's really talking about, though, is the absolute surrender of giving everything we love to Him. We're no longer in control. He is.

Jesus, I give You everything—my house and car, the people I love, my work, everything. I let it all go, knowing You are better able to care for those things and people than I am. Please take control. Amen.

EVENING

I Think I Can

"Do not be afraid; only believe."

MARK 5:36 NKJV

Take a trip through the Bible and you'll see that those God asked to do the impossible were ordinary people of their day, yet they demonstrated that they believed God saw something in them that they didn't see. He took ordinary men and women and used them to do extraordinary things. When you believe you can do something, your faith goes to work. You rise to the challenge, which enables you to go further than before, to do more than you thought possible. Consider trying something new—if you think you can, you can!

God, I want to have high expectations. I want to do more than most think I can do. Help me to reach higher and do more as You lead me. Amen.

DAY 364

MORNING
In the Garden

When the woman saw that the tree was good for food, and that it was a delight to the eyes, and that the tree was desirable to make one wise, she took from its fruit and ate; and she gave also to her husband with her, and he ate.

GENESIS 3:6 NASB

Eve stood beside the "tree of the knowledge of good and evil" and began listening to the seductive voice of the crafty serpent.

And Adam, who loved her, listened to her voice and joined her in eating the fruit of the tree. As a result, Adam and Eve were forced out of this physical garden paradise. Yet the echo of God's loving promise lingered in their ears. . . . A Redeemer would come.

Thousands of years later, Jesus prayed in another garden. And His sacrifice on the cross provided forgiveness, once again allowing access to God's presence. . .now within a spiritual garden of prayer.

Lord, I know I have walked away from You at some point of sin. That's why You sent Jesus to be my Savior. Forgive me, and enable me with Your strength to run from sin and toward prayer. Amen.

EVENING
Owning Your Faith

"But the Helper, the Holy Spirit, whom the Father will send in My name, He will teach you all things, and bring to your remembrance all things that I said to you."

JOHN 14:26 NKJV

Is your faith deeper and stronger than when you first accepted Jesus? While we are responsible for choosing to grow in faith, we can't do it on our own. Jesus promises that the Holy Spirit will teach and guide us if we allow Him to. He will help us remember the spiritual truths we've learned over the years. Fellowship with other Christians also helps us to mature as we share our passions and are encouraged. God wants you to own your faith. Make it real with words and actions.

Jesus, I want to know You intimately. Help me to mature in my walk with You daily. Guide my steps as I seek You through Your Word. Amen.

DAY 365

MORNING
Missing the Target

Those who live only to satisfy their own sinful nature will harvest decay and death from that sinful nature. But those who live to please the Spirit will harvest everlasting life from the Spirit.

GALATIANS 6:8 NLT

The Greek concept for sin is very simple. It means simply "failing to hit the mark." When we let our selfish egos run the show, we are like arrows that miss their target. Our target is life—but unless we surrender our egos to the Spirit, our arrows are all hitting death instead. It's as simple as that.

Spirit of the living God, I want to live to please You, not myself. Keep my thought and actions on target, arrows that speed toward You. Amen.

EVENING
Surprise!

Now that you've found you don't have to listen to sin tell you what to do. . .what a surprise! A whole, healed, put-together life right now, with more and more of life on the way! . . . God's gift is real life, eternal life, delivered by Jesus, our Master.

ROMANS 6:22–23 MSG

We have a choice; we don't have to keep shooting our arrows in the wrong direction! When we choose to aim toward God, our lives are changed in the here and now: they're made whole, all their broken places mended. . .and new life, new blessings keep on coming.

I choose You, Jesus, as my target—in this world and the next. Thank You for the abundant blessings of life and love You keep giving to me, endlessly, world without end. Amen.

SCRIPTURE INDEX

Old Testament

Proverbs

Ecclesiastes

Song of Solomon

Isaiah

New Testament